The Psychology of Criminal Justice

Geoffrey M. Stephenson

BLACKWELL
Oxford UK & Cambridge USA

First published 1992
Reprinted 1993, 1995, 1997

Blackwell Publishers Ltd
108 Cowley Road
Oxford OX4 1JF, UK

Blackwell Publishers Inc
350 Main Street
Malden, Massachusetts 02148, USA

British Library Cataloguing in Publication Data
A CIP catalogue record for this book is available from the British Library

Library of Congress Cataloging in Publication Data has been applied for
ISBN 0–631–14546–X; 0–631–14547–8 (pbk)

Typeset in 10.5 on 12.5 pt Palatino
by Graphicraft Typesetters Limited, Hong Kong
Printed and bound in Great Britain
by Athenæum Press Ltd, Gateshead, Tyne & Wear

This book is printed on acid-free paper

Contents

For Lawrence and Katherine

Acknowledgements

The author and publishers wish to thank the following who have kindly given permission to reproduce figures, tables and extracts: Speech Communication Association, table p. 12, from Beach, W A, (1985), 'Temporal density in courtroom interaction: constraints on the recovery of past events in legal discourse', *Communication Monographs*, 52, 1–18, copyright © by the Speech Communication Association, reprinted by permission of the publisher; John Wiley & Sons Ltd, table 14.1, p. 266–7, from Twining, W (1983), 'Identification and misidentification in legal processes: redefining the process' in S Lloyd-Bostock and I Clifford (eds) *Evaluating Witness Evidence*, copyright © John Wiley & Sons Ltd, reprinted by permission of the publisher; Plenum Publishing Corporation, table 3, p. 93, from Holstein, J A (1985) 'Jurors' interpretation and jury decision making', *Law and Human Behaviour*, 9, 83–100; figure 2, p. 421, Brigham, J C & Ready, D J (1985) 'Own-race bias in lineup construction', *Law and Human Behaviour*, 9, 415–24; Open University Press, figure 3, p. 6, from Allen, H (1987) *Justice Unbalanced: Gender, Psychiatry and Judicial Decisions*; Canadian Psychological Association, table 3 from Doob, A N & Roberts, J V (1984) 'Social Psychology, social attitudes and attitudes towards sentencing', *Canadian Journal of Behavioural Science*, 16, 269–80, copyright © Canadian Psychological Association, reprinted by permission of the publisher; University of Chicago Press, figures 2 and 3, p. 48 Colby, A (1983) 'A longitudinal study of child development', *Monographs of the Society for Research in Child Development*, 48, 1–124, copyright © The Society for Research in Child Development Inc.; *The Independent*, Miles Kington article (31 March 1987), reprinted with kind permission of the author and publisher; British Journal of Psychiatry, figure 1 from Kolvin, I, Miller, F J W, Fleeting, M & Kolvin, P A

(1988) 'Social and parenting factors affecting criminal-offence rates', *British Journal of Psychiatry*, 152, 80–90; Harvester Wheatsheaf, table 1.1, p. 7, from Wagenaar, W A (1988) *Identifying Ivan: a Case Study in Legal Psychology*, copyright © Harvester Wheatsheaf; University of Chicago Press, table 11, p. 56 from Kalven, H & Zeisel, H (1966) *The American Jury*, copyright © University of Chicago Press.

I gratefully acknowledge the contribution of the many friends, colleagues and students who have debated matters of crime, law and justice with me. Noel Clark, Helen Dent, Jim Davis, Harry Hunter, Bromley Kniveton, Ian Morley, Stephen Moston, Brian Perrett, Jan Webb, James White, Jennie Williams and Tom Williamson have been especially important; and I recall with gratitude that Professor W J H Sprott first got me interested in the psychology of criminal behaviour in my undergraduate days at Nottingham University. My thanks also to those I have not mentioned by name and to the many researchers whose writings I have drawn upon in this book.

Charles Blacklock, Ian Morley, Sandra Schruijer and Tom Williamson very kindly read and commented on the entire manuscript. Above all I would thank Tom for his unfailing support and interest over many years. Jan Lloyd, my secretary, has been perceptive, speedy and brilliantly accurate beyond both my deserts and the publisher's expectations. Blackwells have been very patient and consistently professional throughout; thanks especially to Philip Carpenter for his initial encouragement to write the book.

I would like also to thank my colleagues and especially Professor Jim Mansell for taking over my administrative and teaching responsibilities last Michaelmas Term. Also the staff of the Templeman Library at the University of Kent should know I appreciated very much their courtesy and helpfulness during that term and at other times.

Finally, my love and thanks to David and Jennie who have helped me much more than I have let on.

Geoffrey M Stephenson

List of Figures

List of Tables

Introduction

The causes of crime and the functioning of the criminal justice system have both been the object of empirical research and analysis by psychologists since before the end of the last century. They have, for the most part, been separate enterprises, undertaken respectively by psychologists interested in personality and socialization on the one hand, and by social psychologists on the other. It is a central aim of *The Psychology of Criminal Justice* to integrate aspects of these two research traditions within the framework of a single narrative account. The case for synthesis is strong, because the decisions made by suspects, victims, police and those associated with the courts are interdependent, and cannot be neatly separated. This is especially clear in cases where what is under scrutiny is the criminal status of the act that has given offence. The upsurge in prosecution for rape is a good example of this. The increase is commonly held to reflect not an increase in the numbers of men committing the offence, but a change in the evaluation of suspects by their victims, and of victims by the police, and prosecuting lawyers. This book seeks to integrate the two research traditions by describing the interpersonal and group dynamics of decision-making at key stages in the processing of accused persons from the time an alleged offence is committed to the moment sentence is passed.

The criminal justice system has perpetrated dreadful injustices too consistently for this book not to be judged by its relevance to critical debate of the system. However, forensic psychologists have tended to work in something of a social vacuum, and have not become known for their challenges to the *status quo*. Mechanistic descriptions of interesting but isolated features of the criminal justice system have been given in abundance. Criminal behaviour has been attributed to the possession of personality characteristics, mistaken prosecutions to cognitive lapses, perverse verdicts to group polarization and so on, as if these explanations constitute full understanding or suggest their own remedies. They do not, as many lawyers do not hesitate to point out. In my view the failure of psychology sufficiently to challenge the system stems from its failure to recognise the interdependence of decision-makers in the criminal justice system, and hence not to address questions at the appropriate social psychological level. Social identifications and attributions serve to *organize* the behaviour of suspects, victims, police and the courts, even to the point of determining issues of law, as Jackson (1988) points out. There is, as I hope to show, an insidious routine in the creation of criminals fit for sentencing by judges, who normally address the individual convict without consideration of the remarkable contingencies which have brought him or her to that position.

The first four chapters of this book will explore the psychological, moral and social bases of criminal decisions. Criminals do not have distinctive personalities, and their moral reasoning is not especially inept. Processes of social and moral judgement are none the less intimately linked to criminal decision-making, and, indeed, to legal decision-making, an issue explored in the discussion of morality and law in chapter 2.

Chapters 5, 6 and 7 chart societal reactions to alleged criminal wrongdoing, specifically in relation to the behaviour and experience of victims, and of the police, and more generally in an analysis of how blame is attributed to others (chapter 7). This chapter is important for an evaluation of what subsequently happens to suspects in courtroom trials, assuming that the case gets that far. It will be seen that vital components of blaming may receive short shrift in criminal trials, especially when the determination of guilt in a case has assumed high priority in the public mind.

Victims and police between them ensure that some suspects stand trial. At this point social psychology might be said to come into its own with a century's worth of academic devotion behind it to questions of the reliability and validity of investigative procedures. Research on eyewitness testimony has the longest pedigree, but jury decision-making follows closely behind, with systematic studies of courtroom interaction and sentencing more recently coming under experimental scrutiny. Chapter 8 examines studies of interaction in court, and introduces a 'narrative theory' which impinges on the behaviour of all protagonists, from witnesses, victims and suspects, to police, lawyers, juries and judges, both in prospect and as the drama unfolds. It will be seen that for many reasons a jury is not a reliable judge of which version of events to believe.

How fair is our system of criminal justice? The final chapter examines what people want from the criminal justice system, applying criteria derived from social psychological studies of procedural and distributive justice. Problems with our adversarial system have become only too apparent in recent years. It is commonplace now to see the role and operation of the police as being in particular need of urgent reform. It will become apparent to readers of *The Psychology of Criminal Justice*, that the reasons for distrust and disquiet go far beyond the behaviour of just one agent in the organization of criminal justice.

1

Who is the Criminal?

Do criminals have distinctive personalities?

Many reasons have been given for regarding criminals as different from the law-abiding majority, different in ways which explain their criminality. Biological degeneracy, personality malfunctioning and moral imbecility have all been attributed to the law-breaker: in body, mind and soul, the criminal has been said to be distinctive.

The prevailing theory during this century has centred on the idea that criminal behaviour in general is a sign of personality disturbance or malfunctioning. This idea found its richest exposition in psychoanalytic and related practice in the middle of this century. By giving delinquent boys and girls psychotherapy, it was expected that their abnormal hostility to other people – of which delinquency was seen to be an expression – could be replaced by affectionate and loving relationships. William and Joan McCord (1956) described many cases of severely delinquent and aggressive children who in the course of therapy in institutional settings were 'cured' of their delinquency through the medium of newly established relationships with adults. These new relationships served to undo the psychological damage caused by their previously unhappy family relationships. Individual therapy not having proved too successful, the McCords advocated the establishment of therapeutic communities in which children were unconditionally accepted by staff, and provided with an enriched, stimulating environment in which to establish new relationships and interests. The aim was to bring about 'real changes in the boys' personalities' (p. 125) which it was believed would reduce hostility and the consequent impulse to steal and commit other aggressive acts.

The therapeutic approach to delinquency led to a general understanding of delinquency as a personality disorder in need of 'treatment'. This led to some almost hysterical reactions on the part of observers who feared that the fabric of society would be undermined if the theories of these psychologists and social scientists were allowed to undermine the rigours of the law: justice, it seemed, would not be permitted to take its due course because criminals would be mistakenly perceived not to have acted freely, but out of some neurotic compulsion. Daniel Robinson, as recently as 1980, expressed this anxiety in the subtitle to his book on psychology and law: *Can justice survive the social sciences?*

We can answer that 'justice' has, indeed, survived, one reason being that 'treatment' has not been shown to reduce delinquency, whatever its effects on personality might be. Shireman and Reaver (1986), for example, conclude in a sympathetic review of rehabilitation programmes in delinquency that not only have treatment programmes failed in general, but that we have no idea which youngsters will respond well or badly to those programmes. They say that

> this situation seems likely to continue unchanged in the foreseeable future. Through careful research and experimentation we may be able to improve our ability to calculate rough chances that some as yet only vaguely defined types of youngster may succeed or fail. We may become able to define more accurately at least the grosser program elements that lead to success or failure. But prediction on an individual basis in all probability will remain a chimera. (Shireman and Reaver, 1986, p. 93)

Joan McCord, who initiated the well-known Cambridge–Somerville delinquency treatment programme in the 1950s, has recently echoed this conclusion (McCord, 1990). The Cambridge–Somerville programme (McCord and McCord, 1959) aimed to assist delinquency-prone young boys and their families over an extended period of time. Some thirty to forty years later, she concludes:

> The evidence [now] seems to show not only that the treatment programme failed but also that those who provided treatment and those who received it were not good judges of its effects. Although the program was evaluated by recipients of the treatment as beneficial, objective evidence indicated that it was harmful. (McCord, 1990, p. 21)

It goes without saying that the failure of therapy to 'cure' delinquency does not in any way diminish the importance or truth of the finding that many delinquents need psychological treatment of some kind. So, perhaps, do many non-delinquent children.

Other writers have maintained more simply that delinquents have (normal) personalities which may predispose them to delinquency. The search for such attributes has proved tantalizingly elusive (Wilson and Herrnstein, 1985). Farrington (1990) suggests that we might make an exception for 'intelligence' and related cognitive skills. Longitudinal studies have recently shown that a modest relationship exists between self-report measures of delinquency and intelligence which confirm findings that apprehended delinquents average out at slightly below the national average for intelligence (West and Farrington, 1973). Farrington (1990) suggests that a lack of ability to think abstractly may encourage criminal behaviour for two reasons: it prevents the consequences of offending from being anticipated, and it diminishes the capacity to empathize with the feelings and responses of victims. Recent work (Moffitt and Silva, 1988) has indicated that the negative association between delinquency and intelligence is independent of police success in capturing the less well intellectually endowed boys. The association holds also for self-reported delinquents who have had no contact with the police. It is, of course, entirely feasible that the higher the intelligence the less likely are boys to admit to their delinquencies.

Are delinquents difficult to socialize?

Perhaps the most persuasive case for the idea that delinquency is facilitated by the possession of certain normal personality characteristics has been made by Hans Eysenck (see Eysenck, 1964) and later by Hans and Sybil Eysenck (e.g. Eysenck and Eysenck, 1978). Eysenck's theory as stated in the first (1964) edition of *Crime and Personality*, and in other articles (e.g. Eysenck, 1960) emphasized the role of learning in the prevention of criminal behaviour. We do not learn to commit crimes; we learn to avoid crime. It is in the nature of people to be acquisitive and to combat those who frustrate us, but we have to learn to inhibit our immediate desires, and instead to pursue longer-term goals that are socially acceptable.

One implication of this plausible view is that the quality of supervision and training by parents and other carers will be of some significance in the prevention of crime. There is, in fact, an abundance of evidence to that effect. What impressed Eysenck, however, was the possibility that certain personality characteristics might make some people more resistant to discipline than others, and that people possessing such personality characteristics might be more likely to break the law and become delinquent than their more amenable counterparts.

Eysenck's theory of personality emphasizes the importance of dimensions of personality which are said to have a biological basis. Extraversion–introversion is one such dimension. The cerebral cortex of the brain in people on the extraverted side of this dimension (rather than the introverted side) is said to be 'under-aroused' for optimal functioning. Extraverts are likely, therefore, to seek out stimulation from the environment in order to establish and maintain an optimum level of arousal. Introverts have no such need. This biological difference is said to underlie the differences in social behaviour between extraverts and introverts, the impulsive and sensation-seeking individual on the one hand, and the reserved character on the other. A further consequence of the differences in cortical arousal is that extraverts are predicted to 'condition' (in Pavlovian terms) less well than introverts, and it is this bio-social consequence that led Eysenck to believe that extraverts would be over-represented in criminal populations, i.e. amongst people who take what they want and do what they want without regard for the societal consequences. Being difficult to condition, extraverts are said not to acquire those conditional anxiety-avoidance responses which form the basis of 'conscience'. Extraverts, in short, are less likely to feel anxious when contemplating or embarking upon a criminal act.

The theory is tidy, but the empirical findings are not straight-forward. A recent review by Hollin (1989) concludes, 'some studies reported high E [extraversion] scores as predicted in offender samples, others found no difference between offender and non-offender samples, and a small number of studies reported *lower* scores in offender groups' (p. 56). The theory has become more complex particularly in order to accommodate the empirical evidence, but also in acknowledgement of a possible oversimpli-fication in the concentration on only one dimension of personality. For example, unstable people who score highly on N (neuroticism) are said to possess an autonomic nervous system that responds strongly to painful and aversive stimuli. Clearly this might have some effect on the 'efficiency' of conditioning, an argument developed by Feldman (1977) in his influential analysis of Eysenck's theory. Eysenck and Eysenck (1978) have argued that neurotic extraverts would be especially well represented in criminal populations. In practice, 'N' has been found more consistently to be associated with criminality than either 'E' or 'N plus E' (Farrington et al., 1982), when criminal populations have been compared with control groups.

The fact that questionnaire tests of personality do not distinguish as predicted between convicted criminals and the non-convicted population is a drawback for the theory, but does not necessarily invalidate it. Responses to questionnaires measure the conditionability of people indirectly, and are greatly influenced by uncontrollable attitudinal factors derived from experience.

Two other lines of enquiry, however, have produced evidence that makes it hard to entertain even greatly modified versions of the theory. The first relates to the notion of conditionability, and the second to longitudinal studies of the relationship between personality and delinquency. Using measures of physiological conditionability enables the biological hypothesis to be tested *directly*. Are criminals in fact less conditionable than non-criminals? More generally, are poorly socialized people less conditionable? Raine and Venables (1981) studied over 100 15-year-old boys, and measured their level of socialization using, on the one hand, various questionnaire measures of socialization and of psychopathic behaviour and, on the other hand, ratings by teachers of their pupils' destructiveness, swearing, disobedience and fighting. Various personality tests were also completed by the participants. Altogether 18 scales were used to derive mathematically a general socialization factor. Conditionability was assessed using three measure of skin conductance conditioning which it was believed would 'favour' introverts and on which extraverts would 'condition poorly' (Raine and Venables, 1981, p. 277). The results were unsupportive. Socialization scores were not consistently related to physiological measures of conditionability, and the one significant result that did emerge suggested 'if anything that undersocialized individuals conditioned better than socialized individuals' (Raine and Venables, 1981, p. 279). A *post-hoc* analysis revealed, contrary to prediction, a greater difference in conditionability between 'pro-social' and 'anti-social' children in the lower class than the higher social class groups. Unfortunately, the difference suggested that pro-social children conditioned *less* easily than anti-social children. This carefully conducted study contributed further to the bleak picture created by previous attempts to test the conditionability hypothesis.

Comparatively few studies have investigated delinquency longitudinally, starting with a randomly selected but representative group of youngsters, and following them up to see which factors are predictive of delinquency. One study did just that. West and Farrington (1973) reported that at ages 10, 14 and 16, those boys who had been convicted were equal to those in the sample who were not convicted in E, N and 'N plus E'. A later analysis (Farrington et al., 1982) included an analysis of criminality when the boys had become adults, and the picture did not change. Indeed, an item by item analysis of the questionnaire scores indicated that the number of items significantly related to official delinquency at any developmental stage did not exceed chance expectation.

A third dimension – Psychoticism (P) – has more recently been added to E and N in Eysenckian assessment of personality. Scores on P are generally higher in delinquent than in non-delinquent groups. However, the meaning of P and its supposed genetic basis is highly debatable, as reviews by Howarth (1986) and Hollin (1989) both indicate, and its reliability and homogeneity is extremely low (Farrington et al., 1982). Moreover the P scale was constructed using psychopathic and criminal as well as psychotic criterion groups, so it is no surprise that criminals should score highly on the scale. It should also be pointed out that the association, or otherwise, of 'P' with criminality has no bearing whatsoever on the logic and status of Eysenck's long-standing theory of crime as a characteristic of relatively unconditionable persons. Nonetheless, the style of thinking that characterizes 'P', and which is apparently endorsed by criminals, is of considerable interest, and raises questions to which we shall return later in this chapter.

Criminality as a behavioural trait

The search for characteristics that set the delinquent apart from others seems to have proved abortive, but perhaps there were good reasons for initiating the search. Not everyone falls foul of the criminal law, whereas others seem to do so with remarkable regularity. There appears, in other words, to be some consistency about criminal behaviour which demands an explanation. How consistently do people commit crime or, alternatively, go straight? Is delinquency or criminality a behavioural tendency like, say, the tendency to take exercise, something of which relatively few people make a serious occupation – and a few others never even contemplate – but which may characterize the great majority on occasion, with varying degrees of frequency and of seriousness? Although criminals may not have distinctive personality characteristics, nevertheless it may be the case that criminality itself is consistently more a feature of some people than of others.

West and Farrington's longitudinal study (1973) has yielded a number of important and relevant findings which confirm the general thrust of research on this topic (see also Gottfredson and Hirschi, 1988). More than 400 boys aged eight attending six state primary schools in a working class area of London have been investigated into their thirties. Great efforts have been made to maintain contact. All were eventually located at age 32, although eight had died, and 20 had emigrated. Altogether 94 per cent of the total sample were followed up to the age of 32.

There are three aspects of the results of this study (Farrington and West, 1990) that I wish to emphasise: (i) criminality is consistently manifested in time; (ii) it is versatile not specialized; and (iii) it is associated generally with anti-social attitudes. These findings do suggest that there is, indeed, a criminal personality of sorts, albeit not allied to a set of distinctive personality characteristics. Let us briefly describe the evidence for the three conclusions stated above.

Criminality is consistent over time. It is the fond hope of the courts, probation officers, parents and social workers, and maybe of the juveniles themselves, that the first offence will not lead to a second, the second to a third and so on. Punishments, probation, cautions will surely be effective in encouraging desistance or reform. The picture is not so rosy. Whilst it is certainly not the case that first offenders will always re-offend, and whilst new offenders are always emerging from the pool of previous non-offenders, it is nonetheless the case that offending at one age is best predicted by offending at the preceding age. Of those convicted as juveniles (age 10–16) 75 per cent were reconvicted between the ages of 17 and 24, and nearly 50 per cent of the juvenile offenders were reconvicted at age 25 and 32. Those convicted early tend to become the most persistent offenders, a finding that has been confirmed in other studies (e.g. Cambridge–Somerville study, McCord, 1990). In case it might be thought that attention from the police is a factor in these findings, Farrington (1989) indicates that delinquency self-report studies support the same conclusion as do the official statistics.

Criminality is versatile, a point previously well made by Eysenck (1964). Although we tend to think in terms of 'the burglar', 'the rapist', 'the swindler', 'the drug offender', the 'drunk driver' and so on, and probably have more or less detailed images or stereotypes of each, the evidence for specialization is not strong, especially in the late teenage years. Consider the offence of drink-driving. A study by Argeriou et al. (1985) found that in a large randomly selected sample of persons convicted of drunk driving in Massachusetts, more than three-quarters had previously appeared in court, and more than half had been arraigned for non-traffic and non-drink-driving-related offences. Those who steal and commit burglary are pretty much the same people as those who engage in violence, vandalism and drug abuse, who drink excessively, drive recklessly and commit sexual offences. Evidence for this comes from the official statistics and from the self-reports of offenders in the London study (see Farrington and West, 1990). Confirmation of this finding also comes from many other studies. For example, Farrington et al. (1988) report from a large-scale statistical study of 70,000 offenders in the United States that although there is a small degree of specialization, and that this becomes more evident over time, the bulk of offending (in 80 per cent of offenders) is best described as 'versatile'.

Offending is also part of a more general anti-social syndrome. The most serious offenders at each age in the London study were deviant in other respects. At age 18, for example, offenders drank and smoked more, gambled more, had been injured in road accidents, admitted to drinking and driving, had more sex with more partners, used drugs more, and fought more than did the non-convicted 18-year-olds. Of 110 18-year-old males diagnosed as anti-social on non-criminal criteria, 70 per cent were convicted up to the age of 20. This anti-social tendency persists into adulthood. By age 32, 37 per cent of the men had been convicted of criminal offences, and they were consistently more deviant in other ways – more often divorced or separated, more often involved in fights, were heavy drinkers and drug takers, and more likely to steal from work, besides being more likely unemployed, less likely a home-owner and spending more evenings out.

Criminal careers?

The fact remains that the degree to which one is criminally inclined appears to remain fairly constant over time and has led a number of criminologists to encourage the idea that prospective 'hard-core' offenders can be identified at an early age – age six was mooted in a recent *Independent* report (Davies and Crequer, 1991) – and then 'incapacitated' or otherwise treated to prevent the development of subsequent criminal careers.

Blumstein et al. (1985) gave substance to the idea that criminality (or delinquency) could be regarded as a career that attracted some children permanently, others temporarily, and yet others not at all. The *innocents* are never tempted into crime, the *desisters* start on a criminal career but give it up, whilst their comrades, the *persisters*, also start, but continue indefinitely. Of course, it is the potential *persisters* who would be the target of treatment or prevention programmes, projects given some point by figures indicating that, for example 6 per cent of boys born in Philadelphia in 1945 were responsible for 52 per cent of that cohort's arrests (Wolfgang et al., 1972). More recently, Farrington and Hawkins (1991) have suggested that the factors leading to participation in crime before age 20 are different from those that lead to early participation (ages 10–13), and that participation in crime as an adult (21+) has yet another distinct set of predictors.

The finding that different factors are associated with offending at different ages does not, of course, prove that offenders, dissenters and persisters are different types of character. Alternatives to the 'criminal career' viewpoint have been proposed, for example by Gottfredson and Hirschi (1988) and by Rowe et al. (1990), which suggest more parsimoniously that the data we have on participation rates of offending in cohort studies indicate the need to postulate the existence of a latent trait which predisposes people to criminal behaviour. We may describe this trait neutrally, statistically even, in terms say of crime proneness, but the important point is that at no point is there a cut-off between criminals and non-criminals. Even amongst the apparently innocent we must suppose that there are those who are more likely to begin a criminal career than others, and even amongst the persisters there are those who are more likely than others to desist. There is, in other words, a continuum from the most boringly law-abiding at one extreme to the incorrigibly villainous at the other. What we must look for, on this view, is not why some people are villains but what are the causes of villainy, albeit manifested to different degrees as one surveys the continuum from 'innocence' to 'persistence'.

But do criminals think differently?

The idea that criminals have different thinking patterns has been promulgated with enthusiasm (see for example Hampson, 1982) following the description of how treatment may address the problem of how to change 'errors' of thinking (Yochelson and Samenow, 1977). The idea that there is a sub-class of criminals called psychopaths whose offences arise naturally from their affectionless, shameless and remorseless character has been around for a long time, and continues in psychiatric formulations of so-called character disorders. However, it is clear from Samenow's account (1984) that proponents of the criminal mind see criminals *generally* as being prey, through faulty social learning, to faulty ways of thinking which directly cause them to behave in criminal ways. The essential argument is that criminals unrealistically perceive the world as an arena for their self-indulgence, thereby failing to acknowledge either others' rights or their own responsibilities. As Samenow (1984) puts it:

> Despite a multitude of differences in their backgrounds and crime patterns, criminals are alike in one way: *how they think*. A gun-toting, uneducated criminal off the streets ... and a crooked ... business executive are extremely similar in their view of themselves and the world. This is not to deny individual differences among criminals ... But all regard the world as a chessboard over which they have total control, and they perceive people as pawns to be pushed around at will. (p. 20)

Gacono and Meloy (1988) see close parallels between the cognitive style of the criminal as defined by Yochelson and Samenow and classical formulations of the psychopathic personality. What is new is the optimism about the possibility of changing basic thinking patterns (see Finckenbauer and Kochis, 1984; Launay and Murray, 1989).

Way back in 1942, Hathaway and McKinley published the Minnesota Multiphasic Personality Inventory (MMPI), still a diagnostic test widely used in research and clinical practice. One scale was the Psychopathic Deviate (Pd) scale, on which psychiatrically diagnosed psychopaths tend to score high. Cynical disregard for others' feelings bordering on the criminal is a characteristic of many items. For example, 'When someone does me wrong I feel I should pay him back if I can, just for the principle of the thing', and 'I don't blame anyone for trying to grab everything he can in this world' are typically endorsed by psychopaths. Unfortunately, such items are also endorsed by people who have not earned the psychopathic diagnosis, and it is necessary for psychiatric diagnosticians to develop quite a complex profile of scores on different scales if false alarms are to be kept to reasonable proportions (Spielberger et al., 1978). Nevertheless, some of the cynicism characterizing items of the Pd scale is evident and central both in Yochelson and Samenow's formulations, and in subsequent scales, high scores on which have been associated with criminality (see Gudjonsson, 1984). Eysenck's Psychoticism scale is a good example. This scale was developed in part by comparing the responses of prisoners and non-prisoners, and subsequent studies have shown differences in the responses of delinquents and non-delinquents. Delinquents are more likely to answer positively, for example, the questions, 'Do your friendships break up easily without it being your fault?' and 'Do people tell you a lot of lies?'; they are more likely to believe that there is 'someone else who is to blame for most of your problems', and that they 'have had more trouble than most', and that they 'enjoying hurting people you love' (Farrington et al., 1982).

This tendency to blame the world for their problems, to believe, as prisoners do seem to believe, that they have 'had an awful lot of bad luck' as well as 'having had more trouble than most', may well be a reasonable enough response to their circumstances, or at any rate, a means of plausibly rationalizing their experiences (see Farrington et al., 1982, pp 165–6). As social psychologists and sociologists have been pointing out assiduously for many years now, human beings are more *rationalizing* than they are rational and it makes much sense to suppose that the thinking patterns that characterize the criminal personality serve to justify their behaviour to themselves and others. Sykes and Matza (1957), for example, suggested that delinquents 'neutralize' their guilt feelings by finding excuses and justifications for their behaviour, and subsequent studies have provided evidence for such processes (e.g. Mitchell and Dodder, 1983). Neutralization is said to comprise a number of processes: denial of responsibility and denial of injury to a victim, a condemnation of those who would (hypocritically) condemn the criminal, and also what might be termed a glorification of crime. Mitchell et al. (1990) in a study of 694 college students found that agreement with statements reflecting these various processes explained a substantial degree of variance in self-reported delinquency (about 25 per cent), considerably more than did association with delinquent peers (about 5 per cent) or church attendance (no effect). The pattern was broadly similar for men and women, and for different sub-cultural groups. Furthermore, over time, the justification employed to explain past delinquency may subsequently be used to consolidate delinquent tendencies (e.g. Minor, 1984; Thurman, 1984), neutralization being employed in an anticipatory way to justify future, intended deviation (Dodder and Hughes, 1987).

Launay (1987) described a victim–offender reconciliation scheme which aimed 'to deter offenders by confronting them with the human consequences of crime and by challenging the excuses they use to justify their criminal behaviour' (p. 280). He set this work in the context of a more general move in England towards therapies which launch a direct attack on what Yochelson and Samenow described as the errors in criminal thinking patterns. In the context of those bilateral meetings, statements were made by offenders (burglars) justifying and excusing their involvement in crime, and denying the notion that victims were harmed. A so-called JUDEX scale was constructed consisting of Justification (e.g. 'Rich people can afford to be robbed of their possessions'), Excuses (e.g. 'In some neighbourhoods you have to break the law to survive'), and Denials (e.g. 'Most of what people call crime does not harm anyone'). A factor analysis of the full scale (44 items) revealed two subscales of seven DE (Denial that crime hurts) items, and ten JUX (justifications and excuses for crime) items (Launay and Murray, 1989).

Whilst it is no surprise that convicted and incarcerated criminals and delinquents will produce and endorse such denials and justifications, and endorse them to a greater extent than non-convicted

Table 1.1 University students' endorsement of justifications and excuses for crime made by young burglars

JUX (Justification/excuses) sub-scale	Males (N = 91) %	Females (N = 91) %
You can see why young people are driven to crime when there are dishonest policemen	16	12
It is understandable that people should steal from a shopkeeper who overcharges his customers	20	10
It would be foolish to stay honest when everyone else is 'on the fiddle'	14	8
In some neighbourhoods you have to break the law to survive	44	37
Even if he/she comes from a bad area with lots of crime, a youth should still feel totally responsible for his/her criminal behaviour [−ve]	20	20
You can't blame young people with nothing to do, to fill their time by turning to crime	23	9
In this country nobody is so poor that they have to steal [−ve]	59	55
Rich people can afford to be robbed of some of their possessions	39	23
It is only fair when a poor person steals from a rich person	14	3
Even rich people suffer when they are burgled [−ve]	3	1

Source: Pennock, 1988

people, it would clearly be useful to demonstrate that such thinking patterns are also prevalent in non-convicted, 'normal' populations, and linked closely to the practice of criminal *behaviour* in a normal sample. Pennock (1988) obtained responses to JUDEX from 91 male and 91 female university students, and also obtained self-report measures of delinquency from the same students in the context of what purported to be a different study, using a self-report scale devised (for use by university students) by Renwick and Emler (1984). There was a positive association between self-reported delinquency and JUDEX scores ($r = 0.5$, males and females combined), especially for males and especially for the Justification/ Excuses sub-scale. For example, some 30 per cent of the variance in acceptance of the justifications listed in table 1.1 was explained by the number of delinquent acts endorsed. It is apparent that the excuses and justifications made by incarcerated young burglars are familiar enough to university students, both male and female, and that endorsement of those items by University students is strongly indicative of past delinquent activity.

Summary and conclusion

Being criminally active is associated with a strong tendency to justify and excuse criminal behaviour. This is most plausibly accounted for by assuming that when people behave criminally or even merely when they intend to, they seek to rationalize their behaviour in ways which preserve their integrity as moral and socially acceptable beings. We have seen that there is little evidence that delinquents and criminals have distinctive personalities which render them criminal or even necessarily incline them to criminality. On the other hand, the tendency to commit crimes does seem to be a characteristic that is more or less consistently expressed over time, with little evidence for significant specialization in one type of crime or another. Besides the development of characteristic modes of thinking that justify and excuse past, and future, criminal behaviour, the criminal tendency is also associated with the more general expression of anti-social attitudes. Evidence suggests that it is unprofitable to seek to divide the population into criminals and non-criminals, or even to sub-divide criminals into those who persist, those who desist and the like. Criminal decision-making is a foregone conclusion in no one case, and can never be ruled out of another.

We shall explore in subsequent chapters (3 and 4) what causes people to choose criminal options, but in the next chapter we shall broach directly an issue that cannot be evaded in any discussion of criminal justice from a psychological perspective: the relationship between criminality and morality. Those who commit criminal acts may seek to deflect blame from themselves; but are they morally immature?

2

Are Criminals Morally Immature?

There is no hard evidence that traits associated with moral character – moral values, superego strength, capacity for remorse, and so on – are especially deficient in law-breakers. People certainly vary in such characteristics, but criminals are not uniquely feckless in character. Nevertheless, it seems that criminals do reason differently about crime, in a way that many would see as being irresponsible if not wicked. Crime is rationalized as essentially harmless and victimless, justifiable in the context of unequal distribution of wealth, and so on. Such rationalizations may serve initially to justify crime after the event, but may also become in time a motive for continued criminal activity, and thereby indicate at best irresponsibility and at worst a criminally wicked mind. Such an outcome is no doubt on the cards, and does happen, but equally criminals may reform (indeed, most of them do) and non-criminals may follow a similar path to degeneracy – as layabouts, adulterers and bullies, to name but three objectionable conditions.

Despite such objections, it may still plausibly be maintained first, that criminal activity must undermine moral values and second, that highly principled and conscientious people are less likely to be drawn into criminal activities in the first place. We should expect that there would exist a strong correlation between moral reasoning on the one hand, and moral conduct on the other, as exemplified by law-abiding behaviour, and in resistance to those criminal acts which most clearly indicate an unwillingness to fulfil moral obligations.

In the last twenty years or so, a great deal of work has investigated the development of moral reasoning in children and adults, and there is a growing number of studies that have examined the relationship between moral maturity and action. There have also been many social psychological studies which in different ways have explored the situational factors that underlie not only moral behaviour but also the exercise of moral judgement and reasoning. Before describing that work I want briefly to set the stage by describing how legal philosophers and commentators have discussed the formal relationship between law and morality. What they have to say has parallels with the approaches of different psychologists, not surprisingly in that underlying both endeavours is the concern to elucidate the moral basis of rules of conduct, societal in the one case, individual in the other.

Views of the relationship between law and morality

On one view, the law proscribes what ordinary, decent people regard as intolerable behaviour. Clarkson and Keating (1984) quote Lord Devlin as an exponent of this view. What he calls a 'real feeling of reprobation' justifies legal prohibition and criminal sanctions:

> I do not think one can ignore disgust if it is deeply felt and not manufactured. Its presence is a good indication that the bounds of toleration are being reached. (p. 62)

On this view law merely reflects conventional moral standards. Essentially, it reacts to public opinion, seeking neither to lead public opinion nor to lag too far behind. One rather obvious problem with this view is that different sections of the community vary in their views of what behaviour they find unacceptable. Many people find Salman Rushdie's *Satanic Verses* deeply offensive, but many more do not. How intolerable to how many people does a behaviour have to become before the law should step in?

One implication of this view is that the public should have a real say in defining what behaviour should be outlawed. This has its attractions. There are probably many discrepancies between legislators' and the public's views of what should be prohibited and penalized in many domains of activity. For example, there are moves to harmonize criminal legislation across Europe which could well heed public opinion. I.D. Brown (1975) reported data which showed that there was a relatively low correlation (only 0.41) between proposed EEC classifications of the seriousness of offences and the general public's views. One marked discrepancy was between the bureaucratic view that driving without a licence for a vehicle should carry the heaviest penalty of all, and the public's rating of such an offence as trivial. Such discrepancies are disturbing, and lend support to Wilkins' view (1984) that law, and the discipline of criminology itself, should become more oriented towards the consumer, investigating public opinion, not presupposing it.

Another problem with the approach to law via conventional morality, is that many laws are essentially administrative and can hardly be justified in terms of existing moral standards or precepts. They are there to be obeyed merely because they have been enacted. Forgetting to renew a vehicle licence may inconvenience the tax authorities and is duly regarded as an act deserving punishment. It is, however, not regarded as an act of great wickedness by the public at large. Clearly there are many procedural requirements demanded of citizens by their government which people generally accept should compel obedience to the same extent as laws seeking to enforce conventional moral standards. Indeed, there are those in the positivist tradition who argue strongly that law and morality are, or should be, regarded as strictly independent one of the other. Hart (quoted in Clarkson and Keating, 1984) argues forcibly that conventional morality is too subject to fashion, and is too controversial and changing a notion to be a basis for law-making. Harm done should be the criterion for illegality, and laws which when enforced cause more harm than they prevent cannot be justified on moral grounds alone e.g. forbidding male homosexual relations.

Fletcher (1987) outlines a third tradition that rejects both harm done and public repugnance as a basis for proscribing behaviour. On this view laws, to be valid, must legislate for good; the law is, or should be a constructive force in society, pursuing ideals of social organization. This view puts individual conscience above the law, and suggests that the law itself is subject to principled evaluation by its citizens. Laws are valid not by virtue of being validly enacted, as the positivists would argue, nor because they embrace conventional moral standards, but by virtue of the quality of their social justification. The problem with this view would seem to be the lack of agreement on what principles should prevail, of what is for 'good' – the state's welfare, the protection of freedom, the pursuit of social justice, or whatever.

Echoes of the debates that might ensue between representatives of these viewpoints are found in the psychological literature on moral judgement and reasoning, and to this we now turn.

Morality as conformity: the psychology of conservatism

Resistance to change and intolerance of deviation is the hallmark of the so-called authoritarian personality. Although the notion of a distinct personality type whose psychodynamics are rooted in a repressed and unhappy childhood is one which has lost favour for lack of hard evidence (R. Brown, 1965), the finding that conservative attitudes – respect for authority and law, resistance to change, distrust of foreigners, and so on – are an important organizing principle in people's lives has received abundant confirmation. Wilson (1973) argues that fear of uncertainty is a prevailing concern of all of us, and that there is an inexorable tendency towards conservatism and the maintenance of those existing structures which hold out the promise of a predictable and secure future. Factors which create fear of uncertainty – e.g. death, deviance and innovation – encourage generally conservative attitudes towards life, like a rigid morality, and adherence to external authority.

Wilson conceives of conservatism as a general factor underlying the entire field of social attitudes, much the same as intelligence is conceived as a general factor which determines abilities in different areas. Of course, law and morality both prototypically reduce the uncertainty which fuels conservatism, and are rewarding for that reason. They serve the same ends and are functionally linked one with another, a point well made by M.E. Smith (1988) in a quite different cultural context when he describes the techniques used by Pueblo Indians to bring deviants back into line.

Deviation threatens not merely the group's agreement on a particular issue at any given time, deviation is a threat because it may attract followers, become a movement and divert or thwart the achievement of group goals. Many studies have shown how readily individuals conform to the views and will of the majority, as in the pioneering studies of Solomon Asch (1951) which demonstrated that individuals faced by unanimous group decision will deny the evidence of their own senses. More importantly, subsequent work has demonstrated that a majority can be converted by a single individual deviant, and that conversion under such circumstances is more profound and long lasting than the conformity which is the product of majority influence (Moscovici and Nemeth, 1974; R.J. Brown, 1988). When they are effective, minorities are very effective. Their authority must be undermined, their isolation exposed, and their rejection clearly signalled if radical change is to be averted because the very forces towards conformity which successfully resist change can at once be mobilized in the interests of establishing new beliefs as new orthodoxies.

However, conformity is hardly an unmitigated good either when resisting or facilitating change. Atrocities committed in this century by administrators, public servants, soldiers and citizens have frequently been justified by the fact that they were committed in obedience to orders given by a legitimate authority. Kelman and Hamilton (1989) discuss how it is that moral principles can be so readily ignored in such circumstances, a good recent example being the actions of East German border guards shooting down unarmed fellow citizens crossing to the West, an act of obedience for which ex-guards now face prosecution for manslaughter. Why do people think it right to obey immoral orders?

Kelman and Hamilton's answer is important because it is based on evidence from two large surveys of public opinion in the United States following the My Lai massacre in the Vietnam War and the subsequent trial of Lt. Calley. The results certainly demonstrated respect for authority. When asked if they would emulate Lt. Calley by shooting (in response to orders) all the men, women and children of a village whose inhabitants had been alleged to have helped the enemy, a majority of US adults said they would do so. Only 35 per cent thought that Lt. Calley should have been brought to trial. The importance of the findings, however, is less in the documentation of respect for legitimate authority than for their explanation of why people choose to obey, or disobey, immoral orders. Their results suggest that those who support obedience do so either because they are *rule oriented* and respect the power of authority, or because they are *role oriented* and respect the legitimacy of authority. Those who advocate disobedience, on the other hand, predominantly have a *value* orientation; their principles would prescribe disobedience, in defiance of both 'rules' and 'roles'. See table 2.1.

Two important questions arise from this analysis. The first concerns the question of the relation between moral thought and behaviour. Are those individuals with a value orientation truly the

Table 2.1   Rules, roles and values in orientation to authority

Rule Orientation:	Pragmatic obedience e.g. 'If you have doubts about an official order, the best thing is to do what is required of you, so you will stay out of trouble.'
Role Orientation:	Loyal obedience e.g. 'I feel an obligation to support the government even when its policies disagree with my values.'
Value Orientation:	Critical support e.g. 'The most valuable contribution an individual citizen can make is to maintain an active and questioning approach towards government policies.'

Source: After Kelman and Hamilton, 1989

most likely to disobey immoral orders? That is a question we shall try to deal with later in this chapter. The second question concerns the origins of these orientations. The authors suggest that the different orientations represent different levels of 'integration' into society, these levels being *compliance, identification* and *internalization* respectively. At the level of compliance, an immoral order is obeyed because punishment is the consequence of disobedience. At the level of identification, the order is obeyed because obedience is proper. For internalizers, on the other hand an overarching principle – the good of society – may require disobedience. These three 'levels' are strikingly reminiscent of the levels of moral reasoning that psychologists have suggested form a developmental sequence from childhood into adolescence and adulthood. We shall examine that work now.

The development of moral and legal judgement

The average child's knowledge of law and of the operation of the legal and governmental systems is rudimentary until the age of about 13 (Adelson and O'Neil, 1966; Gallatin and Adelson, 1971; Saywitz et al., 1990). This is partly because young children do not generally evaluate or criticize social arrangements in abstract terms (see Dickinson & Emler, 1992), and hence have little incentive for curiosity about how the system works. It may also be that legal and political education is not undertaken in a systematic way in countries where these issues have been studied. That differences between countries do exist is evident from Emler et al.'s (1987) report that French children show a somewhat more deferential attitude towards the exercise of authority by teachers than do Scottish children. Young children do, however, soon come to believe that there is a source of law and order, and a definition of what ought to be, that lies outside themselves. Even the rules of a game for young children have something of an external, even sacred character; the letter of the law must be ritualistically obeyed. According to Piaget (1932) the young child's morality is based essentially upon a sense of lawfulness. It is a morality of constraint in which the unilateral respect of the child for the adult leads to a definition of goodness in terms of obedience.

Piaget believes that it is the child's social relations with adults, based on authority and unilateral dependence, that determines this form of morality, and that it is subsequently the pressure of demands for co-operation with peers that leads to change from the morality of constraint, based on obedience to a morality of co-operation based on reciprocity. What is right and good reflects what is agreeable, and an obligation to stick to the rules follows from shared commitment to co-operative activity. Of course Piaget knew well, as we all know, that the morality of constraint does not disappear as soon as the ability to co-operate is achieved. Adults and schoolteachers continue to exercise authority, as later do employers, and so all along does parliament and should they be required, the police and the judiciary. Indeed, as we noted earlier, conservatism tightens its grip as people grow older. The two moralities of constraint and co-operation seem destined to coexist uneasily in most of us.

Whereas Piaget concentrated on the distinctive modes of thought of the child, his conclusions were based on behavioural observations for the most part. Lawrence Kohlberg (1981) on the other hand (see also Colby, 1983) has looked more abstractly at the question of how we change the way in which we justify our actions as we grow older. He discerned three levels, the first two of which are akin to Piaget's moralities of constraint and co-operation. In the pre-conventional level (stages 1 and 2) we justify our conduct in terms of avoidance of punishment, or achieving practical goals. At

Table 2.2 Kohlberg's six developmental stages of moral judgement

---

Level I: Premoral
  Type 1   Punishment and obedience orientation
  Type 2   Naive instrumental hedonism

Level II: Morality of conventional role-conformity
  Type 3   Good-boy/girl morality or maintaining good relations,
           approval of others
  Type 4   Authority-maintaining morality

Level III: Morality of self-accepted moral principles
  Type 5   Morality of contract, of individual rights, and of
           democratically accepted law
  Type 6   Morality of individual principles of conscience

Source: After Kohlberg, 1981

the conventional level (stages 3 and 4) our aim is to achieve interpersonal concordance, social harmony and conformity. The pre-
conventional and conventional levels are roughly equivalent to
Piaget's moralities of constraint and co-operation respectively, and
for good measure we can also note the parallels with Kelman and
Hamilton's (1989) concepts of rule and role orientations. Kohlberg
suggests, however, that there is a higher level (stages 5 and 6), a
post-conventional stage which we might characterize as the morality
of conscience. At that stage, we judge and justify behaviour by
reference to individually held universally applicable principles of
conduct (see table 2.2).

As with those legal philosophers who believe that law should
implement principles of morality, Kohlberg's problem is to define
what these universal principles should be, and indeed he has been
criticized by feminist researchers for adopting a morality of rights
which reflects the views of those (men) who are in a sufficiently
powerful position to demand privileges and grant rights (Gilligan,
1982). We shall return to that issue. For the moment, let us look in
more detail at the way Kohlberg and his followers came to their
conclusions.

Kohlberg devised a number of moral dilemmas in which hypothetical individuals faced difficult decisions, the ethics of which
were not clear-cut. For example, the following was given originally
to American participants in his studies:

In Europe a woman was near death from a special kind of cancer. There was one drug the doctors thought might save her – it was a form of radium that a druggist in the same town had recently discovered. The drug was expensive to make, but the druggist was charging ten times what the drug cost him to make. He paid $200 for the radium and charged $2000 for a small dose of the drug. The sick woman's husband, Heinz, went to everyone he knew to borrow the money but he could only get together about $1000, which was half of what it cost. He told the druggist that his wife was dying and asked him to sell it cheaper or let him pay later, but the druggist said 'No, I discovered the drug and I'm going to make money from it'. Heinz got desperate and broke into the man's store to steal the drug for his wife. Should the husband have done that? (quoted in Brown & Herrnstein, 1975, p. 310)

This kind of dilemma reflects those posed when defendants in criminal trials plead necessity as a justification for their illegal behaviour, as did Dudley and Stephens in a classic case described at length by Simpson (1984) in his book *Cannibalism and the Common Law*. Their crime of killing the cabin boy in order that they might survive after a shipwreck was one that, on the face of it, seemed unlikely to endear them to the English population. However, on their return in 1884, they told their story to the authorities and expected and received a sympathetic hearing from the public, and indeed from the relatives of the unfortunate youth. The crime of killing the dying boy was justified on the grounds that it was *necessary* to take what action they could to save their own lives, in the interests of their families and dependents. In practice, necessity is a rarely used defence, and is rarely successful when it is used, being regarded somewhat as the thin end of the wedge (Dudley and Stephens were convicted of murder despite public support). Lord Denning, for example, saw fit to remark about the defence that squatting was 'necessary' in the case of homeless people: 'If homelessness were once admitted as a defence to trespass, no-one's house would be safe' (quoted in Clarkson and Keating, 1984). In response to Kohlberg's dilemmas, Lord Denning would un-doubtedly have proved himself to be operating at the pre-conventional level.

It is Kohlberg's view that a decision – either to steal the drug or not – can be justified at any one of the three levels, and at any stage. At the conventional level, for example, respect for the rules regardless of special circumstances may justify not stealing, whilst

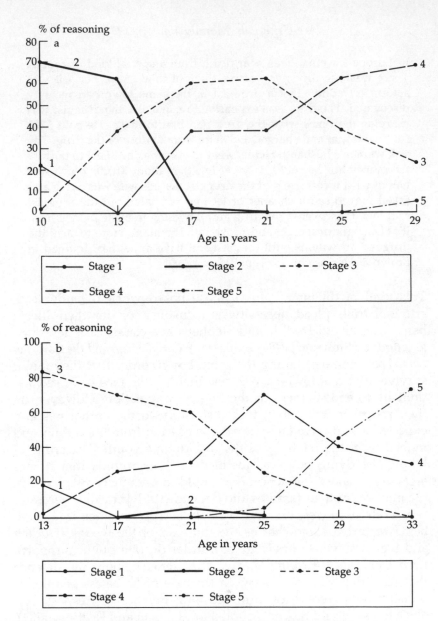

Figure 2.1 Prevalence of different stages of moral reasoning at different ages in two male participants

a Prevalence of moral reasoning at each stage for each age: subject 3 (10 years at time 1)

Source: Colby, 1983

b Percentage of moral reasoning at each stage for each age: subject 37 (13 years at time 1)

Source: Colby, 1983

at the same conventional level, stealing the drug may be justified so long as Heinz is prepared to take his punishment for the crime. Even at the next stage, what we call the morality of conscience, the stage of universal principles, both courses of action may be justified. Preserving life is the highest ideal, and so may justify stealing the drug, whereas stealing the drug may be condemned as potentially unfair because others may need the drug even more than Heinz's wife; not stealing may reflect an ideal concern for justice and not merely respect for the law as such.

The average level of children's reasoning is higher as they grow older, as judged in terms of Kohlberg's scale of six stages (Colby, 1983). This average improvement, however, does not imply that people operate only at one stage, and it disguises considerable variation. A fairly typical result is shown in figure 2.1. This subject was tested six times, starting at the age of 10 and ending at the age of 29. At each age the graph shows the distribution of the subject's moral reasoning between the different stages. Stages 1 and 2, i.e. pre-conventional reasoning, characterize his 10-year-old performance, whereas conventional stages 4 and 3 characterize his 29-year-old adult performance. Post-conventional reasoning is comparatively rare even in adults, and where it does occur it is mostly at stage 5. In figure 2.1(b) the development of another subject's reasoning is portrayed, where the outcome at age 33 is a division between stages 4 and 5, with stage 5 reasoning predominant. The average picture as previously suggested by cross-sectional data has been confirmed by the longitudinal studies reported by Colby. Stages 1 and 2 reasoning steadily decrease with age as stage 3 reasoning increases; as the prevalence of stage 3 reasoning declines, so stage 4 rises steadily to dominate the scene in adulthood, with post-conventional reasoning playing a minor role in most people. Morality for most people is a conventional social morality. When we support others – individually or collectively – we behave morally: role conformity *is* morality for the majority of people.

Legal socialization

Tapp and Kohlberg (1971) coined the term legal socialization as a shorthand for what they imagined was both a descriptive and prescriptive view of the development of the child through the stages

Table 2.3 Example of Tapp and Kohlberg's levels of legal socialization

Question	Level 1 Answers	Level 2 Answers	Level 3 Answers
What if there were no rules?	Laws prevent physical harm, stop crimes and secure physical necessities.	Laws restrain the bad, and guide morals. Promote personal control over greed.	Behaviour is guided by principles; laws are distinguished from moral principles.

Source: After Tapp and Kohlberg, 1971

of moral development. They asked a large sample of boys to state what they thought the purpose was of rules and laws, and had no difficulty classifying answers in terms of Kohlberg's three main levels of development. Table 2.3 briefly describes the quality of answers to the question, What if there were no rules?. Echoes of Piaget's morality of constraint are found in the characteristics of reasoning at level 1. Laws are immutable and must be obeyed because they exist and are backed by the threat of punishment. At level 1, there is a rule-obeying perspective, but at level 2 the child or the adult is concerned that the rule should be maintained in the interests of restraining potential offenders and promoting good order. In the post-conventional stage, however, we are led to challenge the existing order, and to judge it in terms of abstract principles of morality. The authors assume that a stage by stage progression is desirable and ask 'what procedures seem key or instrumental in moving individuals toward principled legal development?' (p. 85). They recommend opportunities for role playing and participation in conflict resolution in family, school, legal, and non-legal institutions, and they assert, without much evidence, that 'interaction with just socialising agents in both the school and legal systems – the teacher and the policeman, the principal and the judge – is crucial to legal development' (p. 88). The experimental results of Morash (1982) do not suggest that such optimism is justified.

Should it be assumed (e.g. Snarey et al., 1985) that the principal measure of success of moral or legal education programmes is the extent to which pupils shake free of conventional morality and advance through to post-conventional reasoning? Recent critics have included not only Gilligan from a feminist perspective (1982), but others who point out that the philosophical content of the different levels reflects contrasting political biases and orientations (Markoulis, 1989; Emler and Hogan, 1981). Emler and Hogan (1981) suggest that moral reasoning is a social skill which we learn to vary according to the context. This is an idea that Piaget broached: the child's morality of constraint is an appropriate strategy for dealing with the relationship of unilateral dependence and respect that is imposed by parents. Similarly, as competence in social relationships with peers increases, so the rules become a focus for negotiation and agreement, and the morality of co-operation emerges. Respect for arbitrarily imposed rules is reinforced at school, where the bureaucratic organization becomes the prototype for subsequent dealings with authority. Sensitivity to authority (Kohlberg's stages 1 and 2) is second nature to the child, and transfers easily into the organizational context. Sensitivity to re-lationships arises for the most part in peer relationships based on equality and mutual respect and so a relationship-oriented morality emerges characteristic of Kohlberg's stage 3. As adults become part of the social system itself they may wish to sustain it, and adopt an appropriate law and order mentality characteristic of stage 4. Stage 5 reasoning is more characteristic of higher status persons in powerful roles. Such people can influence the business of law-making and may more readily adopt the privileged critical approach characteristic of stages 5 and 6. So we see that the types of moral reasoning as defined in Kohlberg's stages may reflect attunement to the demands and privileges of different social roles as the person develops from infancy to adulthood. Lower status and relatively powerless working class roles give rise to stage 4 reasoning, re-flecting a rule-following emphasis on law and order and general conservatism. On this view of Emler and Hogan, moral reasoning reflects the degree of social competence and success achieved by the individual in society.

Nevertheless, the use of different levels of reasoning by different political groups is highly context-specific. For example, at the time of the year-long miners' strike in Britain, Conservative voters used highly principled moral arguments when reasoning about the need for a national ballot of mineworkers, but were less principled than Labour supporters when it came to reasoning about the police use of road-blocks to prevent secondary picketing (Sparks and Durkin, 1987). The implication is that our level of reasoning has less to do with a consistent orientation to society than it has with the demands of the situation which faces us. If that is the case, we should be less than optimistic about finding a consistent relationship between level of moral reasoning and the morality of our behaviour.

Moral reasoning and moral action

One of the stranger findings of Kohlberg's research is that women, when they are employed as participants, are, by comparison with men, found to be morally 'immature'. They seem to function predominantly at the conventional stage 3 level and ascend the heights of stage 6 even less frequently than do men. As Kitzinger (in press) indicates, this prejudicial finding echoes a tradition (in criminology and in psychoanalytic theory) justifying charges of moral inferiority against women. Gilligan (1982), on the other hand, suggests that women speak and reason morally 'in a different voice' from men. Women's responses to Kohlberg's dilemmas are said to reflect 'care and compassion' for individuals more than a concern with universal principles of justice and rights, women focusing on 'connectedness', men on 'separateness' from others. According to Gilligan, the different voices of care and compassion on the one hand and of individual rights on the other are associated with gender (women and men respectively) but are not defined by gender. Both concerns are legitimate bases of moral thought and action, it being regarded as unfortunate that Kohlberg's preoccupation with the view of male participants has led to preoccupation with individual rights. Kitzinger's more challenging view (in press) suggests that from their dominant position in society men can afford to adopt a law-making perspective, leaving women to ensure that social and family relationships are unimpaired, and the women themselves accessible to their menfolk. Certainly people will vary their level of response according to how greatly they need to justify the choice they have made. When forced to justify a choice they did not prefer, the participants in Nisan and Koriat's experiment (1989) produced responses at a lower level than when defending their proposed choice of resolving a dilemma. Inclination not incapacity leads people to operate at one stage or another, including the 'higher' stages, a conclusion that echoes that of Sparks and Durkin (1987).

The association of gender with level of moral reasoning is but one indication of the tenuous connection between moral reasoning and moral action. There is little doubt that women act more morally than men. It is predominantly men who murder and pillage, men who cheat on their income tax and drive their cars too fast, and it is predominantly boys, not girls, who break into houses, play truant, and avoid paying their bus fares. The fact that men adopt the high moral ground in response to Kohlberg's questions should fool no one. Kohlberg admits that moral behaviour cannot be predicted from moral judgement alone, and allows for the role of situational and personality factors. He nonetheless assumes that the higher the stage of moral reasoning, the greater is the ability to rise above situational and other pressures. An essential reciprocity is assumed between moral reasoning and moral action. This is seen in Snarey et al.'s (1985) belief that the moral and political quality of the social structure in which one participates will determine the moral reasoning of the actors.

Blasi (1980) reviewed the literature on the relationship between moral thought and moral action, and did find some evidence for the proposition that moral reasoning is implicated in moral behaviour. For example, the moral maturity of delinquents has been shown consistently to be below that of comparable groups of non-delinquents, using Kohlberg's conventional method of scaling moral maturity. However, Emler et al. (1978) showed that although Borstal boys in England did, indeed, score lower than non-delinquents on a standardized test of moral reasoning (based on Kohlberg's scale), there was no correlation between moral behaviour and moral judgement within the delinquent sample. This finding was also true of the so-called non-delinquent boys whose degree of self-reported delinquency was unrelated to stage of moral reasoning.

Blasi suggests that 'moral reasoning is an important aspect of delinquency', but the results of Emler et al. suggest that the reasons for this remain unclear. It may be that apprehension and incarceration lead to a use of causes and justifications for their behaviour which influences the way delinquents in general respond to the test materials used by investigators. It should also be borne in mind that the full range of moral reasoning stages is found in delinquent populations, a point made by Jurkovic (1980) in his extensive review.

The issue of the relationship between moral reasoning and behaviour is certainly not finally resolved. It has been found, for example, that those with a reputation for being moral, helpful and honest, do have a tendency to score higher on tests of moral reasoning (Harris et al., 1976). There is also a handful of studies which suggest that those whose characteristic reasoning is at the post-conventional level tend to resist temptation to cheat (Malinowski and Smith, 1985). Most interestingly, McNamee (1977) shows that such high level moral reasoners are prepared to disobey an experimenter in order to respond to a cry for help from a supposed fellow student in distress. This suggests that moral maturity may interact with type of moral choice faced by the individual. There is evidence for such interactions.

Van Voorhis (1986) found that level of moral maturity did not predict which offenders complied with restitution orders – i.e. a requirement to personally compensate the victim of one's crime. Indeed, high maturity offenders – who tended to be of higher social status than low maturity offenders – were in some ways rather less moral in their behaviour than low maturity offenders. For example, they were more likely to carry weapons and they committed more serious offences. In relation to restitution, however, it seemed that high and low maturity offenders responded differently to the demands made upon them and were susceptible to different features of the situation. Low maturity offenders were more likely to pay up to a personal than an organizational victim and were more susceptible to possible sanctions for non-payment. High maturity offenders, on the other hand, were adversely affected by high amounts of restitution and by factors affecting their ability to pay – like unemployment status. The authors suggest that low maturity offenders responded to sanctions and supervision; high maturity offenders to the justice of the requirement to pay in the prevailing circumstances.

Cohn and White (1986) also found a differential response to circumstances of high and low maturity offenders. They carried out an interesting study of the effect of maturity level of students on attitudes towards rule-breaking in their residences. In one residence the students ran their own 'judicial' system, whereas in another residence discipline was externally imposed by the residence staff who strictly and routinely enforced the rules. When there was general agreement on the appropriateness of rules, high level reasoners responded better, it appears, to the participative regime, and the lower level reasoners to the external authority. This applied, for instance, to the frequency of engaging in disorderly behaviour and with attitudes towards destructive behaviour.

People and situations: the case of drink-driving

People behave in socially appropriate ways and hence in similar circumstances they frequently behave in remarkably similar ways. Should their behaviour result in subsequent embarrassment, guilt or shame, a variety of face-saving devices or techniques are available to salve the conscience or restore esteem and social acceptance, techniques which social psychologists and sociologists have described variously, for example, as 'dissonance reduction' (Aronson, 1972) or 'aligning actions' (Stokes and Hewitt, 1976). Why else do those in a crowd – regardless of moral philosophies or level of moral reasoning – walk by an injured stranger (Kidd, 1985)? Why else is a majority of subjects (regardless of personal moral philosophy or moral reasoning level) prepared to give electric shocks to a heart patient when instructed to (Milgram, 1974)? Why else, of course, in so many wars, have so many soldiers (regardless of personal moral philosophies or level of moral reasoning) been prepared to acquiesce or join in the committing of atrocities?

Driving home when near or above the legal level of blood alcohol is less prevalent than it used to be, but is still not an uncommon criminal activity in many Western nations. An interesting recent study carried out in Canada shows not only what an effective moral leveller drinking can be, but also how powerful is the social situation in which the drinking takes place. Denton and Krebs (1990) twice assessed the moral maturity of 40 male and 40 female adults, recruited individually from lively bars and parties: once in the bar or party context, and again a few days later at the university. After each interview blood alcohol level was assessed using a breathalyser, and the bar/party alcohol readings provided the basis for a division into high and low blood alcohol groups. The groups were equally sober at the university. Figure 2.2 shows a strong effect of situation on Moral Maturity scores, especially for those subjects who drank heavily in the social drinking setting. Of equal importance for our present purposes was the finding that all but one of the subjects

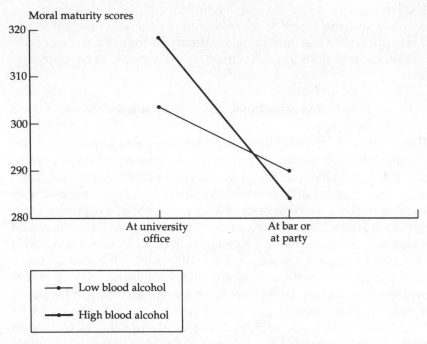

Figure 2.2   Moral maturity scores of 40 university men and 40 women
tested in a social drinking setting and at university
Source: After Denton and Krebs, 1990

who had driven to a bar or party also drove home, however badly
impaired by alcohol. As the authors state:

> This finding was surprising because subjects had just been inter-
> viewed about the values of life and law and the wrongfulness of
> impaired driving, had been given the results of a breathalyser test,
> and had been cautioned about the effects of driving while impaired.
> (p. 247)

Nevertheless, this finding apparently confirms those of earlier
studies suggesting that people will drive home when intoxicated,
despite knowing of their intoxication, and despite cautions from
the investigator. To compound the self-serving hypocrisy of it all,
Denton and Krebs also found that an independent group of subjects responding hypothetically believed predominantly that they
themselves would not drive when drunk, whereas – in their opinion – 'others' no doubt would!

Concluding thoughts

Empirical findings indicate that the relationship between moral reasoning and moral action (of which criminality is but one measure) is not especially close. One important reason for this is the susceptibility of the measurement of moral maturity to contextual factors. This has been amusingly illustrated by a recent study (Krebs et al., 1989) in which the anticipated *audience*, a Philosophy Department or a Business Studies Department, determined the level of moral reasoning elicited by Kohlberg-type dilemmas: higher levels for the philosophical audience, of course! As a number of investigators have suggested, people may 'turn on' different styles of moral reasoning as appropriate to their needs, thus rendering the very measure, if not the concept, of 'moral maturity' open to question.

There are, nevertheless, some interesting indications that individuals reasoning consistently at a post-conventional level may reveal their distinctiveness not so much by obedience to laws, as by their willingness to challenge lawful authority when appropriate. This was first noted by Haan et al. (1968), who in a large scale study of students at the University of California found that those scoring consistently in the Principled Morality category of Kohlberg's scale were significantly more likely than those scoring consistently in lower categories to be arrested during a civil liberties ('Free Speech Movement') campaign. This tendency was especially true of female students, as figure 2.3 indicates. McNamee (1977), in a study referred to above, found that nearly all of her participants with a moral maturity average score of 5 or 6 were prepared to overrule the experimenter in response to a plea for assistance from a suffering fellow subject. For the majority (at the lower levels) who did not intervene, the experimenter's authority was the deterrent. As one of them put it: 'I was your subject, like under your control, under your ruling force' (p. 30). The authority of the experimenter could be used effectively as a reason for non-intervention by those who were rule or role-oriented (to use Kelman and Hamilton's terms (1989)), but not by those with a value orientation who perceive it their duty to give only qualified and critical support to authorities, or who, in Kohlberg's terms, have progressed beyond conventional towards a principled morality.

The issue of moral thought and moral action in relation to

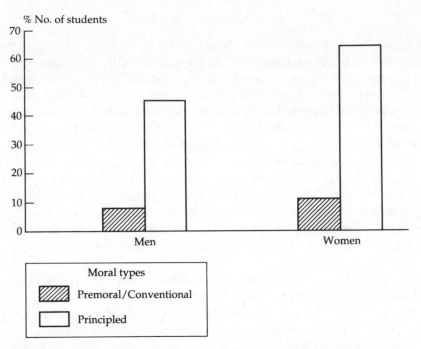

Figure 2.3 Percentage of students in different moral reasoning categories arrested in University of California Free Speech Movement Campaign
Source: After Haan et al., 1968

criminality has been explored in only a limited way. Criminal participants have been predominantly male, working class and incarcerated, and as such hardly representative of those who participate in criminal activities. A study of female delinquents by Krebs et al. (1989) suggests that the finding of somewhat lower moral maturity scores in delinquents than in 'controls' is not gender-specific, but the research by Emler et al. (1978) effectively disposes of any explanation of this in terms of an intrinsic, relation between the variables of criminal behaviour and moral maturity.

In psychology, as well as in the popular imagination, 'criminals' have been viewed as a type of personality or a character type. Of course, many people have pointed out the fallacies behind such thinking but the habit has persisted and distinctions have been made, for example, between 'real criminals' and those who occasionally commit crimes 'out of character' (Yochelson and Samenow,

1976). The evidence we have examined in this and the previous chapter has betrayed the lack of wisdom in this approach. Why people make criminal decisions, and why some make consistently more than others, will not be explained primarily in the search for common personality types or defective moral characters. The next two chapters explore traditions that have long come to terms with that conclusion.

3

Preparedness for Crime

What determines the extent to which we are prepared to commit criminal acts? Embracing a delinquent identity is an option that is considered and found more or less attractive by most young people. It is an option that never entirely loses its appeal – even if only in fantasy – as an alternative to the rewards of conventional achievement. People vary in their preparedness to commit criminal acts. The greater the preparedness, the more energetic a person will be in responding in a criminal way to needs and temptations as they arise. The distinction drawn is between preparedness for crime – the subject matter of this chapter – and criminal decision-making itself, which is discussed in chapter 4. A similar distinction is made by Cornish and Clarke (1986) between 'involvement' and 'event' decisions in criminal decision-making. Their emphasis on involvement decisions, however, implies the validity of making a categorical distinction between those who decide to become criminal and those who do not, a distinction we rejected in chapter 1. My preference is to distinguish between the continuum of preparedness to be criminal and the varying circumstances which induce people to commit criminal acts. Let us now turn to the first issue: preparedness.

Age, gender and criminality

Being accused of crime and suffering the indignities of prosecution and punishment is largely a prerogative of the male of the species and especially of young males. Figure 3.1 portrays crime in the under-21s in 1987. The peak age for offending overall is 15 years.

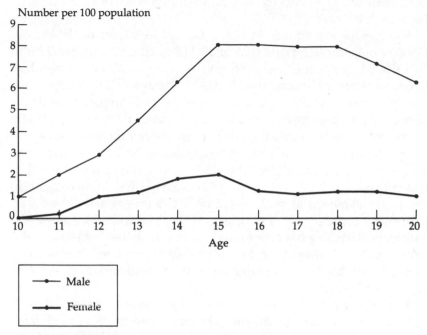

Figure 3.1 Offenders under 21 in 1987 in the UK per 100 of the population
Source: Home Office, 1989

Another striking contrast between the two trends is the remarkable difference in the number of males and females who contribute to the criminal statistics. This is at its peak in later teen years when male offending continues at or near the peak level, while female offending declines.

Imagine a continuation of the two trends to show the figures in adulthood. You would see a radical decline to very low levels of criminal conviction. The number per hundred of men being convicted declines to an average of about 1.4 after the age of 21, the equivalent figure for women being about 0.3 (Home Office, 1989). Nevertheless, the numbers involved in criminal behaviour at some point in their lives should not be underestimated. For example, in the United Kingdom, nearly 31 per cent of men born in 1953 had been convicted of a 'standard offence' by the age of 27, and the figure for those born in later years is likely to be substantially higher. The figures for females born in 1953 are lower – about 7 per cent – but the gap between men and women is narrowing for those born in later years.

The figures are similar in other European countries. Wikström (1990) for example reports that of 15,117 people born in Stockholm in 1953, 31 per cent of the men and 6 per cent of the women had been convicted of at least one crime by the age of 25. The Swedish data also demonstrate the high association of delinquency with the teenage years, the number of new first offenders falling off gradually as the cohort moved into the adult years. Given the low conviction rate, especially for theft and related offences, and given that those who offend infrequently will be additionally under-represented in the official criminal statistics, it is evident that involvement in criminal behaviour at some stage of life, but especially in adolescence and especially in males, is very high indeed. Moreover, the numbers offending have increased considerably over the years. For example, the numbers of 14–16-year-old convicted males have virtually doubled, and females more than quadrupled, in the past twenty-five years or so.

The observation that delinquency is so closely associated with age and gender by no means indicates that these factors *cause* delinquency. Consider the association with adolescence. Does adolescence *cause* delinquency? To the extent that a given level of intellectual, physical, financial and social independence is required to commit crime (indeed, 14 is the accepted age of criminal responsibility in the UK), then adolescence, and the relaxation of parental supervision that adolescence brings with it, may be said to be a *prerequisite* of delinquency. However, not all adolescents become 'young delinquents'. Most become predominantly law-abiding young men and women. As for gender, it is tempting to see, as many have done, the evidence for greater aggressiveness in males as the principal factor underlying sex differences in criminal behaviour. However, it may also be noted that female under-representation in delinquency is matched by under-representation in other activities, for example, the legal profession and the judiciary. Any biological or quasi-biological explanation of observed sex differences in criminality needs to meet the objection that the social position of women in society may be influencing their performance in criminal as in other aspects of life. We have seen that in criminal behaviour – as in some areas of professional attainment – the gap between the sexes is narrowing. In 1961 the ratio of boys to girls (aged 14–16 years) cautioned or found guilty of an offence was

Table 3.1 Childhood predictors of criminality up to age 32

	General Predictive Factor	Most Salient Aspect*	At Age
A	Socio-economic deprivation	Poor housing	8–10
B	Poor parental childrearing	Separated	10
C	Family deviance	Convicted parent	10
D	School problems	Low junior school attainment	11
E	Hyperactivity–impulsivity– attention deficit	High daring	8–10
F	Anti-social child behaviour	High troublesomeness	8–10

* as revealed by multiple regression analysis
Source: Farrington, 1990

approximately 10:1. By 1984 this ratio had been reduced to 4.5:1 (Central Statistical Office, 1986). If the biology of sex differences was so important in crime, such historical variation would defy rational explanation.

The associations with age and gender are two substantial facts about crime which it is difficult to explain purely by reference to biological maturation or biological sex differences. Some of the factors associated with adolescence and maleness are no doubt conducive to the development of criminal behaviour, but the origins of a life-style which incorporates criminal tendencies must be sought in more general aspects of social performance, circumstances, and development.

Early predictors of criminality

Longitudinal studies suggest that troublesome and difficult behaviour in quite early childhood is predictive of delinquency and criminality later in life. Indeed, Farrington (1990) reports on analysis which indicates that 'troublesomeness' as reported by parents and teachers at age 8–10 is an independent predictor of adult offending up to age 32 (see table 3.1).

His conclusion that this association reflects, 'continuity in an underlying construct of anti-social personality which has different behavioural manifestations at different ages from childhood to adulthood' (p. 102) nonetheless exaggerates the significance of the modest association that exists between early troublesomeness and later criminality. Early troublesomeness may have other antecedents. For example, it is closely associated with a syndrome most commonly known as Attention Deficit Disorder (ADD) comprising poor attention, impulsivity and hyperactivity. Known as ADHD (Attention Deficit/Hyperactivity Disorder) in the Diagnostic Manual of the American Psychiatric Association (1987), it is understood to be an organically based learning difficulty (see Weiss, 1990). The behaviour of children with this disorder is said to lead to 'chronic success deprivation' and consequent behaviour problems especially in school. The complications have been said to extend into adulthood with unemployment, marital instability and criminal behaviour as common findings (e.g., Levine, 1987; Willander, 1988; Weiss, 1990). Farrington (1990) found that ADD in 8–10-year-old boys independently predicted adult criminality, along with a number of other factors – convicted parents, academic problems, poor parenting, socio-economic deprivation and 'troublesomeness'. Troublesomeness itself accounts for about 7 per cent of the variance in later offending, the other variables accounting for a further 13 per cent in total.

An important longitudinal study by Moffitt (1990) shows clearly that delinquency at age 13 has a quite different developmental pathway for boys with ADD and those without. Children who are diagnosed ADD and are delinquent at age 13 have adverse family backgrounds and have been consistently anti-social from the age of 5 (the age of first assessment) onwards, thereby contrasting markedly with ADD (non-delinquent) children in whom both antisociality (more or less) and family adversity were consistently low at earlier ages. Those with delinquency only at age 13, however, had shown *no* anti-social tendencies at earlier ages (5, 7, 9, and 11), although family circumstances had shown signs of deterioration in late childhood. This apparent interaction of ADD and adverse family circumstances suggests the wisdom of Joan McCord's note of caution (McCord, 1990) that although different parenting factors may be consistently associated with criminal behaviour, the mere fact that such correlations exist does not itself eliminate the possibility that parental behaviours themselves are a response to circumstances which pre-date the collection of longitudinal data and which may also underlie the anti-sociality of their offspring. It may be noted incidentally that ADD is rarely diagnosed in girls.

Early 'troublesomeness' is not necessarily an early expression of a self-conscious 'anti-social tendency', as Farrington rather suggests. More plausibly, it is a response to the circumstances faced by the child which may well provide the child with a model for later deviance. Simply put, being difficult at an early age may become a persistent coping strategy for dealing with highly unfavourable circumstances, both personal (e.g. ADD), social (e.g., adverse family circumstances including physical and sexual abuse) and educational (e.g., poor academic progress).

Certainly the association of criminality, both early and late, with unfavourable family backgrounds is undeniable and has been demonstrated in many studies in different countries. One of the first comprehensive comparisons of delinquent boys and matched control subjects was by the Gluecks in the 1940s (Glueck and Glueck, 1950). The homes of delinquent boys revealed greater poverty and squalor, with unfavourable family history of mental illness and crime. Moreover, the treatment the boys received from parents was less consistent and more punitive, to mention but a few of their findings. Two recently published studies employed more methodologically sophisticated prospective longitudinal designs. Kolvin et al. (1988) reported on the criminal fate of 1142 infants born in Newcastle (UK) between 1 May and 30 June 1947. The infants came from 1132 families, and those families were regularly investigated since they were first studied at the time the babies were born. Naturally, there are many interesting and varied findings but I shall concentrate on the main effect of social deprivation. Figure 3.2 shows the number of criminal convictions of males in successive two-year age-bands from the age of 10 to 33. There are three lines, for 'multiply deprived', 'deprived' and 'non-deprived' groups of males.

Deprivation was measured in terms of five factors: marital instability, parental illness, poor domestic provision and care of the children and homes, social dependency, overcrowding, and poor mothering ability. A child in a house with three or more indices of deprivation was described as 'multiply deprived', with one or two as 'deprived', and 'non-deprived' with no such indices. There is, as figure 3.2 shows, a very strong association between number of convictions and degree of deprivation with a tendency towards earlier offending in the multiply deprived group.

Mean no. of convictions

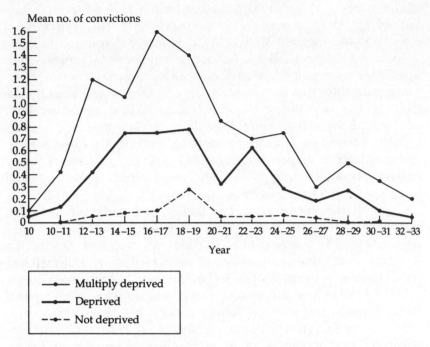

Year

—•—	Multiply deprived
—•—	Deprived
– •– –	Not deprived

Figure 3.2   Number of convictions for a) 53 Multiply deprived, b) 178 Deprived and c) 226 Not deprived males
Source: Kolvin et al., 1988

'Social deprivation' in this Newcastle study incorporated a measure of maternal supervision. A recent study by H. Wilson (1987) confirmed what Kolvin and many others have found, that independently of other measures of social deprivation, including parental criminality itself, lax parental supervision is significantly associated with delinquency in boys. The importance of poor parenting also emerged strongly in the London study of Farrington, poor parenting being assessed by various measures including harsh or erratic discipline, parental disharmony, poor supervision or monitoring of behaviour and separations of child from parents for reasons other than death or hospitalization.

Kolvin's variables of social dependency and overcrowding reflect not so much parental childrearing but acutely unfavourable family circumstances, a factor that emerged as a major predictor of delinquency and adult criminality in Farrington's study. Low family income, large family size, poor housing and low socio-economic status at age 8–11 were all associated statistically with subsequent delinquency and criminality (Farrington, 1990). However, Larzelere and Patterson (1990) suggest that in a smaller longitudinal study of 206 boys from Oregon, the association of socio-economic status (SES) with delinquency in young boys was mediated entirely by parental management, a measure which reflects consistent discipline and close monitoring of the child by the parents. Social class in itself was not a determining factor in delinquency.

A third family background factor that has repeatedly been shown to exert an independent influence on the child's anti-social tendency and subsequent criminality and that came out strongly in the London study, is parental criminality and sibling misconduct and delinquency. This factor was reported by the Gluecks and is not a surprising finding in view of the important role that modelling plays in a child's learning and development.

School achievement

A study by Ferguson in 1952, *The Young Delinquent in his Social Setting*, pointed significantly to the role of academic achievement in boys' delinquency, a finding that has been consistently replicated. For example, a recent review (Graham, 1988) concludes that 're-search findings on the relationship between failure at school and delinquency are . . . relatively conclusive. Pupils who fail at school are more likely to become involved in delinquent activities than those who succeed' (Graham, 1988, p. 47). This, combined with the results of a recent study showing the immense variation between schools in their effects on the academic attainments of their pupils (D.J. Smith and Tomlinson, 1989), leads to the conclusion that the achievement of schools as well as the achievement of pupils in schools may play a causal role in the encouragement of delinquent achievement. Whilst most studies of school achievement have focused on the performance of the adolescent, Farrington (1990) emphasizes that poor academic performance is evident in the junior school, and is highly correlated with low verbal ability and low intelligence generally. The single most important educational predictor of delinquency in the London study was, in fact, low junior school achievement at age 11 (see table 3.1).

Explanation of the findings

It is possible to give a highly individualistic explanation of all these principal findings in terms of the psychology of individual motivation and development. Farrington (1986) and Farrington and West (in press) explain the findings in terms of individual motivation and beliefs. Thus children from poorer families who fail at school will be motivated to achieve their (economic) goals illegally. Children whose parents discipline them ineffectively fail to develop internalized controls over their behaviour, and children with criminal families learn anti-establishment attitudes and a belief that delinquency is 'justifiable'. Delinquency peaks in late adolescence because motivation for material and social success peaks at that time of their lives, at a time when they are least able to fulfil their desires in a legal manner. More generally, the catalogue of 'causes' listed by Farrington can plausibly be thought to induce boys to turn to crime to fulfil their needs. Children from poorer families who because of an unstimulating and unsympathetic family environment are of low intelligence tend to fail in school and to have erratic employment histories. They are, in Farrington's words, 'less able to satisfy their desires for material goods, excitement, and social status by legal or socially approved methods, and so tend to choose illegal or socially disapproved methods' (p. 103).

Those authors follow up their findings that economic deprivation, school failure and poor parental childrearing behaviour are causal factors by suggesting that (a) economic resources should be targeted on the poorer families, (b) it is desirable to offer free high quality pre-school enrichment programmes to children 'at risk', and (c) parents could be trained to use more effective childrearing techniques. Moreover, Farrington (1990) cites evidence from a number of studies in the United States that pre-school enrichment programmes have been shown to improve problems arising from low intelligence and school failure. Not only were academic and employment prospects improved, but delinquency was reduced in those receiving the pre-school enrichment experience. Behavioural training of parents aimed at improving their childrearing practices effectively reduced stealing by their offspring, over the short term at least. Studies of such innovative programmes should be replicated. Attempts to target financial benefits to those families most at risk have apparently not yet demonstrated a beneficial effect on delinquency. This is not surprising. The multiple socio-economic deprivations associated with poor housing, for example, are not so easily isolated and rectified.

The need for caution in such targeting programmes is stressed by White et al. (1990). In a longitudinal study of New Zealand children, some ability of behavioural ratings of children as young as three years old to predict anti-social conduct at age 11 was demonstrated. There was, however, a very high false positive rate when using discriminant factor analysis to predict anti-social disorder at age 11 and delinquency at 15, employing five variables obtained from ratings at age 3 and 5. They state:

> Of the 209 children predicted to have anti-social outcomes at age 11, 84.7 per cent did not develop stable and pervasive anti-social behaviour of the severity required for diagnosis in this study. Thus, the prediction does not yet appear to be accurate enough to provide the basis for any intensive intervention program that is designed to prevent stable and pervasive conduct disorder. (pp. 521–2)

Is delinquency merely compensatory?

One implication of the view that criminality represents an attempt to compensate for deprivation (broadly defined) is that self-esteem should be lower in delinquent children. Tests of that notion have consistently failed to demonstrate low self-esteem in delinquents, thereby reflecting again the findings that personality characteristics do not differentiate between groups of individuals who vary in their degree of criminal behaviour. Indeed, a typical finding has recently been replicated by Oyserman and Markus (1990) showing that more severely delinquent children, if anything, have higher self-esteem than less delinquent children. What Oyserman and Markus did find to be strongly associated with delinquency, however, was an inappropriate match between the sort of person that a boy or girl *expected* to become and the sort of person they *feared* becoming. For example, a non-delinquent youth might expect to 'get along in school' and to fear 'not getting along in school', to take just the most frequent responses in both categories. The equivalent responses for the most delinquent group were 'Be happy' and 'Be a criminal'.

Oyserman and Markus argue that a feared self which comple-
ments the expected self enhances the motivational significance and
effect of the decried state of affairs. Delinquents are in the unhappy
position of not having an appropriate match between possible and
feared selves, 63 per cent not having one match out of three possible
matches, compared with only 19 per cent of the non-delinquents.
Their major problem was a lack of appropriate expected possibilities.
The authors concluded:

> Although these delinquent youths have the type of feared selves
> that might be associated with the avoidance of delinquent activity,
> many of them seem to be missing the expected possible selves that
> could provide the organizing and emerging vision of how they
> might avoid criminal activity, and what they might expect if they
> do. (p. 123)

The authors also report that imbalance was associated with future
delinquent behaviour during the three-month follow-up period.

It is important to take into account the social context in which
delinquent aspirations and motivations are constructed. Indeed,
early troublesome behaviour itself may develop initially as a strategy
for obtaining the recognition and control that in better-endowed
and better-resourced individuals might be achieved by other means.
The attempt to 'predict' delinquency has led investigators resolutely
to seek the causes of delinquency in early childhood. This has
detracted from the role of social motivations inherent in the organization of school and social life in later childhood and adolescence, and it has also created an image of the delinquent as
an inadequate, unfortunate, essentially passive and reactive misfit.
In fact delinquents – or some of them – may have remarkably
positive qualities and may use their talents in a creative way to
achieve their wayward ends, in ways which elicit admiration if
not awe from delinquent and non-delinquent peers alike.

Agnew (1990) used data from a longitudinal study of Youth in
Transition conducted by the Institute of Social Research at the
University of Michigan. The subjects were all boys, 2213 in total.
He showed that the correlation between possession of a resource
– like money, or intelligence or (cognitive) flexibility – and delin-
quency was different for those 'at risk' (who went out frequently
for 'fun and recreation') than for those lower on that variable.
For those at risk, take-home pay was positively associated with

delinquency, whereas for those not at risk, it was if anything negatively associated with delinquency. Intelligence was negatively
associated with delinquency for those not at risk, positively associated for those at risk. 'Flexibility' was increasingly associated with
delinquency the more the boys were at risk. The possession of
resources is, they conclude, positively associated with delinquency
for those who place themselves at risk, those who are, in the author's
view, 'delinquency-prone'. The variables involved – money, intelligence and flexibility – enable the boys to overcome the barriers to
delinquency by helping them evade supervision and control and
by providing them with the means to engage in many delinquent
acts.

Schools may reinforce the divisions between the conventionally
successful and the deviant 'failures'. Hargreaves (1967) published
a detailed study of social organization of teaching and social
relations in the fourth year of a secondary modern school he called
Lumley. His main finding was that the fourth year was divided
socially into two sub-cultural groups which he called the academic
and delinquescent respectively. These groups were based on streams
which had been created over the years from successive promotions
and demotions from the first (aged 11+) to the fourth (aged 15+)
year. The academic sub-group came largely from the successful
boys in the A and B streams, and the delinquescent from the
unsuccessful C and D streams. Evidence for the sub-cultures came
first from friendship patterns which clustered within the As and Bs
on the one hand, and separately within the Cs and Ds. Second, the
two groups had different and opposed norms, with A and B being
predominantly pro-school, and the Cs and Ds largely anti-school.
Academic success was valued by A and B boys but derided by the
Cs and Ds, and 'messing about' was highly valued by the Cs and
Ds and scorned by the As and Bs. The organization of the school
reinforced the pattern of schoolboy intergroup relations, with the
most incompetent teachers being allocated to the delinquescent
streams, whilst rewarding the better teachers with the more co-
operative A and B stream boys.

Hargreaves (1980, 1981) has subsequently argued that schools
may be 'criminogenic', and that the school may be the mechanism
by which contrary values in the social backgrounds of pupils from
academically-oriented pro-social homes, and those from delinquent
and anti-social families are brought into collective opposition. As
Graham (1988) puts it: 'Through their capacity to motivate, to

integrate and to offer each pupil a sense of achievement irrespec-
tive of ability, schools would seem to possess the capability to
prevent some pupils from being drawn into the juvenile justice
system. The converse is also true (p. 47).' The converse is what
Hargreaves observed at Lumley. Delinquent acts served to establish the credentials of boys in the anti-academic C and D streams.

A number of observers have tried to locate what it is about schools
that prevents the emergence of an anti-authority oppositional ethos
in a school. Reynolds (1976), for example, suggests that the more
effective schools call a 'truce' whereby the more irksome of school
rules are abandoned and a negotiated compromise is achieved,
rather than the rigid and discriminatory enforcement of rules that
is observed in the criminogenic schools. Hargreaves (1980) has
attempted to summarize what he sees as organizational options
facing school managers and heads when trying to deal with six
main problems areas. These are listed in table 3.2. All the non-
delinquent options are said to promote the perception of fairness,
and hence to create the conditions in which a common cultural
climate might flourish. The alternative options, on the other hand,
promote the development of organized opposition to the school
and its values. In the climate thus created, delinquency may become
normative, bringing status and prestige to those who would
otherwise be deprived of such rewards. Whilst Hargreaves'
description of the options that determine which schools become
criminogenic is speculative, it serves to summarize our current
social psychological understanding of how the known predictors
of delinquency – poverty, family criminality, inadequate parenting
and poor academic attainment – may interact with school structure
to create delinquents.

A recent study by W.P. Robinson (1990) has indicated that
an emphasis on competitive academic assessment is not in itself
sufficient to enhance the attraction of the delinquent alternative
in those who are least successful. His study of school children in
Japan, France and England compared the most academically successful 25 per cent of pupils with the least successful 25 per cent,
but there was no evidence that the 'failures' generally become anti-
school, nor that they prized smoking, drinking, excitement, sex etc.
more than the successful pupils. Moreover, the country which had
the least competitive educational system (England) and should
hence have generated such processes less than, say, France – the
most competitive example – had the most delinquescent attitudes

Table 3.2 Alternative school organizational strategies in relation
to delinquency

Problem area/ Organizational options	Delinquency-prone	Non-delinquent
Streaming	Flexible: pupil demotion and promotion	Rigid and stable: setting and streaming
Teacher Assignment	Discriminatory	Non-discriminatory
Discipline and Curricula	High teacher autonomy	Strong control and supervision by Head of Department
Rule Enforcement	Rigorous enforcement of minor rules	Creation of 'truce'
Attitude to pupils who are difficult to teach	Leave to own devices provided not disruptive	Expect them to work and behave like all other pupils
Attitude to deviant pupils	Distrusted and categorized as irresponsible	Optimistically given trust and responsibility

Source: After Hargreaves, 1980

amongst their failures. In addition, French failures, unlike the Japanese or the English, were as high in self-esteem as French successes.

It appears from Robinson's research that the English school system does tend to generate less positive enthusiasm for school amongst its so-called academic failures, but this fact appears to do little or nothing for their self-esteem and there is no particular enthusiasm for anti-social behaviour amongst the failures. Moreover, the cross-cultural comparison indicates very clearly that failure as such is not sufficient to create an opposition to school or to the academic values it represents. This is consistent with the findings of Hargreaves (1967) at Lumley. The boys who led the delinquescent subculture were themselves able, resourceful characters whose followers were more dutiful than enthusiastic about establishing their delinquent credentials.

Delinquency as 'reputation management'

Academic failure may not necessarily lead to the development of anti-social attitudes, but it may fuel an existing anti-social tendency. Delinquency happens to peak at a time when academic demands are at their greatest and it may well establish an alternative, and additional, source of satisfaction to academic success. Emler (1984) spells out the negative implications for self of not being part of the successful, pro-school set of pupils who are rewarded and praised by teachers as they move seemingly inexorably towards acquiring their qualifications and achieving a stable position in the world of work. Delinquency offers a clear-cut behavioural dimension in terms of which success may be measured and a position of prestige acquired.

Emler's arguments employ a number of findings we have already touched upon when describing the work of Farrington and colleagues. For example, he shows (Emler, 1984) that delinquency is a 'scaleable' characteristic, ranging from very mild or negligible law-breaking to the committing of quite serious offences, the serious offenders admitting to the lesser varieties of offence as well. Again, echoing the work of Farrington, Emler reports that delinquents are 'versatile', there being little specialization. The argument that delinquent activity serves to establish a valued identity (see Reicher and Emler, 1985, 1987) is fuelled by the findings that delinquent attitudes and delinquency itself are strongly associated with anti-authority statements in general against police, teachers and parents. Delinquents are generally at odds with officialdom, believing that, for example, 'most school rules are petty' or 'the police pick on working-class people too much'. As Reicher and Emler (1987) say, by expressing certain attitudes we align ourselves with certain identities and distance ourselves from others. The correlation between delinquency and anti-authority attitudes is in the order of 0.7 indicating that the delinquent tendency is intimately related to hostility to all forms of authority.

The final argument used by Emler is crucial and concerns the implications of regarding delinquency as a means of securing the admiration of others, albeit for conventionally unacceptable behaviour. Such admiration is most effectively secured when others have had the opportunity to observe the deeds in question. West and Farrington's study (1973) reported that delinquency in adolescence is an especially social matter, invariably committed in groups. Such findings are substantiated in the study of Emler et al. (1987) in which the whole gamut of offences – drugs, theft, aggression, vandalism – was strongly associated with group involvement. Interestingly, girls were even more likely to report group involvement in crime than were boys. A recent study by Morgan and Grube (1991) on illicit substance use confirms the importance of social factors in both the initiation and maintenance of the habit.

Gender and crime: a final note

There must be few boys who do not at least dabble in delinquency in a more or less daring way, thereby distancing themselves to a greater or lesser degree from conventional (and boring) conformity. Delinquent involvement for girls (and women) is much less pervasive; criminality does not seem to have the same attractions as it does for boys. There is no evidence, however, that the factors predisposing boys to delinquency are any different for girls. Where girls have been studied alongside boys, the same pattern of findings has always emerged (e.g. White et al., 1990). Girls, it would appear, merely have a higher threshold of resistance to those circumstances that persuade boys to opt for the material and social rewards of criminality. Similarly, a recent study (Windle et al., 1989) shows that causal relationships between alcohol, marijuana and hard drug usage are identical for adolescents of both sexes.

Allen (1987) has observed that the Courts act as if women's crime is different from men's, and should be responded to differently, in ways which undermine the principles of equal treatment. Morris (1987) seeks to undermine the view that women's criminality is so very different from that of men. She points out that although women are convicted less frequently, experimental studies reveal them to be as aggressive and as likely to steal small amounts as are men. Women are involved in trivial crime and as trivial crime is underreported, women's crime is likely to be under-reported. Morris also points out that stereotypes of women's crime as predominantly involving shoplifting and sexual behaviour overlooks contrary evidence. A recent study of CID interrogations in London (Moston et al., 1992), for example, showed no gender difference in the pattern of crimes allegedly committed by suspects.

It may be suggested that the perceived role of women as the passive observer of men's achievements is changing as a result of social changes which have brought women into the workforce and accelerated the advance of feminist ideology. If this is the case, criminal activity may become as much a feature of women's experience as it is of men's. Something like this view was advanced by Adler (1975) who sought to document 'the rise of the new female criminal'. McCord and Otten (1983) found, however, that attitudes to sex roles and women's rights were totally unrelated to self-reported female or male criminality, and Losley et al. (1985) failed to find that 'nontraditional' aggressive female criminals were characterized by more non-traditional feminist attitudes than the 'traditional' non-aggressive female criminals. Indeed, the reverse was the case. Nonetheless, female criminality is increasing faster than that of males – and it is hard to believe that this is not related to the fact that girls and women are competing more extensively in social, economic and political life. Hence, increasingly, the desire to achieve these if necessary by illegitimate means may well become akin to that in boys.

Whether one adopts what might be called the compensation theory of Farrington, or the reputation management theory of Emler, what should be clear is that it is perceived social and material deficits, and perceived available social identities that motivate individuals. We know from many past studies that such perceptions are not directly related to actual material and social circumstances, but are mediated strongly by expectations. In the case of both men and women, the point to be made is that preparedness for crime arises from perceived frustrations, deprivations and disappointments. Although it may lie dormant in those for whom respectability has been or is a chosen way of life, it may surface dramatically in the most respectable of people, and is an ever-present available resource when the circumstances are sufficiently compelling.

4

Calculating Criminal Behaviour

Introduction: from preparedness to decision-making

Does threat of punishment deter potential offenders? Paternoster and Iovanni (1986) twice interviewed nearly 1200 boys and girls in their tenth grade at high school, 15 months apart, aiming to predict future delinquency from the assessments of attitudes in the first interview. The results indicated that neither certainty nor severity of expected punishment had a deterrent effect, and nor were attachment to school, educational sanctions, or attachment to parents related to subsequent delinquency. Important factors were for the most part those one might have predicted from the findings reported in chapter 3, and the interpretation given in terms of the development of a delinquent identity. As the results reported in table 4.1 indicate, those who commit delinquent acts tend to have friends who do likewise and who would not disapprove of their own delinquency. They do not think that minor delinquency is particularly wrong, and they are unconcerned about career consequences. They also tend to be boys. What seems to be important is the extent to which a delinquent social identity and network has emerged providing good friends who reinforce a carefree attitude towards the future, with that life-style being further facilitated by lack of parental supervision.

Paternoster and Iovanni's finding that deterrents to crime did not predict subsequent involvement in juvenile delinquency confirms the results of many other studies: in general researchers have consistently failed to find an inverse relationship between perceived severity of punishment and criminal involvement, whether juveniles or adults have been studied. This general finding has caused some

Table 4.1 Attitudinal predictors of subsequent delinquency in 1173 high school children

Significant Factors in order of Diminishing Magnitude	Non-Significant Factors
Friends' behaviour	School attachment
Moral beliefs	Educational sanctions
Paternal supervision	Attachment to parents
Gender	Certainty of punishment
Social sanctions	Severity of punishment
Occuptional sanctions	

Source: After Paternoster and Iovanni, 1986

alarm because it seems to undermine faith in that commonsense understanding of human motivation which lies at the heart of penal policy. The problem is resolved, however, when we distinguish clearly between those factors that predispose us towards criminality and those factors that might induce us to commit a particular crime. The extent to which we come to identify with a delinquent or criminal life-style is largely a product of childhood and adolescent socialization and will in a general way determine the level of criminal involvement. The process is largely devoid of rational calculation. The decision to commit a particular crime, however, is quite another matter. Then, as one would expect, anxieties about apprehension and punishment – based at least in part on our expectations of punishment in the event of apprehension – will play a very important role in determining our behaviour.

The 'rational choice' perspective

The potential rewards of criminality are so apparent – maintaining a desired life-style, social success, excitement, and a range of personal, interpersonal and social satisfactions and pleasures – that we need to be clear why, when given appropriate opportunities, many people do not succumb to the pervasive temptations, never mind not actively seek out opportunities. The answer is, of course, that people deal with the temptation to rob or murder as they would deal with the 'temptation' to borrow money to go on an expensive holiday, or to take a job abroad or to have a risky operation: that is, they reason their way through the pros and cons, the justifications and objections, they consider what their loved ones advise, they consider what obstacles might be put in their way, they try making up their mind one way or another to see how they feel about the possible consequences, and so on. Criminal behaviour is no exception to the rule that human social behaviour is *reasoned*.

Tuck and Riley (1986) put forward the view that the Theory of Reasoned Action (Fishbein and Ajzen, 1975), which has been successfully applied in the prediction of a variety of social behaviours in the medical, health, political and educational fields, can be successfully applied to criminal behaviour. Intentions to perform a particular behaviour are said by the authors to be determined by our own attitudes and our understanding of, and motivation to comply with, the expectations of significant others in our lives (the Subjective Norm). Attitudes themselves are a product of beliefs about the consequences of behaving in a particular way and our evaluation of those consequences.

Let us consider briefly what might go into the belief side of the equation. Beliefs about the consequences of actions – probability of getting caught, the rewards to be expected, and so on – and how much we value these consequences are of obvious importance in determining our intention to commit a particular act. Such beliefs may be determined by highly circumstantial factors, like the physical location of a particular house to be burgled in a busy street or an isolated country road, or may be the consequence of considerable experience or specialized knowledge (e.g. how to disable alarm systems). On the normative side, the extent to which the expectations of significant others exclude criminal behaviour is clearly important, but of equal or greater significance is the regard in which others' expectations are held. As we have seen, the justifications and excuses that criminals develop – their criminal preparedness – may well serve to immunize them against any normative expectation of others.

Ajzen and Madden (1986) incorporate a third variable, perceived control, into a revised version of the model (see figure 4.1), termed Planned Behaviour. Perceived control is potentially important for our understanding of why people might hesitate to perform certain criminal behaviours. Its addition to the model recognizes the fact

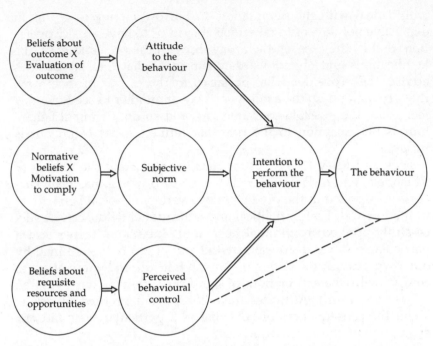

Figure 4.1 The Theory of Planned Behaviour
Source: After Ajzen and Madden, 1986

that circumstances or abilities might prevent the effective perform-ance of the behaviour in question. For example, the adolescent might not be able to give her parents good enough excuses for absence from home late at night, or a potential burglar might not know of a suitable intermediary through whom he could dispose of the property he would like to steal.

As formal theories, Reasoned Action and Planned Behaviour have been successfully applied in a variety of contexts and especially in the field of health behaviours. For our present purposes it provides a framework for the presentation and discussion of diverse studies all of which point to the importance of calculation in criminal decision making. I shall be describing a range of studies that illustrate what Cornish and Clarke (1986) call the rational choice perspective on crime. The studies mostly illustrate the fact that as circumstances render crime personally more profitable and/or justifiable to oneself, so the individual will be more likely to commit a particular criminal act. First, however, let us examine some views from outside psychology that are congruent with the rational choice perspective but which deal for the large part with aggregate data rather than the responses of individuals to particular circumstances. The thrust of the argument is that crime is a commodity for which demand varies, and that variations in the level of demand will determine the rate at which it is supplied in accordance with established laws of supply and demand.

The economics of crime

Ehrlich (1982) suggests that there is a market for offences in the same way as there is a market for any other commodity or service. People commit crimes, he suggests, because they are expecting a given return for their labours. In terms of the theory of planned behaviour, they have beliefs about the outcome of their behaviour that induce a positive attitude towards intention to commit it. In economic terms again, they expect to gain from their illegal behaviour because their expected profits (rewards minus the costs of committing the crime) are high. Ehrlich points out that the more suppliers of crime there are, the less profit there is in it and vice versa – for example, your wage as a get-away driver will be high if there is no competition for the job – and that the market for crime, as for other commodities, is in equilibrium when the supply or flow of crime is equal to that demanded.

Psychologists have on the whole concentrated on the supply side of the equation, imagining that by changing people so that committing a crime no longer serves a psychological function for them, the problems of crime can be solved. Ehrlich's views put paid to that line of reasoning. Whilst the demand continues, there will be those forthcoming who wish to meet that demand. Indeed, Ehrlich argues that for all those who are put away in prison there will be others ready to take their places, if necessary by learning the trade anew or from scratch. After all, the less competition there is, the greater the profit to be expected and therefore the greater the incentive to acquire the appropriate skills.

Those who literally employ others to commit crime create a straightforward demand. The demand for contract burglars or for contract killers is no doubt fairly consistent and predictable. Ehrlich points out, however, that in the market for offences there are not just two parties for we are all parties to the flow of crime. At least, we are all purchasers of crime. We take out insurance so that we may be careless with our possessions and thereby encourage others to appropriate them. It is easier not to lock the garage door at night or not to lock the car door when one is soon to return than it is to be obsessionally careful: our insurance cover then finances those crimes we thereby induce. Demand for crime is also created by advertising, by tempting displays in supermarkets, and by flamboyant life-styles which advertise wealth. When crime is supplied, its cost is offset against the gains – of increased sales, or of social esteem, or notoriety.

A number of investigators working within this economic framework have examined directly, using macro-economic data, the suggestion that changes in opportunities for legitimate employment affect the demand for and supply of crime in a predictable way. Phillips and Votey (1981) argue that reduction in employment opportunities reduces the rewards that may be expected from seeking the employment option, and thereby increases the relative attraction of the criminal option. Their large-scale macro-economic data confirm that unemployment is reliably associated with an overall increase in crime, in the same way that Farrington et al. (1986) confirmed the hypothesis in his longitudinal study of individual men. Phillips and Votey suggest, interestingly, that the increasing number of young women entering the labour force will, by increasing competition, put increasing pressure on young men to adopt the criminal option. This view receives indirect support from White (1989) who considers that the increase in youthful crime seen in a number of advanced industrial countries can only be understood in relation to changes in the contemporary economic context which have had the effect of excluding large numbers from the formal waged economy.

The economic approach has stimulated the examination of some interesting hypotheses. Lott (1987) argues that the provision of public (state) education in the United States should lead to an increase in crime. This is because the 'cost' of crime is greater in proportion to the amount of money that has been invested in the offending youth's education. Free education reduces the capital investment by parents and their subsequent concern to ensure a return on their investment. Both the model and the results of Lott's analysis of time-series data on educational expenditure, confirm the notion that decreased parental investment in schooling facilitates delinquency. More conventionally, Corman et al. (1987) provide longitudinal data suggesting that arrests provide a strong deterrent to crime, presumably because the rate of arrests provides incontrovertible evidence of the relative certainty of apprehension and punishment, a factor which is of critical importance in the calculation of the likely gain for criminal behaviour.

For social psychologists the economic analysis of criminal behaviour has confirmed the importance of paying close attention to those beliefs that may influence the perceived attractiveness of a given criminal act.

Criminal calculations

Studies of the decision to desist from crime are part of an increasing trend towards the longitudinal study of so-called criminal careers (Blumstein et al., 1988), and interview studies of the decision to give up crime have thrown light reflectively on the reasons for continuation. The decision to give up crime seems generally to be precipitated by some 'shock' – an event that highlights the costs of criminal behaviour and leads to a reassessment or recalculation of the relative gains of crime and going straight. Cusson and Pinsonneault (1986) say of their study of 17 Canadian ex-robbers:

> It was often during the commission of their last crime that our subjects suffered this shock. One of them was wounded by the police during a shoot-out as he was leaving a bank. Another saw his partner killed by police bullets. A third told us that his accomplice had tried to kill him to get his share of the loot. (p. 74)

Shock is said to combine with 'delayed deterrence' to bring about a reassessment of the value of crime. Estimates of the likelihood of punishment, dread of further time to be lost in prison, and of longer sentences being imposed in the future, and fear of the uncertainty of it all, all increase with age itself and with first-hand experience of the ruthlessness of the penal system. The grinding awfulness of it gets through and desistance, following a reappraisal of goals, becomes at last the more attractive alternative.

The chances that a robber will get caught are on average quite low, and it is no surprise that Feeney (1986) found in his study of active robbers then under arrest that getting caught had not been of great concern to most of them. Only 14 per cent of juveniles had thought about getting caught before committing the offence that had brought them to court, the equivalent figure for adults being 24 per cent. These results reflect the general nonchalance of this sample of robbers who on the whole did not go in for careful planning, and most of whom 'feel that they can handle away any situation that arises without specific planning' (p. 67). However, experience did not make these robbers more circumspect. Quite the reverse, in fact, with 30 per cent of first-timers thinking getting caught a problem, and only 19 per cent of the more experienced. Such imperviousness to risk seems justifiable in the light of the reported experience of one of those interviewed who had apparently committed 1000 robberies by the age of 26, having been convicted only once. The impression is gained from these interviews that the evaluations of risk by these robbers are highly determined by the immediate context, with the decision to rob frequently being taken casually, and for the flimsiest of social and personal reasons:

> 'I get a kick out of it really. Watch people's faces when they see you. They scared. I robbed because he gave me a smart answer.'

> 'I don't know. It sounded easy and I guess we needed the money. We didn't really need it but we wanted to do something.'

> 'Because he asked me to help him out. He had done a favour for me before. I didn't really want money.' (Feeney, 1986, p. 58)

The contrast with burglary appears to be considerable. Bennett and Wright (1984) argue that burglars are on the whole a circumspect lot; at least, that is true for those with experience, as was the case with those interviewed by Bennett and Wright. 'Opportunistic' burglars constituted only 7 per cent of their sample. This contrasts strongly with the 55 per cent of Feeney's robbers who said that they did no planning at all, and another 33 per cent for whom planning was minor. The planned offence was characteristic of 59 per cent of burglars, a particular house being targeted and burgled if the conditions were right at the time. If the conditions were not right, the planners did not tend to displace on to another target, whereas those who were searchers tended to persist if prevented from burgling the chosen house and to seek another target the same night. What is quite clear from this study is that all burglars seem to have decided that the time is right to go burgling and go

Table 4.2 Cross-tabulation of burglary victimization risk by household family composition and percentage single-adult households

| Household Composition | Percentage Single-Adult Households | | |
	Low (0–8%)	Medium (9–18%)	High (19–36%)
Single adult, no children	.020	.039	.051
Two adults, no children	.009	.002	.031
Single adult, with children	.077	.128	.143
Two adults, with children	.027	.031	.044

Note: Cell entry is proportion victimized by household burglary and theft.
Data were weighted to correct for the over-sampling of inner-city areas.
Source: *British Crime Survey*, 1982

about their business in what to them is a determinedly rational way.

It appears to be crucial for burglars to recognize that competence and planning is required and to believe that they do, indeed, possess the requisite resources for successful burgling, and can create appropriate opportunities. For example, Deusinger (1986) reports that burglars are well able to comment on the extent to which particular houses 'induce' them to break in. They distinguish more accurately than non-burglars between those houses which have suffered break-ins, from those which have not, and generally the burglars distinguished sharply between those houses which invite burglary and those which inhibit burglary. How well founded the distinctions are cannot be judged, but clearly there is knowledge to be gained from experienced burglars about where the break-ins may be expected!

There is, indeed, good evidence that household features do affect the risk of victimization by burglars. Sampson (1987) shows that in areas where the percentage of single adult households is high, so the risk of burglary increases across all types of households. Thus the character of your neighbours' households affects the probability that yours will be burgled. Table 4.2 cross-tabulates the risk of burglary in areas where the percentage of single adult households varies (low, medium and high), with households of varying composition. The community effect operates not only for single adult households, but for other household combinations as well.

Beliefs that some neighbourhoods are better bets by virtue of the predominant household composition are clearly in operation here.

What emerges from these various studies is evidence of a degree of purposeful intent and rationality in the activity of criminals, consistent with the view that their beliefs about the opportunities and benefits of crime determine their attitudes and intentions. Weaver and Carroll (1985) confirmed this general finding, using the technique whereby experienced criminals – in this case, shoplifters – are compared with novices on their first training session with an experimenter. Weaver and Carroll used a method of data collection they call process tracing whereby the shoplifters accompanied the experimenter on an hour-long trip around a supermarket with a view either to shopping or shoplifting. A hidden tape recorder served to record their stream of thoughts throughout the expedition. The main finding was that expert shoplifters said rather different things from novices, betraying a greater sense of strategy in their offending. Novices were more concerned with motivation – with what they wished to steal. Experts, on the other hand, concentrated on the technical problems of the shoplifting itself, such as security devices; motivation was taken for granted. Novices were deterred by fears of apprehension and guilt; experts were deterred by strategic problems like size of items. Experts regarded security devices and the like as problems to be surmounted; novices were readily deterred by any problem they perceived. The lesson from this study in relation to the model of Planned Behaviour (figure 4.1), is that experts have a repertoire of skills which enables them easily to justify their optimistic approach to theft and their many calculations of the benefits of stealing. Novices lack those skills and their cost-benefit analyses are hence readily dominated by fear of capture and subsequent humiliation.

The social calculus

Beliefs about the propriety and acceptability of offending to those whose opinions we value play a more or less important role in our calculations according to the concern we have for our reputations. Increasing attention is being paid to such subjective norms (see figure 4.1) in the genesis of offending. Norms are particularly important in certain crimes of violence, but are also well illustrated in the justifications and excuses developed by property offenders and also in relation to a number of so-called white-collar crimes. Action taken against insider trading and legislation to permit the more extensive inspection of bank accounts by police officers in the UK, have perhaps helped to change attitudes somewhat to criminal behaviour in business and commerce (see Levi, 1991). That normative pressures are influential is strikingly illustrated in research by Berger and his colleagues (Berger et al., in press) on drunk-driving. The incidence of drunk-driving varies enormously between the three countries they studied – Australia, Norway and the USA, with the greatest contrast being between Norway and the other two countries. Drinkers in Norway drink quite heavily, 35 per cent of them usually consuming four or more drinks on each occasion. However, they infrequently drink away from home, and only 2 per cent admit to driving after having consumed four or more drinks. Twenty-three per cent of them know someone who was jailed in the last year, and 70 per cent support imprisonment as a punishment for first offenders. Australians also drink fairly heavily (30 per cent consuming 4 or more drinks on each occasion), but they frequently drink away from home and 28 per cent drove home after consuming four or more drinks. A mere 5 per cent knew someone jailed for the offence in the past year and only 19 per cent support jail for first offenders. The striking differences in norms and attitudes between people in those countries leads the authors to suggest that Norway has progressed to a situation where drunk-driving is prevented by moral pressure rather than being merely deterred by the prospect of punishment.

Wilson and Gorring (1985) point to the importance of normative beliefs in the criminal fraud perpetrated by doctors in Australia. Medical fraud apparently costs the country far more than burglary and it occurs, according to the authors, partly because being in a position of trust doctors have the opportunities to commit crime. More important, however, are the factors that serve to legitimate crime as merely an appropriate pursuit of self-interest. The authors cite training which orients doctors away from altruistic towards strictly professional concerns, career expectations of high rewards, and medical unions which pursue the financial self-interest of doctors rather than the interests of people's health.

Where the definition of crime is unambiguous then as we have seen perpetrators may rationalize and excuse their offences sometimes by what amounts to a process of redefinition of the crime as something other than criminal or immoral. Pogrebin et al. (1986) studied a sample of 62 persons found guilty of embezzlement and suggest that the very position of trust that embezzlers usually enjoy within an organization is itself used to justify their theft: as trustees they can be permitted to make appropriate use of the money entrusted to them, even if that involves paying off personal debts (the usual starting motive for embezzlement). As one would expect, the more resources available to the embezzler (as indicated by the higher status of the job in question) the greater were the sums of money involved, indicating yet again the importance of behavioural control in criminal behaviour, a factor also recently illustrated in a quite different context by Lester (1991). He showed that the differential availability of firearms in different European countries was directly related to murder using firearms but not to the incidence of murder by other means.

Reasoned action and crimes of violence: the case of rape

It is one thing to argue that property crime is a calculated activity but many crimes of violence do not seem at first glance to fall into that category. Stereotypically, most violent crimes are seen to be relatively spontaneous, impulsive crimes of passion, not based on reason. In fact, much recent work thoroughly undermines such stereotypes and male violence against women is a case in point. Stets and Pirog-good (1987), for example, report that one major determinant of male violence against their female dating partners was a tendency of the men to accept a range of violent tactics as non-violent. No such relationship existed for violence perpetrated by women against men, suggesting that the justification of violence by men but not by women is normative in our culture. This notion recurs in many other studies. Smeaton and Byrne (1987), for example, report that the more a male had 'hypermasculine' beliefs the more likely he would be to justify raping a dating partner.

At what stage of development 'fear of unmanliness' becomes a salient force in males' lives is unclear. Davis and Leitenberg (1987) in a review of work on adolescent sex offenders report that no work had then been carried out on relevant attitudinal characteristics of male adolescents who have raped females. Relevant studies of adults and of adult sex offenders have been conducted. Fischer (1987), for example, has demonstrated that permissive attitudes towards rape are correlated positively with traditional attitudes towards women. Scott and Tetreault (1987) have shown that rapists, more than other violent offenders, and more than non-offenders, have more conservative attitudes towards women. Rapists, they suggest, hold exaggerated versions of stereotyped views about what is appropriate behaviour for women – letting males take the sexual initiative, staying at home to look after the children, etc. – that are typical of men in general. A similar conclusion is reached by Burt (1983) who claims that rapists use to their own advantage justifications for violence against women which are already prevalent in society.

Scully and Marolla (1984) interviewed 114 convicted male rapists incarcerated in seven Virginian (USA) prisons. About 40 per cent of the men denied they had committed rape, and justified their behaviour by a combination of discrediting and blaming the victim, thereby leaving themselves free to put their own behaviour in a benign light. The woman might be portrayed as willing, a luring seductress whose behaviour led the men unsuspectingly into sexual exploits. 'Women mean "yes" when they say "no"', 'most women eventually relax and enjoy it', 'nice girls don't get raped' were other predominant themes in the interview responses.

By way of contrast those admitting their offences were prone to excuse their behaviour, for example by blaming alcohol and drugs, referring to their emotional problems and projecting an essentially 'nice guy' image beneath it all. One young man who had raped at knife point and subsequently killed five women stated: 'Physically they enjoyed the sex. Once they got involved it would be difficult to resist. I was always gentle and kind until I started to kill them. And the killing was always sudden, so they wouldn't know it was coming' (p. 541).

The authors allege that convicted rapists 'have learned the attitudes and actions consistent with sexual aggression against women', including the 'acquisition of culturally-derived vocabularies of motive which can be used to diminish responsibility and to negotiate a non-deviant identity'.

Precisely because rape can be so readily 'justified' or 'excused' it can be used to serve multiple purposes. Scully and Marolla (1985) report further on the interviews with their sample of rapists, showing that, from the rapists' perspectives, rape can serve a variety of quite conscious motives in their lives. A number of rapists saw their activities as inflicting appropriate punishment or revenge, sometimes against the victim's male partner. Rape was sometimes a bonus to a routine burglary; or to gain sexual access as a presumed right; or to achieve sexual fulfilment through control and domination, which for some represented the ultimate in sexual experience. It is perhaps not surprising that few of the men reported feeling guilty after raping their victims. Predominantly, it elevated their self-esteem, and made them feel good.

Lisak and Roth (1988) examined the role of motivational factors in sexual aggression in two studies involving a total of 261 male university students. Questionnaire data were used to classify the men on a seven-point scale of sexual aggresssion from non-aggressive (1) to rape (7). The data from the first study of 184 men permitted a classification of the 141 heterosexually active men in that study as follows:

		No.	%
1	Non-aggressive	32	22.7
2	Fantasy rape	17	12.1
3	Manipulative sex	38	27.0
4	Coercive sex	33	23.4
5	Sexual assault	9	6.4
6	Attempted rape	3	2.1
7	Rape	9	6.4

The views of these men were obtained on the anger they felt towards women (for example, women act seductively in deliberately teasing way; feelings of being betrayed or manipulated by women); on the desire for power over women (for example, 'Have you ever felt the urge to assert yourself with a woman because she was getting a little too "pushy", a little too domineering?'); and on feelings of disinhibition (for example, holding cynical views about conventional morality).

Analysis of their views revealed a major divide between those men in categories 5, 6 and 7 on the one hand, and those in categories 1, 2, 3 and 4 on the other. The dividing line is between those admitting to coercive sex, in which the man admits to persisting with sexual intercourse without using force even though the woman tried verbally to stop him, and those admitting to sexual assault in which physical force is used to make a woman engage in kissing or petting when she did not want to. The use of force, or its threatened use, is a pointer to views about the nature of women and of sexual morality which sets these men apart from others, whose ranks nevertheless include those whose behaviour overrides the woman's wishes in the matter, short only of being physically violent. The two studies were consistent in demonstrating highly significant differences between the sexually aggressive and the sexually non-aggressive men on all the variables of underlying power, underlying anger and disinhibition, with sexually aggressive men scoring higher in each case.

The importance of such work on samples of non-convicted sexual aggressors is illustrated by the results of a national survey in the US reported by Koss et al. (1987). This large-scale study of male and female higher education students revealed that 56 per cent of the women, whose mean age was 21, reported having endured forced sexual contact since the age of 18. Rape itself was reported by 15.5 per cent of the women surveyed. The respective admissions for men were 25 per cent and 4.5 per cent. In a one-year period, 18 per cent of the women reported that they had been coerced into intercourse or into oral or anal penetration; 9 per cent of the men admitted such offences. The total number of incidents reported and admitted suggests that some misperception exists on one side or another; many men did not perhaps recognize the degree of violence in their behaviour. The authors suggest that many men see their aggressive behaviour as congruent with consensual sexual activity. The prevalence of rape and sexual violence suggests to these authors that sexual violence by men against women is part of the 'normal' pattern of relations between men and women, and that we must no longer think of rape as a crime committed by a small number of sexually psychopathic males. Rather, it is a crime committed by a substantial minority of men whose behaviour is implicitly condoned in the language and use of traditional reasoning.

The environmental calculus

Aspects of the immediate environment have frequently been linked to crime rates. One of the most interesting is the association between violent crime and temperature, increases in temperature and high temperatures being linked to the incidence of violence (e.g.

Cotton, 1986; Anderson, 1987), mediated presumably by the influence of temperature on mood (at least in working environments);
higher temperatures increase negative arousal which then becomes
directed towards provocative people or circumstances. Recently
much work has been directed towards the idea that the built
environment may similarly have an indirect effect on victimization
by its effects on the evaluation of different targets, for example
residences (see Brantingham and Brantingham, 1981).

In 1972 Oscar Newman claimed that crime flourished in some
urban areas because residents could not exercise sufficient informal
control over their environment; they lacked 'defensible space'.
Coleman's book, *Utopia on Trial*, echoes this theme and opera-
tionalized the notion of defensibility in blocks of flats by reference
to 15 design variables, for example number of dwellings per entrance, storey height, presence of overhead walkways, a front
garden and gate etc. Blocks of flats (4099 of them) were coded on
design features presumed to facilitate crime (its lack of defensibility),
and design was then correlated with measures of abuse of the
physical environment: litter, graffiti, excrement and vandalism, and
in later studies, crime itself. The expected correlation between 'good'
design and low abuse was found (Coleman, 1985).

Sommer (1987) has recently tested the defensible space hypothesis
across differently designed university halls of residence, and found
that the hypothesis stands up well in relation to the incidence of
a number of criminal acts. Brown (1985) and Brown and Altman
(1983) also found in relation to single family houses that non-burgled
houses were more visible to observers from the road, were better
maintained and had more signs of personalized care (e.g. symbolic
barriers, ornaments) than did houses that had been burgled.
However, Macdonald and Gifford (1989) point out that the characteristics of the burgled houses may have been the product of
owners' response to being burgled, not a cause of the burglary
itself. In their carefully conducted research, burglars rated photographs of houses that varied systematically in supposed dimensions of defensibility. Surveillability from the road was an important
predictor of vulnerability, occupants' surveillability of the outside
slightly less so. Symbolic barriers, however, seemed to encourage
burglars to burgle, probably because estimates of house value were
strongly correlated with vulnerability.

There is, then, some discrepancy between the results of laboratory
experimental studies with burglars and observations of where crime

actually takes place. What is needed are predictive or prospective studies to clear up the confusion, although it should be noted that all studies point to the importance of one or more design features characterizing the defensible space hypothesis. There is little doubt that by manipulating the environment we can control to some extent the degree if not the type of crime. Car theft has been reduced since locking devices made cars more secure, although there may be some displacement of that form of criminal activity on to some other form.

Laycock in two studies (1984, 1985) shows that both perceived difficulty or danger and actual increased difficulty of breaking into premises will prevent break-ins. It would appear to be sufficient merely to advertise property marking to secure a reduction in theft of such property. In Ehrlich's terms, by manipulating the environment we affect the demand for crime (Ehrlich, 1982). A novel example of this is Moser's study of vandalism of telephone boxes (1988). A notice explaining what to do in the event of telephone breakdown (e.g. by a map showing the location of the nearest alternative telephone) was sufficient to reduce considerably the incidence of retaliatory vandalism by frustrated callers.

Notwithstanding the arguments of those like Hope (1986), who denigrate the notion of architectural determinism, the evidence we have briefly reviewed suggests that people do, indeed, adapt their behaviour according to environmental features in what is clearly a reasoned fashion. For example, it is safer to break into a flat from which there are a multiplicity of escape routes than from one to which access is through one entrance serving the whole block (Coleman, 1985). The environment may not create crime, but it may facilitate crime by affecting the calculations of those – that is, all of us – who are exposed to criminal opportunities.

5
Criminal–Victim Interaction

The stereotypical victim of crime is the vulnerable individual, most likely female, very old or very young: someone who is typically innocent, passive and blameless. Paradoxically, becoming a victim may undermine in the eyes of others the claim to possess those qualities required of victims. A vulnerable individual should not be so reckless as to venture into situations where their vulnerability might be exploited. Howard (1984b), for example, shows that a woman's character will be called into question much more than will a man's if she or he is sexually attacked whilst hitch-hiking.

In practice, victims are not generally especially vulnerable people, certainly not in terms of gender or age, and they are not always innocent. Indeed, we shall see that Black's (1983) notion of crime as social control – whereby vengeance is achieved by those who themselves have been victimized – is an accurate portrayal of the circumstances of some types of crime. Nor is it true that the victim is always an individual. Groups and organizations, corporations and the state itself are also victims of a great deal of crime; indeed, these are the most frequent victims, according to Freiberg (1988): 'Through customs offences, social security frauds, sales, income, payroll, gift, death and other forms of tax evasion, the state is probably the most frequent victim of crime' (p. 23). In turn, the public itself is the victim of countless corporate 'crimes' or injustices, both financial and against the person, for which none may necessarily be censured, blamed or punished even when responsibility has been apportioned (Cullen et al., 1983).

The overwhelming role of the state in prosecuting criminals keeps victims relatively inconspicuous during the process of criminal investigation and any subsequent prosecution. The victim's role is limited to that of providing for others whatever evidence is sought or accepted as a basis for prosecution. Such public imperceptibility may serve to mask the crucial role that victims play in ensuring that the criminal justice system has its quota of cases to process. Although the stereotype suggests a minimal role for the victim – who as an essentially mild, passive, defenceless individual is offended against and on being so discovered is instantly championed by the police and the courts in a successful prosecution of the criminal culprit – the reality is quite different. In this chapter there are three aspects of victims' behaviour that I wish to bring forward for discussion that determine the quantity and quality of criminal justice: in what respect do victims contribute to their own victimization? What prompts victims to report their crimes? How does fear of being a victim affect behaviour of potential victims? Let us take those questions in order.

How do victims contribute to their own victimization?

Some social psychologists have suggested that it brings comfort to people to have faith in a just world, and that one necessary price of support for this enabling proposition is the belief that, by and large, victims get what they deserve (Lerner, 1980). If others deserve their victimization, we deserve our immunity! Points of law may sometimes turn on whether or not the victim is 'truly' a victim or not. Jackson (1988) describes strictly comparable cases of fraud which gave rise to contrary judgements, seemingly because the worldly innocence of two elderly sisters was more truly apparent than that of a male postgraduate chemistry student (pp. 101–6). Blaming the victim does not these days always have such intuitive appeal. A judge who in England recently gave a light sentence for rape of a female hitch-hiker because of her 'contributory negligence' received short shrift from most of the press.

In may be, as Maxfield (1987) points out, that it is little more than commonsense to argue that what people do and how they behave may affect the likelihood of victimization, just as it affects the likelihood of other misfortunes like having a car accident. Certainly, it is undeniable that those whose lifestyles increase their availability for victimization suffer most from personal assault, theft or robbery: men more than women, the young rather than the old,

single and divorced more than married or widowed, and the unemployed more than the employed. Gottfredson's (1984) examination of the British Crime Survey data shows clearly that night-time
behaviour which increases exposure to likely assailants is strongly
associated with victimization: for example, going out at weekends,
going to parties, travelling by public transport, rather than say,
staying in, visiting friends or going to church, and travelling by
car. Even more interesting is the strong association between victimization and self-reported drinking and self-reported offending.
For example, 42 per cent of those who confessed to assault and
violence reported being victimized, compared with 6 per cent of
those who did not so offend. The difference in level of victimization
for those committing theft and those not committing theft was not
so great (13 per cent versus 6 per cent) but still substantial. The
deviance of victims with respect to alcohol consumption at least
was convincingly demonstrated by Budd (1982) who demonstrated
that 100 homicide victims in Los Angeles in 1980 had levels of
blood alcohol that were substantially higher than would be expected
from a sample of the population.

A study by Hassinger (1985) indicates how a perpetuating cycle
of criminal–victim–criminal interaction may ensue. He questioned
those who legally carried guns in public places and discovered
that fear of crime in one guise or another accounted for the main
reasons given by 96 per cent of the sample interviewed. The
respondents were particularly anxious for the protection of a gun
when moving through downtown commercial and rundown city
areas, areas where indeed victimization would be more likely to
occur. Of course, potential assailants in those areas are unlikely to
remain unmoved by the prospect that substantial numbers of their
potential victims will be armed. It is likely to be as potent an
incentive to armed robbery as it is a disincentive.

Kennedy and Forde (1990) using data from a Canadian study
confirm that a lifestyle that takes people away from home increases
the risk of property crime victimization, but they also show that
a lifestyle typical of young males that exposes them to potential
interpersonal conflict increases their chances of being assaulted or
robbed. For example, young unmarried males who frequent bars
and also are out walking or driving around are those who are most
likely to be robbed. And they are most likely to be robbed because
offenders themselves are drawn from the same pool of people who
are attracted to such a lifestyle: here is a convergence of potential

victims and offenders in space and time. The importance of lifestyle is highlighted by analyses of Miethe et al. (1990) showing that changes in lifestyle were accompanied by (mostly) predictable changes in the risks of victimization.

A recent study in Sweden suggests, however, that the hypothesis that criminals and victims are drawn from the same population because of their shared lifestyle, is too simplistic. Kühlhorn (1990) examined the cases of all those sentenced in the Stockholm region in 1975 for murder, manslaughter and aggravated assault, and one in every ten cases of assault. He tested the hypothesis that there would be systematic differences in the status of offenders and victims. These differences would, he thought, on the basis of a previous study, lead to misunderstandings and misperceptions which lie at the root of interpersonal violence. There were, indeed, consistent differences between offenders and their corresponding victims: the offenders are more likely to be male, and to be younger and less wealthy than their victims. They were also more likely to have criminal convictions and a history of violence, to be in receipt of welfare assistance, to drink and use drugs. That said, the victims were also not drawn from a 'normal' population, especially with regard to income, criminality, alcohol and drug abuse. In these respects, they were clearly intermediate between the offender and a 'normal' population. But there were also similarities between offenders and their individual victims in lifestyle variables. The biggest drinking offenders were matched with the biggest drinking victims, despite the overall differences between the two groups. And the same kind of matching occurred with respect to welfare benefits, drug abuse, sex and age. The author suggests that lifestyle may, indeed, bring the two groups together, but that asymmetry between people in critical encounters 'facilitates violence from the direction of the most socially deviant' (p. 56).

People's jobs and people's communities independently affect the likelihood of victimization. Collins and Cox (1987) show that jobs which involve dealing frequently with members of the public – for example, delivery and sales jobs – are associated with violent victimization. Lynch (1987) reports on USA Crime Survey data which specifically addressed work-related victimization, and which showed clearly that exposure to risk by virtue of work-related activities was more important than demographic characteristics of employees in determining victimization.

Sampson and Wooldredge (1987) confirm that lifestyle routine activities are associated with victimization, but in addition they demonstrate that community variables operate to increase victimization independently of the lifestyle of its members. Social cohesion, for example, militates against burglary, social cohesion being defined in terms of mobility and density of friendship networks. More prosaically, it was found that owning a VCR does not itself increase your chances of being burgled, but being in an area where many possess VCRs does increase the risk. Hough (1987) presents an unflattering portrait of burglars' abilities and points out that over half attempted burglaries are total failures. His conclusion is that quite minor precautions, like leaving lights on when out at night, may be sufficient to reduce the risk of burglary.

Women as victims

The lifestyle of women, it has been claimed, has changed more dramatically than has the male lifestyle. Their role has become less domestic, and more work-orientated; and more women live alone, have more possessions and carry more money than they used to. This being so, it seems reasonable to suggest that women should now feature more as victims of crime than they used to in the past. Moreover, there seems to be little reason to suppose that this would not be evident for most crimes. Competing more with men, and living at work and at home more like men, their representation as victims both of property crimes and of assaults should have risen. M.D. Smith (1987) examined the proportion of different types of victimizations experienced by women in the US over a nine-year period from 1973 to 1982. His results show that the representation of women as victims of robbery and larceny increased by a significant amount, comparable figures for violent crimes showing no increase.

It is, of course, to be expected from a lifestyles analysis that property crimes directed against women would show a proportional increase. The virtual absence of a comparable increase in crimes of violence is harder to explain. Without knowing more about the circumstances in which violence occurred, it is not possible to say with any certainty why women should apparently prove the exception to the availability rule with respect to crimes of violence. It might be that as public violence against women increased proportionately, so the proportionate level of domestic violence decreased, leaving the average about steady. Only more detailed studies can provide the answer.

The contribution of victims to sexual abuse

West (1984) suggests that many sexual assaults are assaults in law only, and that the active consent and co-operation of the victim is often given, the event sometimes being initiated by the victim. He cites evidence suggesting that 80 per cent of homosexual offences against minors are consensual, the equivalent figure for hetero-sexual offences being 34 per cent.

West is confident that a significant proportion of children initiate sexual relationships with adults, and that adult-child relationships are frequently 'positive' for the child. To be set against West's complacency, Berliner and Conte (1990) and Conte et al. (1989) describe a study of 23 abused children and their abusers which makes it apparent that children's belief in the relationship as positive can coexist with the use of coercive tactics by adults which the children found impossible to resist. Three stages in the abusive relationship were apparent: sexualization of an existing relationship, justification of the abuser's behaviour, and finally co-operation, in which the offenders seek to keep the child involved in the relation-ship but prevent them from telling others about it. The process is clearly manipulative and in the interests of the offender not the child, yet both the children and the professionals involved were often reluctant to condemn the behaviour as sexual exploitation. The abusers themselves had no such illusions. In their interviews (Conte et al., 1989) , the abusers describe clearly how they targeted children, secured their co-operation, and exploited their needs to keep them available.

Not all sexual abusers are as subtle in their manipulation of the victims as were those described by Conte and his colleagues. Silbert and Pines (1983) describe a study of 200 female street prostitutes aged 10 years to 46 years. Sixty per cent of the women reported having been sexually exploited as juveniles by an average of two males each. Nearly 70 per cent had been physically damaged and virtually all reported severe emotional damage. It is evident from this study that severe physical and sexual childhood abuse has been the experience of many females who end up as prostitutes, but it is equally clear from the work of Conte and his colleagues, that the so-called collaboration of the child in less obviously coercive instances of sexual abuse is no more a matter of informed consent than is the collaboration of any other victim of a confidence trick.

As Goffman (1952) so well described it, tricksters learn to 'cool the mark out' in order to minimize the chance that damaging complaints will be lodged against them. In the same way that the 'mark' is led to accept his or her victimization, so young children may come to believe that their seducers meant them no harm: 'From a psychological perspective, perhaps, it is too painful and humiliating for the child to face the possibility that what was taken for a misguided or "sick" misuse of the relationship or even for real love was in fact an elaborate strategy to manipulate and use him/her without regard for his/her feelings or benefit' (Berliner and Conte, 1990, p. 38). The fact that children may even fail to perceive themselves as victims should not blind us to the process by which they have been victimized, any more than the failure of a victim of a gambling swindle to realize it was not his fault that he lost a fortune should lead the police to ignore the activities of the successful swindler (see Snyder, 1986).

The belief is frequently expressed that women contribute to their victimization by dressing and behaving in ways that evoke sexually aggressive behaviour in men. Krahé (1988) in an experimental study obtained typical results, but shows in addition that subjects who endorsed rape myth beliefs were especially likely to use behavioural information to denigrate a women who alleged she had been raped, the rape myth being a set of sex-role beliefs which lead to attribution of responsibility for the rape to the victim herself. In Krahé's study, the manipulation of the victim's pre-rape behaviour took the form of the variation of a single sentence in the description of the case. The introductory sentence started either, 'After having finished work in her office, the victim was on her way to the car park where her car was parked', or 'After having had a drink on her own in a pub, the victim was on her way to the car-park where her car was parked'. The role-discrepant drink in the pub led men and women who scored high on rape myth acceptance to attribute responsibility for the rape to the victim herself.

The tendency to blame the victim has been linked to other features like attractiveness and the relationship between the victim and accused. For example, Gerdes et al. (1988) show that less attractive victims and victims who were acquainted with their attacker were more likely to be deemed responsible for the rape attack. Such general endorsement of sexual aggression, at least in certain circumstances, helps condone assaulters' distorted perceptions of their activities. Dutton's study of 75 persistent wife-batterers (1986) found not only that the wife's behaviour was used to excuse or justify the assault, but that those who blamed their wives were also inaccurate in their descriptions and recall of the assaults. Specifically, they described the assaults as less frequent, less severe and less consequential than was actually the case.

Some support for the view that women's behaviour may render them more likely to be attacked comes from a study by Koss and Dinero (1989) of 2700 college women in the USA. They assessed the women on variables which have been said to put women at risk of sexual attack, with a view to assessing the relative importance of those factors in bringing about the past victimization of the women. There were three sets of risk variables: (a) traumatic experiences in childhood – e.g. family violence and sexual abuse – which are said to create vulnerability; (b) social psychological characteristics, including measures of sexual attitudes, adversarial sexual beliefs, and rape myth acceptance; and (c) situational–behavioural variables, like alcohol use and frequency of sexual activity, factors that could be said to facilitate victimization by a sexually aggressive man.

Retrospectively using the statistical technique of discriminant analysis, a composite 'predictive' model was developed which correctly classified only 25 per cent of the 396 rape victims, and failed entirely to discriminate amongst lesser categories of sexual aggression, and wrongly predicted that 61 non-victimized women would be rape victims. Four variables represented virtually all of the discriminating power: sexual abuse in childhood, present sexual attitudes, alcohol abuse, and sexual activity. However, sexual attitudes and behaviour assumed importance only in the context of a sexualized childhood.

Principally, this study found that there was a main effect of childhood sexual abuse; and amongst those who had been abused, those with more liberal sexual attitudes, who were more active sexually and who drank more tended to be those who reported having been raped. Nonetheless the limited strength of these associations led the authors to conclude that: 'In future conceptual work on rape vulnerability, a valid interpretation of the present

results that should be considered is that most of the sexually assaulted women were dissimilar to unvictimised women primarily
in that they had encountered a sexually aggressive man' (p. 249).
Given that conclusion, it is surprising that the authors go on to
suggest that 'clinical interventions . . . targeted at the reduction of
risky behaviours might be warranted among clients who are potential targets of sexual assault' (p. 249). These two contrasting
conclusions reflect the authors' ambivalence towards results which
confirm that who will be raped is to some extent predictable from
behaviour and attitudes of the victim, but which overall demonstrate
that most women who are raped are indistinguishable in character
and background from those who are not. Moreover, such
associations as were found retrospectively between characteristics
and victim status may (a) be themselves a product of victimization,
and (b) say nothing about what determined the offence or offences
in question.

The authors are on sure ground when they conclude that the
results offer 'no justification for continuing to focus on gender role
behaviour or rape-supportive attitudes as risk factors by which
some women are rendered uniquely vulnerable to victimization'
(p. 249). Neither femininity on the one hand nor feminist attitudes on the other increased or decreased vulnerability to sexual
assault.

According to Walker (1989) the traditional sex role 'script' incorporates the belief that men have the right to control the women in
their lives, if necessary by violent means. Of course, not only men
but women also are socialized into this way of thinking, as a recent
study of token resistance to sex clearly indicates. Muehlenhard and
Hollabaugh (1988) discovered that of a large sample of sexually
active women in their university, 61 per cent reported having
engaged in token resistance to sex; that is, they had indicated they
had not wanted to have sex with a man when in fact they had
every intention to and were willing to engage in sexual behaviour
with the man concerned. A variety of reasons was given by the
women for engaging in this behaviour but most importantly it
was related to belief in a sexual script which emphasizes the role
of the man's aggression in overcoming an insincere display of
reluctance by the woman. As the authors indicate, such behaviour
may be 'rational' for women in this culture but it is also the case
that the widespread practice of token resistance can only encourage men to ignore women's refusals.

What prompts victims to report their experiences?

Were it not for victims reporting their experiences to the police, little conventional crime would be investigated or prosecuted. As it is, the police have no shortage of crimes reported to them, most of which goes uninvestigated and remains unsolved. For all that, Sparks et al. (1977) calculated that about two-thirds of victimizations are not reported to the police. The degree of reporting varies with type of crime. Car theft is nearly always reported whereas assault is rarely reported. Of course, theft of a car needs to be reported for purposes of prosecuting insurance claims.

Objective seriousness and subjective estimates of seriousness influenced people's willingness to report crimes committed against them, but just as important was an evaluation of whether the police would or could do anything about the situation: With 'trivial' crime, people quite rightly are pessimistic on both counts. Indeed, it is common knowledge that police prioritize crimes in terms of their seriousness and their ease of solution, for they are disinclined to waste their time on trivial crimes or even more serious crimes that are unlikely to be solved.

Victim crime surveys carried out by national governments have clarified considerably the answers to questions about which crimes get reported to the police. The recent report by Webb and Marshall (1989) confirms many findings of earlier, smaller studies. They analysed 44,593 reports of personal victimization in relation to three sets of factors: socio-demographic, including age; incident variables relating to the severity of offence; and contextual variables concerning the locale in which the incident took place. Their particular study excluded those incidents where there was no contact between offender and victim, thereby leaving them to draw conclusions about what action different victims would take to defend themselves against the offenders.

Table 5.1 presents a summary of the main factors determining the level of resistance to the aggressor. Fight (or flight) is most characteristic of better-educated, young, white victims, particularly in cases of rape and assault, living in predominantly white communities with male heads of household. It should be said that gender was related to mode of defence: women were more likely to attempt non-violent resistance whereas men were more physically aggressive towards the offender. However, none of the factors

Table 5.1 Factors determining level of resistance (physical and non-physical) to assailants

	Moderately Important Factors	*Of Little of No Importance*
Socio-demographic factors	Age: younger more resistant Race: whites more resistant Education: better-educated more resistant	Gender Family income
Incident factors	Type of crime: victims of rape and assault most resistant; victims of robbery and especially armed robbery least resistant	Weapon present Multiple offenders Bystanders present
Contextual factors	Percentage Black neighbourhood: higher the less resistant Percentage Female headed households: more, the less resistant	Age range of population Level of unemployment Poverty level of community

Source: After Webb and Marshall, 1989

studied was of overwhelming importance in determining resistance to victimization.

That is even more true of the findings for reporting to the police (table 5.2). Socio-demographic variables in particular were only weakly associated with reporting, with no consistent association with age; 62 per cent do not report in the youngest age group (12–24), down to 46 per cent in the 25–34-year-olds and 43 per cent amongst 35–54-year-old group and up to 47 per cent but the 55+ group. As for gender, the difference is a mere 56 per cent non-reporting for men and 50 per cent for women. Contextual factors

Table 5.2 Factors associated with reporting to police

	Moderately Important Factors	Of Little or no Importance
Socio-demographic factors	Age: the very young (12–24) report less Sex: more women report	Race Family income Educational level
Incident factors	Weapon present increases reporting Multiple offenders increases reporting Type of crime: greatest for rape and armed robbery Bystanders present: report more	
Contextual factors		Age range of population Household head male/female Racial mix Educational level Unemployment Poverty

Source: After Webb and Marshall, 1989

were of minimal significance but incident factors, which are associated with severity of offence, were as a whole of considerable importance. Reporting by the individual was greatest when the offence was grave, when a weapon was in evidence, and there were multiple offenders. The failure of socio-economic and community variables to influence reporting is replicated in a study by Biblarz et al. (1984) where a composite measure of 'social integration' failed to predict reporting of serious crimes in a survey of nearly 20,000 households.

The immediate social context of the victimization is an important incident factor that is directly related to type of crime. Victimization within the family is notoriously under-reported, and notoriously kept at arms length by the police who have in the past been reluctant to challenge a husband's or parent's rights to chastise as they think fit. A recent study by Singer (1988) indicates that 5 per cent of victimizations involving direct contact between victim and offender are not reported primarily from fear of reprisal. This reason is given especially by women, by single people, by the less educated, the poor and by children and teenagers. More significantly these victimisations took place predominantly in the house as part of a series of offences by someone known to the victim, frequently their spouse. The power relationship with the offender is a critically important aspect of the social context of the victimization.

Experimental social psychology has confirmed some aspects of the survey results and given a plausible explanation for some of the findings. Extensive work on bystander intervention in emergencies, including when a crime has been committed, suggests that crime reporting is not the result of an especially rational process of calculation of the costs and benefits of such action, any more than is bystander intervention in any kind of emergency. Intervention – and crime reporting – occurs on an impulse, as Kidd's review indicates (Kidd, 1985). If people intervene, they do so within seconds, depending on the clarity of the situation (e.g. someone calls for help), prior contact with the victim (e.g. a friend) and seriousness. Kidd's model of crime reporting suggests that seeing a crime being committed creates emotional arousal which leads to relatively unthinking, habitual reactions, with intervention (or reporting) being the chosen response when the victim's suffering is more salient than the apparent potential danger of the situation. Intervention is also more likely when the individual concerned is a naturally impulsive person. People who impulsively or recklessly intervene are apparently generally impulsive individuals and above average in 'aggression'.

Experimental studies by Greenberg et al. (1979, 1982) rather confirm aspects of Kidd's model for reporting by victims as well as bystanders. In one ingenious experimental field study of theft from part-time job applicants, it was shown that anger was associated with the victim's decision to report a theft, and that advice from another to report had no effect on the decision to report, although advice not to report was heeded. Reporting was clearly determined by strong arousal, it occurred quickly and was not overly influenced by rational considerations.

More detailed analyses of the circumstances in which crimes are committed and subsequently reported or not are required if we are to have any hope of developing a reasonably adequate account of why the police are kept in ignorance of the bulk of crime.

So far in the discussion we have considered crime reporting in general, and the type of crime has merely been entered as one factor in the equation. However, type of crime is probably the single most important factor determining the response to victimization, and that is true not merely because more serious crimes tend to be those that are reported to the police. A vital ingredient in crime reporting is the individual's expectation about the response they will receive from representatives of the legal and judicial system. Ford (1983) reports that in two-thirds of cases where women complained about their husband's violence towards them, the matter was 'solved' by telephone when the woman rang the police. Uncertainty, indecision, inefficiency and complacency by officials characterized the processing of those cases that were pursued by the police, with some prosecutors even refusing to treat wife battery as a criminal offence until the wife had petitioned for divorce. Naturally, no such uncertainty and prevarication occur over the definition of crimes such as burglary, or crimes of violence occurring outside the family. Interestingly, Ford's analysis showed that 70 per cent of women who managed to get as far as having the man arrested then declined to continue with the prosecution. Far from this justifying official complacency, this figure indicates the extent to which in many cases taking matters this far had been necessary to enable the woman to negotiate an acceptable arrangement with the man. In other cases it reflected a fear of reprisal if matters were proceeded with. The number of cases in which loving relations had been restored was slight but exaggerated by court officials.

The importance of beliefs about the response to be expected from the police and the legal system for reporting a victimization is well illustrated in the case of rape. Feldman-Summers and colleagues (Feldman-Summers and Norris, 1984; Feldman-Summers and Ashworth, 1981) have shown both in actual cases, and with respect to hypothetical intentions, that reporting to the police by victims is strongly related to the belief that they would be treated in a positive way by police and subsequently in the legal process. However, the most influential factor was the social expectations variable: those who reported were apparently under more social pressure from friends to do so than were those who did not report the offence. If physical injuries had been sustained, then reporting was more likely, and it was more likely if the assailant was a stranger, both of these factors reflecting the common stereotype of rape, and hence, no doubt the victims' beliefs in the credibility of their accounts when told to others. The study by Williams (1984) of a large sample of women who attended a rape crisis centre also confirmed the importance of acquaintance and physical injury in determining whether or not the police were informed.

Psychological consequences of victimization

Fear of crime

Fear of crime may emphatically influence quality of life, principally in its impact on the social life of the community, including problems with the supervision of children, and also on the sense of personal safety when walking or going out for entertainment (Hale, 1988). Crime victimization, in other words, has a collective impact affecting many everyday decisions people take regarding their families' and their own activities.

Those who commit least crime, and who are least likely to be victimized – the elderly, and women – are the most fearful, as measured by standard questions like, 'How safe do you feel walking alone in this area after dark?' Box et al. (1988) show that the gap between men and women tends to narrow in old age, as men become relatively more fearful. Those who have been victimized are, not unnaturally, more fearful than those who have not been robbed or assaulted in public. However, the difference between victimized and non-victimized varies according to the type of neighbourhood. The effect is generally reduced in threatening areas: where neighbours are rowdy, where there are graffiti on walls and buildings, where teenagers hang around street corners, and drunks and tramps frequent the streets, where rubbish and litter are noticeable, and houses are boarded up or windows smashed. Where neighbourhoods are threatening in this kind of way, previous victimization becomes almost irrelevant to fear of crime.

From such findings, we can deduce that the critical factor in fear of crime is estimate of perceived personal risk. As men grow older they perceive themselves to be more vulnerable, in a way which women may always have felt about themselves. In high threat neighbourhoods, perception of risk based on personal experience of victimization becomes irrelevant in the light of the manifestations of crime and disorder all about the neighbourhood.

A number of researchers have investigated social and environmental factors which make people more sensitive to risk. Bankston et al. (1987) take up the question of why people in remote rural areas (where crime is low) have sometimes regarded themselves as at greater risk of victimization than city dwellers. They investigated fear of victimization and perceived likelihood of victimization in relation to specific offences. While there were important differences between offence category types, the results generally showed that the effect of a perceived increase in risk disproportionately increased fear in rural farm populations. Generally speaking, perceived risk is lower in rural farm than in urban population, but when the perceived risk was high, the country dwellers become disproportionately fearful. Take, for example, the level of fear of being beaten up by an acquaintance at different levels of perceived risk for rural farm dwellers and for small city dwellers. Fear rises much more steeply in rural farm dwellers than in urban dwellers when they perceive the risk of being beaten up by an acquaintance as high. Rural farm dwellers are more sensitive to risk, perhaps for the good reason that such an event could have more profound consequences for them should it occur. Generally speaking, sensitivity to perceived risk varies with the seriousness of the crime. Warr (1987) shows that fear of victimization rises more steeply with increases in perceived risk, the more serious is the offence. Thus, women are more fearful of being raped than being hit by a drunken motorist whilst driving their own car. However, increases in perceived risk of these two offences leads to a steeper increase in fear in the case of the more serious offence – rape – than in the case of the less serious driving offence.

Skogan (1981) points out that fear of crime may be fuelled by a general tendency to overestimate the frequency of its occurrence, with violent crime and burglary being especially badly overestimated. Fear of crime had steadily increased in the USA over a 16-year period to 1981, and 86 per cent of the population believed that crime was increasing throughout the US as a whole. Interestingly, only 46 per cent of the sample thought that crime was increasing in *their* area, and only 6 per cent thought their neighbourhoods more dangerous than other neighbourhoods. As a result, although 87 per cent thought that others generally were taking more precautions against crime, this applied to only 67 per cent when 'people in their neighbourhoods' were at issue, and reduced to only 48 per cent of the sample who said *they* were taking more precautions. One may speculate on the reasons for this bias in favour of own neighbourhood, but Heath (1984) adduces interesting evidence that the amount of sensationalism, and the apparent randomness of the crime, in media reports of local crimes, both affect the fear of crime in a population. Specifically, people benefit psychologically (i.e. their fear is reduced) when sensational and random *non-local* crimes are reported, but their fear is increased when similar reporting of local crime prevails, and is read about in the media.

There seems little doubt that fear of crime may seriously affect behaviour, but Liska et al. (1988) make the important point that behaviour may also affect the level of fear. In their analysis of large-scale crime survey data in the USA they demonstrated that there is, indeed, a reciprocal effect whereby constrained behaviour increases fear which may in turn lead to further restrictions on behaviour. Relations with age are particularly informative, indicating that for the very old, constrained behaviour still increases fear, but fear does not further constrain behaviour. The results also confirm the finding that males' vulnerability increases more with age than does females'. Interestingly, age itself is associated with fear only through its effect on behaviour, whereas gender operates by its direct association with fear which in turn serves to constrain behaviour.

Adjustment to victimization

What are the consequences of victimization for individuals? The consequences will vary, of course, according to type of crime, although in one of the few reported comparisons of victim reactions to different types of crime Resick (1987) reports that robbery victims show a similar pattern of response in terms of anxiety, self-esteem and adjustment to work as do victims of rape. However, they improved somewhat quicker. Rape-robbery victims were the most deeply affected of the three groups, suffering more from nightmares and flashbacks, various sexual problems, chronic distress and depression. Consequences vary also with the age of the victim. The appalling consequences that may ensue for victims of child abuse are becoming increasingly well documented (e.g. Miller, 1991), and

they arise in part because of the acute cognitive conflicts and behavioural dilemmas that persistent abuse by a trusted adult imposes
upon the child (e.g. Summit, 1983).

We may assume that on average the problems of adjusting, say,
to a traumatic physical attack are greater than those associated
with burglary of an unoccupied residence, but that does not mean
to say that the effects of the latter are negligible. Virtually all victims
of residential burglary are distressed by the event, and many require
extended clinical support and treatment (Hayward, 1981). Months
after the event, suspicion, paranoia and a sense of disillusionment
are common, and some victims resort to moving house and burning
furniture to escape the sense of pollution and violation (Maguire,
1981). The variety of measures taken by victims of burglary (and
also of assault and robbery) are significantly less than those taken
by victims of rape, but they nonetheless constitute an imposing
list, although taking these measures may do little to alleviate stress,
and changing the telephone number appeared to increase stress
(Wirtz and Harrell, 1987). Such an outcome would, of course, be
expected from the analyses of Liska et al. (1988, above), which
showed that behaviour directly influences levels of fear.

An important study by Brown and Harris (1989) used interviews
with female victims of burglary in a suburb of Utah to evaluate the
extent to which the depth of territorial intrusion was associated
with adverse psychological reactions to burglary. A number of
writers, including Maguire (1981) had noted that 'ransacking'
seemed to be especially traumatic, and the authors reasoned that
extensive intrusion would upset victims more and induce greater
long-term insecurity than would less extensive intrusion. The results
showed clearly that both short-term distress and feelings of
vulnerability (including distrust of the police) were related to degree
of devastation, not so much in terms of damage to property, but
more in relation to the number of rooms entered, and the extent of
disarrangement of property. The value of goods stolen bears little
relation to emotional upset. Curiously, the monetary value *per se* of
goods stolen was negatively related to fear of further burglary, but
if valuable property with sentimental value had been stolen, fear
and feelings of vulnerability were increased. These investigators
also found that short-term coping strategies – talking to neighbours
more frequently, checking locks more often, etc. – were unrelated
to fear of future victimization, and did little or nothing to alleviate
distress in the short-term.

Table 5.3 Illustrative items from three attributional factors in views of female victims of rape

Poor Judgement	Societal Factors	Victim Type
Poor judge of character.	Never police around. People don't get	Can't take care of myself.
Made a rash decision.	involved.	Got what I
Too trusting.	Too much pornography.	deserved. Victim type.

Source: After Frazier, 1990

Tyler and Rasinski (1984) used both interviews and experiments to discover what aspects of a burglary led to long-term fear of victimization. Three different cognitive models of social reasoning were employed to suggest that the perceived *informativeness*, *memorability* and *emotionality* of the event would be important determinants of fear and attempts to cope. In the event the results showed that only informativeness – how much the victims felt they had learned from the crime – and emotionality or 'affect arousal' – how frightened and shocked they had been – were implicated in long-term fear of crime. It is easy to see that territorial invasion as described by Brown and Harris would be strongly associated with the emotionality factor.

The depressive symptoms associated with the aftermath of victimization have been more frequently studied in victims of sexual violence than in victims of burglary and following the pioneering work of Seligman (e.g. Abramson et al., 1978), a number of investigators have sought to relate our understanding of what caused the event to subsequent adverse reactions and adjustment. Meyer and Taylor (1986) for example found that the tendency to blame oneself for the victimization – either one's behaviour or character – was strongly associated with poor adjustment. Frazier (1990) found that so-called 'behavioural' and 'characterological' self-blame were not meaningfully distinguished by the victims of rape that she interviewed, and that self-blame generally led to post-victimization depression. Moreover her careful study showed that blaming both self *and* societal factors was associated with poor adjustment. A factor analysis of 15 attributional statements yielded three factors as described in table 5.3. Of the three factors, societal factors were most strongly related to depression as measured by the Beck Depression Inventory three days after the event, and a regression of those test scores on the three factors accounted for 67 per cent of the variance in scores.

Support for the view that blaming others may be as psychologically counter-productive as blaming oneself for misfortune comes from a review of 25 studies which have examined the relationship between blaming others and adjustment to a variety of misfortunes, including criminal victimization (Tennen and Affleck, 1990). In nearly all cases, the evidence suggests that blaming others does not improve the prospects of successful adjustment or, more likely, has a negative impact. What does seem to be associated with successful adjustment or recovery from traumatizing events is having a feeling of control over one's future life (see Frazier, 1990), coupled with a view of the event itself as a visitation from fate ('it couldn't have been avoided') (see also Frey et al., 1985) that has no implications for efficacious decision making in the future.

Victims in the system

There is an increasing concern that the role of victims within the criminal justice system should be reconsidered. The concern is firstly that the sensitivities of victims should be better considered so that, for example, they should not inadvertently come face-to-face with the defendant outside the courtroom (Shapland and Cohen, 1987). But the concern extends further than this, reflecting a feeling that the state now inappropriately prevents victims from exercising a proper discretionary role in the prosecution of those who have offended them. For example, Resick (1987) suggests that victims 'should be allowed and encouraged to participate in the prosecution of cases as much as possible' (p. 475), taking part, for example, in any process of plea bargaining that might take place and being consulted about sentencing.

Those who call for victim participation need to be clear about the advantages that such participation might bring. Would it consistently improve decision-making? Would it help victims adjust to their circumstances? It is not clear that victim participation would help in either process. Whilst it is entirely reasonable that the needs of victims should be carefully met by the police and the courts, calls for their participation in decision-making go beyond what is self-evidently desirable. It is, of course, necessary that sentencers should be aware of the experiences and sufferings of victims, for without that information it is not possible properly to assess the blame that should be attributed to the offender. To that topic we now turn.

6

Social Psychology of Criminal Liability

Victims who report an offence are inviting the police and the courts to share their view that the harm committed against them was the responsibility of an individual or individuals who should be sought out, publicly blamed and punished for their transgression. The laws governing this process state in an apparently precise manner the circumstances in which blame may be attributed. First, all offences are defined in terms of the act (the *actus reus*) that must be committed before any question of blame arises, for example the appropriation without permission of someone else's property in the case of theft. The concept of *actus reus* conceives the behaviour or conduct of an individual abstracted from the motives, intentions or other mechanisms which may bring it about. However, mere appropriation of the property is not sufficient to justify a charge of theft. There must also be an intention to deprive the other of their property on a permanent basis.

The attempt to separate the behavioural and mental elements of an act is not one that all psychologists welcome (Blackman, 1981), and it leads to many problems in law. The mental element in crime (known as the *mens rea*), is, not surprisingly, the more problematic aspect in many prosecutions. Not that the act itself is always unproblematic. For example, is a failure to act (e.g. not switching off the gas, or not leaving a child in the care of a person over 12 years' old) a positive act or not? Further complications arise from the fact that the mental requirement is relaxed in cases of strict liability, where the *actus reus* alone is sufficient for conviction, drunk-driving being a notable example. Negligence and recklessness may also be sufficient in many circumstances to justify blaming someone who may not have intended the act but could have reasonably fore-seen the harmful consequences of the act. Yet more complications arise from the possibility that planning but not committing a crime may in certain circumstances be an offence in itself, e.g. criminal conspiracy. Moreover, in other circumstances merely being associated with someone who commits a crime may render one liable to prosecution for a secondary offence of, say, aiding and abetting. Even having proved the combination of *actus reus* and *mens rea* the prosecution may yet be thwarted by general defences advanced by the accused. The crime may be justified by 'necessity', for example, or excused because of provocation, threat, 'automatism' or mental illness.

Of course, the law is usually presented by lawyers, and even more certainly by judges, as having coherence and certainty in principle, and consistency and fairness in practice. Yet evidence to the contrary comes at us day by day in reports of truly gross miscarriages of justice and in debate of the need for truly fundamental reform of the adversarial criminal justice system. Textbooks of criminal law now acknowledge that, in the words of Lacey et al. (1990), it is 'the *appearance* rather than the reality of certainty, coherence and fairness' (p. 43) that is the significant element in the official account of the system's rationality.

Why is the reality so different from the rhetoric? Political reasons are emphasized by Lacey and her colleagues. The operation of law is said to legitimize existing power structures, and criticism of the law's bases in rational theory and consistent practice undermines the ability of the powerful to maintain their privileged position. Whatever the cultural truth of such an analysis, we may still ask why people do not make a better job of operating the existing system, and how, if at all, things might be changed to enable the system to work better. One problem is that the individual actors in the system who wish to assign blame, starting with the victim and working through the police, prosecutors, lawyers and magistrates and juries, have their own agendas which do not coincide with the formal task of applying legal criteria in the judgement of individual actions. The child may not want her father to be locked up in prison, the police may have knowledge of the accused person's criminal activity that they are not permitted to put before the court, the lawyers are concerned to demonstrate their persuasive skills to potential clients and jurors might wish to seize this remarkable opportunity to make a telling political point. Even if the protagonists seek genuinely to do justice, some are required to perform impossible tasks and unreliable evidence is routinely demanded and provided, as will become evident in later chapters on the performance of witnesses and juries. Hence the information which constitutes the basis on which judgements of blame may rest is frequently suspect but deemed acceptable because it has passed formal tests of 'admissibility'. More fundamentally, it will become apparent that the adversarial system of justice frequently demands not an evaluation of blameworthiness against formal criteria, but a choice between two versions of reality both of which have been constructed with an eye to advantage rather than truth.

Such problems with 'the system' may become clearer as in later chapters we examine the decisions taken by different actors – the police, the witnesses, juries and judges. It is nonetheless necessary at this stage to look carefully and in general at the processes by which blame is deemed to be attributed in social life and in legal justice. The rhetoric of legal justice is what commands our allegiance as passive or active participants in the process by which the blameworthiness of fellow citizens is assessed, and punishments meted out to proven offenders. Rightly or wrongly the attribution of blame is the originating and vindicating activity in the whole criminal justice process. Change and reform of the criminal justice system requires that we understand as fully as we can the requirements of determining criminal responsibility. Victims have provided us with suspects. Who amongst those suspects can be blamed?

A formal model of blame

There can be no blame without its first being established that harm has been caused. Figure 6.1, which is a highly simplified portrayal of Shaver's analysis of the psychology of blame (1986), indicates that Harm Done initiates the process which might end in blame. Of course, harm might occur as an act of God, as when lightening strikes and kills, for example, an unfortunate player in a football match. In that case no human agent could be said to have caused the death so there is no question of blame, unless it could be said that one person – the referee, for example – had recklessly or negligently allowed the game to continue in dangerous weather conditions. More conventionally in criminal justice systems it will be alleged that some one individual caused the harm that has been done. By that is meant that at the very least an antecedent action of the suspect had been sufficient and necessary to account

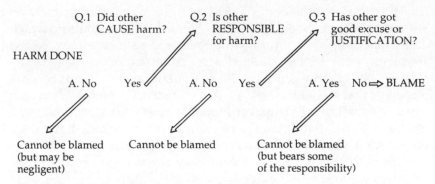

Figure 6.1 Blaming another for Harm Done: the sequence of questions and answers
Source: After Shaver, 1986

for the observed harm. The suspect had fired the gun or thrown the punch or broken down the door, thereby causing the wounding, the assault or the unlawful entry. Mere causality, however, does not imply that we can blame that person for the offence in question, nor even hold them responsible for their actions. In defence, it may be suggested that the punch thrown by the man at the bar was wildly directed in the air in the course of an innocent conversation with a fellow drinker and was not directed deliberately towards the landlord who innocently stepped into its path when collecting empty glasses. If so, such an accidental wounding would be apparent as such to any observer of the incident, just as a deliberate act of punching another would be equally and instantly recognizable as deliberate. Our very language – he punched X, he fired the gun at Y etc. – implies intention in the actions we describe (see Gauld and Shotter, 1977).

Purely accidental assaults or killings even do not imply responsibility for the consequences of the action. Apart from accidents, other automatic actions or reflexes which cause harm occurring as for example in an epileptic fit, may be counted to lack the *mens rea* and hence not to qualify as actions for which people may be held responsible.

Only when intention is established may we ask whether or not the individual should be 'blamed' for the harmful consequences. It is at this stage, strictly, that questions of moral responsibility for actions crop up. 'Voices' may send someone on a crusade of vengeful killing, or to take a more conventional example, someone may deliberately kill another in a rage when blind drunk. In these cases there may be no doubt that the individuals concerned had the intention to cause harm (i.e. *actus reus and mens rea*), but there is an argument to be made that they should be excused blame. Both the mad person and the drunk may in some jurisdictions reasonably attempt to excuse themselves on grounds of motive or lack of control. Shiner (1990) argues cogently that drunks should not be deemed to lack *mens rea*, as does happen apparently in many cases at trial in the United States, but that does not prevent a defence on the basis of excuse.

Peele (1990) thinks little of some of the excuses increasingly mounted by 'addicts' of varying descriptions but undoubtedly a case can be made for the argument that some people, whilst being responsible for their criminal actions, are not morally responsible for the harms they cause and should not be blamed. A traditional distinction is made between justified actions (in which there is an obligation to commit the act which causes harm), and actions which remain wrong and regrettable but which may nonetheless be 'excused'. Stealing to feed one's child may be justified. Stealing because you are being blackmailed may be excused. In practice, the distinctions between excuse and justification are hard to draw and indeed Morawetz (1986) suggests that if we are to make distinctions then we need to distinguish between (a) acts which are totally justified (*tout court*) – acts of self-defence, for example; (b) acts which are wrong but justified – killing a policeman having mistaken him for an intruder ('justified wrongs'); and (c) 'excused wrongs', into which class would come the criminal acts of madmen and indeed children who may be said to lack the capacity for appropriate moral judgement by virtue of their age, but who may nevertheless have known what they were doing.

Psychological issues lie at the heart of many debates about justification and excuses. The issue of the criminal liability of children is one which is frequently addressed by those who wish either to see it lowered because too many criminals (young though they may be) are escaping prosecution and thereby distorting the criminal statistics, and are quite likely not being effectively dealt with by other means. It is also addressed by those who wish to see the age higher in order that children may not be contaminated by exposure to the personnel and procedures of the criminal justice system. The issue has come to the fore in Canada where a new Act has raised the age of criminal responsibility to 12, and also changed the status of juvenile delinquent from that of 'being in a condition of delinquency and thereby requiring help and guidance' to being 'young persons ... [who] should nonetheless bear responsibility for their contraventions' (Dalby, 1985). Leschied and Wilson (1988) discuss the policy issues involved in the treatment of children under 12 who commit crimes, and question whether decriminalizing the 7–12-year-olds is appropriate, given the seriousness and prevalence of offending in that age group.

Dalby (1985) discusses the evidence from cognitive developmental studies, studies of moral development and studies of the development of self-control, and concludes that, indeed, 'children at about the age of seven meet at least minimum criteria for criminal responsibility' (pp. 142–3), though given variations in rate of psychological growth, he concludes that 14 is the age by which an assumption of criminal responsibility for all young persons could be made. The minimum criteria, however, are limited to what Shaver would call the criteria of causality and responsibility. It is inappropriate that a child of seven should be regarded as blameworthy in the sense that an adult might be deemed blameworthy because they are far from having the knowledge or capacity to take responsibility for their lives, a criterion that would make the age of 14 or even 16 more appropriate.

Making a clear conceptual separation between responsibility and blameworthiness would aid the discussion of this issue, and possibly raise the question of other categories or people, apart from children, who might be deemed responsible but not blameworthy. For example, Ewing (1990) has recently raised the question of those battered women who kill their husbands or partners. He argues that the psychological evidence for the existence of a 'battered woman syndrome' (Walker, 1989) should lead us to recognize a justification based on psychological rather than physical self-defence. Most women who kill in such circumstances fail to establish self-defence as a justification because they were not at the moment of the killing in defence of their lives. They were, however, according to many accounts, in the desperate condition of defending their (psychological) existence as human beings. Although this viewpoint elicited a vigorous legal counter-attack (Morse, 1990) it is likely that as data accumulate, pressure will grow for a revision of the law which broadens justification for homicide along the lines suggested by Ewing.

Shaver intends his model (figure 6.1) to be prescriptive, meaning that before we blame someone for harm committed, we must verify that the criteria for blaming have been fulfilled at each stage of the process (Shaver and Drown, 1986). We might, therefore, use it as a model against which the 'efficiency' of criminal investigation and trial are evaluated. The English system might not fare well, I regret to say, given so many important trials in recent years in which the wrong people have been arrested, charged, prosecuted and found guilty. A systematic application of the model in cases like those of the Guildford Four and the Birmingham Six and the Maguire family might well have ensured that the cases collapsed at the stage of establishing that the suspects caused the harm in question.

Shaver maintains that the principal distinctions in the model – between attribution of cause, responsibility, and blame respectively – are not only demanded by moral and legal philosophers (e.g. Hart and Honoré, 1978) but are generally drawn by men and women in their everyday judgements. Critchlow (1985), for example, asked participants in his study to judge or explain a variety of behaviours performed by people who were either 'drunk' or 'sober' at the time, and who were either 'social drinkers' or 'chronic alcoholics'. Judgements of the extent to which individuals were said to have caused, been responsible for, to be blamed for and finally to be punished for the act in question were positively related to one another but were clearly not regarded as one and the same thing. Coherent distinctions were made based on the available contextual information provided.

Other studies have also demonstrated that, in the abstract, people combine information relevant to harm done, causal and personal responsibility and available justifications, in order to make ratings of blameworthiness or culpability which rationally reflect variations in the available information. West (1986), for example, asked subjects to rate 25 aggressive acts like a youth hitting a policeman, a woman stabbing her drunken husband, and a student tackling a thief, on a number of dimensions, e.g. illegality of the action, sympathy for the action, degree of harm inflicted, relative social power of those involved, degree of acquaintance of aggressor and victim, and so on. Analyses indicated that three factors were particularly important in determining how people grouped the various acts: the degree of harm inflicted, the amount of provocation, and how well acquainted the people were. Of these, the degree of harm inflicted and the extent of provocation were the most telling factors predicting ratings of moral condemnation or blameworthiness. Horai and Bartek (1978) also show that independently of actual harm done, intended harm was an important factor influencing recommended punishments.

In other words, judgements of blameworthiness, at least in the abstract, reflect the level of harm caused, the degree of responsibility and the availability of excuses in predictable and comfortingly rational ways. In practice, the picture is not so rosy, as we shall now see.

Deviations from rational attributions of blame

Over the last twenty years or so, attribution theory in social psychology has sought to elucidate the conditions under which we assign responsibility and blame to an individual for his or her behaviour. This work is directly relevant to the way in which individual actors in the criminal justice system – victims, suspects, police, lawyers, magistrates, jurors and judges – make up their minds about the culpability of suspects, and it has implications for questions of both responsibility and blameworthiness, as the important discussion by Fincham and Jaspars (1980) makes clear.

Fincham and Jaspars centre their analysis on Heider's (1958) portrayal of *levels* of responsibility attribution (see table 6.1). These levels reflect different degrees of contribution of 'environmental' and 'personal' factors to the outcome of an action, from 'guilt by association' (level 1) to 'intention' (level 4), with 'justification' (level 5) serving to mitigate responsibility. It should be apparent that these 'stages' are not developmental stages. Both adults and children are likely in some circumstances to use, for example, mere 'association' as a criterion of blameworthiness. Some two or three years ago in South Africa, mere by-standing members of a crowd were found guilty of murder by virtue of their supposedly sharing a common purpose with a crowd, some other members of which had actually killed a man – a clear example of Heider's level of Association. Although not reflecting developmental stages, the levels do constitute a psychological scale of responsibility attribution. Given numerous examples of wrongdoing, people will order them in a way which reflects the distinctions made by Heider in his rankings of levels of attribution.

It may be noted that these levels implicitly recognize the three core questions in Shaver's model of blame attribution. The first two levels provide the conditions necessary for answering the question 'Did other *cause* the harm?'. Levels 3 and 4 define the

Table 6.1 Heider's levels of responsibility attribution

Level	Description
1. Association	'the person is held responsible for each effect that is in any way connected with him or that seems in any way to belong to him.' (Heider, 1958, p. 113)
2. Causality	Anything 'caused by [a person] P is ascribed to him. Causation is understood in the sense that P was a necessary condition for the happening, even though he could not have foreseen the outcome however cautiously he had proceeded ... the person is judge ... according to the actual results of what he does.' (Heider, 1958, p. 113)
3. Foreseeability	'P is considered responsible, directly or indirectly, for any after effect he may have foreseen even though it was not a part of his own goal and therefore still not a part of the framework of personal causality' (Heider, 1958, p. 113)
4. Intention	'Only what P intended is perceived as having its source in him' (Heider, 1958, p. 113)
5. Justification	'P's own motives ... are seen as having their source in the environment ... responsibility for the act is at least shared by the environment.' (Heider, 1958, p. 114)

Source: After Fincham and Jaspars, 1980

conditions of what Shaver calls responsibility, and the fifth level indicates the conditions necessary for withholding blame, despite causality and responsibility having been established.

Social psychologists have for a number of years addressed themselves to issues raised by Heider's fifth stage, of responsibility. The question of when we attribute responsibility for an action to the individual or to the environment has been frequently tackled. Research has tended to verify Kelley's (1973) covariation principle, which suggests that attributions are determined by three behavioral attributes: consistency, distinctiveness, and consensus. Let us consider the case of someone who is caught in the act of (apparently) stealing something. If that person is consistently dishonest, if there is no distinctive environmental event to which dishonesty in the present instance is a response (e.g. rampant storm damage – creating unique opportunities for pillaging), and if dishonesty is not a characteristic (consensual) of his or her group, then the suspect's theft in this particular instance will unequivocally be deemed the responsibility of that individual and not of circumstances.

In observing trials at the local Canterbury Crown Court, I have sometimes wondered on what basis the police and prosecution have decided to prosecute one party or another that has been involved in a brawl: who, one might say, was 'responsible' for the brawl, and who was 'reacting to circumstances'? Stereotyped notions, for example of what is typical behaviour of persons of different ages, race or social class backgrounds, undoubtedly enter into such decisions, affecting as they do judgements of likely 'consensus', 'consistency' and 'distinctiveness'. In responding to particular incidents of this kind, the prejudices of the police and prosecutors may lead them to 'discount' (Kelley, 1973) one or other set of causes for particular groups or individuals. Such discounting may lead to errors of attribution and to systematic bias in the judicial process.

There are various other errors of attribution leading to unsympathetic judgements of those who have caused untoward events or harm. To begin with, we may be defensive in our judgements. Walster (1966) told subjects the tale of one Lennie who left his car parked at the top of a hill. Regrettably, Lennie did not make a good job of it, or he had not checked his brakes, and the car rolled down the hill and caused damage to itself and to other property and people. Participants in these experiments were found to criticize and blame Lennie more, the greater the damage and the more severe the consequences. It is suggested that by blaming Lennie, rather than fate, people defend themselves against the thought that they might cause similar damage.

Somewhat better substantiated is the Fundamental attribution error, which leads observers to minimize the role of situational factors and to exaggerate the role of personal characteristics when explaining someone's behaviour. Interestingly, Miller (1984) has suggested that this general tendency to attribute behaviour to personal dispositions – 'he steals because he's wicked' – is not something that children in all cultures learn to do to the same extent. Hindus were much less likely than Americans to attribute anti-social behaviour to personal dispositions, being rather more likely to blame contextual factors.

Naturally, the suspect in a criminal trial has a distinctive viewpoint on his alleged misconduct, and is likely as the 'actor' to attribute responsibility differently from the judge or magistrate. Whilst observers and judges may commit the fundamental attribution error, the suspect is more likely to reverse the bias in favour of environmental or contextual factors. Indeed, 'actors' generally attribute responsibility for their behaviour more to the environment than to themselves, a tendency which was emphasized by Jones and Nisbett (1972). A variation on this tendency is the 'self-serving bias' (Bradley, 1978) in which people try to enhance their self-esteem by attributing their successes to themselves and their failures to the environment, a tendency which has clear and rather obvious applications to judgements and attributions in the trial process.

Character of the victim

The factors determining blame in Shaver's model are general, and other particular circumstances of the case should not be permitted to affect attributions of blame, according to Shaver's prescriptive model. Thus, the fact that a dangerous driver has killed a drunk rather than a sober person should not other things being equal, influence the jury's assessment of the guilt of the defendant. But such factors appear to be very influential in jury decision-making. Kalven and Zeisel (1966) document many cases where the jury's verdict of not guilty surprised the judge who would have returned a guilty verdict. This happened in 20 per cent of the 2979 cases where the judge would have convicted, a total of 596 cases in all. The judges' reasons for these discrepancies were examined in some detail by the authors. In a very significant number of cases the judge reasoned that it was the jury's feelings about the defendant that was crucial in determining their decision. The authors suggest that American jurors redefine the crime of rape by taking any excuse that presents itself to perceive an assumption of risk by the female, for example, by drinking with the defendant, by having had sex with him on a previous occasion, by having been previously married and divorced, and so on. Even in some cases where rape was aggravated by gross violence, a Not Guilty verdict was returned, because of previous acquaintance and drinking together on the night in question (see Kalven and Zeisel, 1966, pp. 249–57). The jury in such cases appears to be taking the view that previous behaviour or the victim's character disqualifies her from complaining. Similar biases were experimentally demonstrated by Pugh (1983), especially for male 'jurors'.

An unusual and important demonstration that the character of the victim may be crucial to the determination of the guilt of the accused – despite what the law, and rational models of blaming might say to the contrary – comes from a recent study of the hindsight effect by Alicke and Davis (1989). The basic scenario described a man shooting an intruder whom he mistakenly thought was carrying a gun. In hindsight, different groups of subjects were told variously that the dead man was in fact the boyfriend of the killer's daughter, a dangerous criminal intruder, a non-dangerous criminal intruder, an attractive non-criminal, an unattractive non-criminal, or they were told nothing about the man. The results suggest clearly that subjects blame the killer more when the victim was innocent than when he was a criminal of any description or when no details were given. Recommended sentences were also significantly longer for killers of those victims who were subsequently proved innocent. Of course, such hindsight bias is unfair to the killer whose mental state and awareness of what he was doing at the time of the shooting did not vary across any of the conditions.

To the extent that victims can take some of the responsibility for their victimization, the suspect can hope for a corresponding improvement in the chances of being exonerated by the fact-finders. It is, therefore, alarming to find that in an experimental study of attributions of blame to victims of rape or robbery when either jogging or hitchhiking, Howard (1984) found a general tendency for female victims to be blamed more than men. This applied especially to 'characterological' rather than 'behavioural' blame, and was a feature of both male and female attributions of blame. There appears to be a general belief that women especially are foolish not to keep themselves out of harm's way.

The importance of role responsibility

Lloyd-Bostock (1983) found that many accident victims whom she interviewed were reluctant to blame others, or their employers, for the accident, even when such blame might well be justified. It was as if it were not perceived to be appropriate for them to accuse others, or for others to take the blame. For example, people were not inclined to blame those they knew personally, say the owner of a small business, or a fellow employee when the injury occurred at work. On the other hand, victims of road accidents frequently attributed blame, whereas victims of domestic accidents rarely blamed anyone else at all. Lloyd-Bostock related these differences (67 per cent blaming another in a road accident, 37 per cent blaming another in an industrial accident, and 4 per cent in a domestic accident) to the perceived availability of compensation.

Hamilton (1978) would probably be more inclined to fashion an explanation in terms of the role responsibility of the varying parties. For example, the status and authority of a boss in a large firm makes that person a more legitimate target of an action for damages than would be the case in a small firm. The owner of a large company may be perceived to have greater responsibility by virtue of his or her impersonal contractual authority. In a small firm authority depends more upon the interpersonal relationships that have been established between employer and employee. Hamilton's 'model' makes a distinction between role variables and deed variables. It is not only what you do that determines illegality. Role variables also enter into legal dimensions of responsibility; for example a teacher or parent is directly responsible for a pupil or child's welfare in a way that is more compelling than in the case of other adults without such role responsibility. By the same token, a ferry company owner is more responsible than a friendly yacht owner in the event of an accident in a Channel crossing. Most work in the field of attribution theory, however, has been concerned more with deed variables, viewed independently of the social context.

Hamilton and Sanders (1983) suggested that there would be cross-cultural differences in the tendency to emphasize either role or deed variables in the attribution of responsibility. In a complex experiment, they presented stories to a large number of Japanese subjects. The stories were constructed in such a way as to vary systematically two role variables and four deed variables. The two role variables they called Status and Hierarchy, reflecting the type of relationship (interpersonal or contractual) and position power (with or without any) respectively. Four main deed factors were also varied – intentional mental state, consequences of the action,

encouragement (influence from another), and past pattern of behaviour. In all the stories some harm was sustained – e.g. in an
accident at work – and responsibility had to be assigned by the
subjects to the one who caused the harm. It was found that Japanese
subjects gave more weight to role relationships than did subjects
from the US, and they were more inclined to excuse someone
who was influenced by another's advice or example. Americans
emphasized the mental state more than the Japanese. However, in
general all subjects were inclined to blame more those in authority
and those under contract; to take intention into account; to be
influenced adversely by a history of such wrong- or harm-doing;
and to be more sympathetic when another's influence was in
evidence.

Hamilton and Sanders make a number of points about the legal
implications of their work, but two are of particular importance to
later discussions. The law does not take position power into account
in its dealings, for example, with disputes between individuals and
corporations, and it has difficulty operating outside contractual
relations. Corporations, for example, are treated as persons, but
because of their power will invariably win contests with individuals.
The tendency of the law to assume 'equal-contract' relations also
means that crimes committed within intrinsic relationships (e.g.
within families) remain outside the law in many cases. The crime
of marital rape, for example, has only recently been acknowledged
as a crime in England.

Informal resolution: accounts and remedies in everyday life

A number of findings have suggested that Harm Done is the most
salient consideration in blaming, a conclusion that is fortified by
the finding that in everyday judgements people conclude more
about another's character from their bad than from their good deeds.
McGraw (1985) found, for example, that an improbable immoral
act calls forth a greater increase in condemnation than a correspondingly improbable moral act elicits praise. Shultz and Wright
(1985) found that whilst people are deemed to be responsible for
negligent harm, there is no corresponding credit for benefits arising
from their negligence.

Whilst evidence of evil intentions or carelessness or negligence may exacerbate our estimate of the degree of harm, evidence that a criminal is well-intentioned does little to mitigate blame. A very interesting child developmental study by Walton (1985) indicated that in classroom disputes between children, or between a child and a teacher, the question of intention is rarely an issue in the interchange between the parties. In fact, denials of intent by an accused child was characteristic of only 1.4 per cent of the 1718 'remedies' (responses to accusations) in the fourth-grade children observed. The importance given in the literature, both in attributional studies and in cognitive-developmental studies, to the supposedly increasing use of intention with age in the evaluation of blameworthiness is ascribed by the authors to the prevalence in laboratory studies of the damage to property scenario. Intention is clearly an important component in the characterization of 'accidents' which by definition rule out intention as a causal factor. In fact in Walton's study, the majority of 'intention remedies' were given in cases of physical damage to property or people. Walton also failed to find many instances of reference to norms of reciprocity or even fairness in the everyday classroom disputes between children. Most children (47 per cent) when accused of an offence complied with the challenger, acknowledging in one way or another that the complaint was justified (see table 6.2). We shall see in the next chapter that suspects in police custody are similarly compliant.

Twenty-six per cent of the children denied the charge, claiming to be quite innocent of the charges, and 17 per cent attempted to justify their behaviour, by asserting in one way or another that the act was appropriate in the circumstances. They might deny the existence of a rule, suggest that the behaviour serves a higher purpose, suggest that no harm was done or suggest that the act was one of retribution or a demand for equal treatment. Excuses constituted 10 per cent of the remedies, when children claimed either to have been too ignorant to act any differently, to have been unable to act differently, or, finally, not to have intended to produce that particular effect.

Walton suggests that in such dispute resolution children were negotiating a 'definition of the situation', although her analysis focuses primarily on the immediate response to a challenge, rather than the total interchange whereby agreement is reached. The point to be made, I think, is that children in the classroom have a continuing relationship with their accusers, and what is being negotiated are the terms of the relationship. The challenge indicates

Table 6.2 Classification of remedies in response to accusations in classroom disputes

Type of Remedy		Example	Frequency
I.	Compliance	The accused cleans up paint spilled on the table	47.0%
II.	Denial	'I never took your eraser'	26.0%
III.	Justification		
(a)	Deny the rule	'It's allowed to tell secrets in games'	11.0%
(b)	Appeal to higher goals	'I'm just trying to keep my promise'	3.5%
(c)	Deny damage	'That picture was ugly anyway'	1.5%
(d)	Appeals to reciprocity	'Well, you hit me first'; 'If Jenny can sit here I can sit here'	1.4%
IV.	Excuse		
(a)	Deny knowledge	'I was absent when she told us to bring jars'	4.3%
(b)	Deny control	'I didn't have enough paper'	4.0%
(c)	Deny intent	'I didn't really mean to hurt you'	1.4%

Source: After Walton, 1985

that one person at least thinks the terms have broken down. When that person is the teacher, compliance naturally enough was a more frequent response to challenge then when the challenger was another child.

Shaver (1986) recognized that blaming is a social process in which harm done, causality, responsibility, justifications and excuses may become the subject of debate and controversy, but always with the assumption that at each stage a correct answer is in principle forthcoming. Moreover, Shaver assumes that it is necessary to progress from one stage to the next in the prescribed order, the questions at each succeeding stage becoming relevant only when those in preceding stages have been answered. Analysis of everyday challenges, remedies and accounts reveals on the contrary that

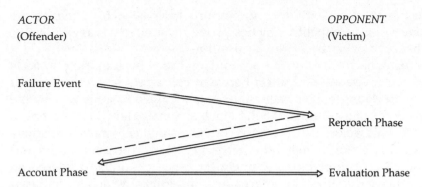

Figure 6.2   Structure of an Account Episode
Source: After Schönbach, 1987

the social process is *initiated* by blaming, and is followed by a negotiation of the remedy. A general account of this process is given by Schönbach (1987, 1990), who has examined the structure of what he calls account episodes. Figure 6.2 portrays the structure of an account episode between an 'actor' and 'opponent', who from the perspective of criminal justice we may prefer to call 'offender' and 'victim'. The interaction starts with a Failure Event – an offence whether of commission or omission – which elicits the Reproach Phase: the victim's response. This may be neutral or even sympathetic in tone, as well as or instead of being critical. The victim may, for example, merely ask why the failure event occurred. In the Account Phase, offenders may seek to justify or excuse their conduct or otherwise deny their guilt, which may lead to further 'reproaches' from the victim and subsequent account before an evaluation by the victim brings the interaction to an end, for the time being at least.

Note that Schönbach's analysis does, indeed, reverse the order of events prescribed by Shaver's stages. Whereas in Shaver's model blame is the end-product of a lengthy analysis of behaviour, motives and circumstances, Schönbach's model has the actor assuming guilt, and leaving the opponent to search for antecedent conditions which will serve to exonerate or excuse him or her. Although it might be thought that the criminal trial should approximate more to the analytic procedure incorporated in Shaver's model, in practice, the reverse process in which suspects search for means of undermining the accusations made against them may be much nearer the truth. Our system of justice is termed 'accusatorial' for good reasons, and justice too frequently fails to be done because victory goes to the side whose competitive tactics prove most effective, regardless of the truth or falsity of the accusations.

Schönbach investigated account episodes by requiring subjects to improvise an altercation between characters in a story, one of whom claims to have been injured or wronged in some way by the other. In one example of Schönbach's, a man had promised not to reveal his workmate's previous conviction and jail sentence to others at work. Unfortunately, at a party, he let slip the information and the friend suffered greatly in consequence. Schönbach devised an extensive classification of 'accounts' in terms of which he analysed the interaction of accusers and accused in such cases. He found four major (cardinal) categories of accounts: (1) Concessions – e.g. an expression of regret; (2) Excuses; (3) Justifications; and (4) Refusals – e.g. denial of responsibility. In practice, however, justifications are hard to categorize unequivocally, because they share a common core – with excuses. In both, some norm is held to warrant the behaviour in question – say a violent act of self-defence. This leads to its not being regarded as an offence at all (justification), or to the offence being admitted with lessened responsibility (excuse). This distinction cannot be reliably determined by the common man, if Schönbach's results are typical. This may be in part because opponents are negotiating the best possible interpretation of their conduct and are inclined to keep their options open, such that failure to justify one's conduct does not rule out the possibility that it may subsequently be excused.

Gender played a large part in determining offenders' response to reproach, reflecting a difference in men's and women's understanding of the very concept of responsibility. Schönbach suggests that for men, the concept of responsibility is linked closely to that of the power and position of the 'holder' of responsibility. Men, therefore, are more concerned with explaining the causes or origins of a problem than women. Women, on the other hand, are less concerned with who is responsible for causing the problem than they are with who is responsible for seeking solutions to the problem. In consequence, men are readier to accuse *and* readier to defend themselves against accusation by denying responsibility. Schönbach notes that whilst excuses and justification are evenly proffered by male and female offenders, there were large differences in refusals, with men much more likely to deny guilt, especially in those cases where causal responsibility is most clear-cut. By way of contrast, women are more likely both to admit responsibility and to make offers of help and restitution. Needless to say, our criminal justice system emphasizes the male preoccupation with establishing the cause of crimes or 'problems' more than it promotes the search for solutions to the consequences.

In the subsequent chapters we shall examine the decision-making of the key protagonists following the victim's complaint: the police, witnesses, fact-finders and sentencers. How, in practice, are the accuser's claims evaluated, and how effectively is blame established? In the decisions made by the respective parties we may expect to find abundant confirmation of departures from the prescriptive ideal described in this chapter.

7

Police on Crime

Police role in the adversarial system

The English system of criminal justice is appropriately termed adversarial or, alternatively, accusatorial. Defence and prosecution promulgate opposed accounts of the suspect's blameworthiness, and it is left to the jury in the higher court, or the magistrates in the lower courts, to pick the winning version. The 'fact-finders' – the jury or the magistrates – wait to be persuaded, by one side or the other, of the truth of the matter. It would be hard to think of a system better designed to encourage the presentation of distorted or lying versions of reality.

The police play the central role in the construction of the prosecution's campaign to persuade the fact-finders that the accused is blameworthy. The police respond to complaints, initiate enquiries, interview witnesses and suspects, bring charges and recommend prosecution. Their role in the construction of evidence is not an impartial one, and it is only in the last 15 years or so in England that it has been necessary for the police even to inform the defence of evidence which is of advantage to the case for the defence. Needless to say there is no reciprocal responsibility on the part of the defence who may for example make highly selective use of the results of forensic examinations it has commissioned.

One natural consequence of this structural bias is that police have views which reflect their prosecutorial role. It is commonplace to point to the greater authoritarianism of the police as a group, or to point to the cognitive gap between the police and the policed. Rafky's results from the USA (1977) are a good example. Police, compared with students, have an exaggerated 'respect for the law', and in terms of their moral stance are unequivocally on the side of traditional values. Police, for example, are less likely than non-police to agree with the statements that 'It is all right to evade the law if you do not actually violate it' and 'A person who reports minor law violations is only a trouble-maker'. On the other hand, they are more likely to agree with statements like 'All laws should be strictly obeyed because they are laws' and 'A man should obey the laws no matter how much they interfere with his personal ambitions'.

This was as predicted by the author. Interestingly, however, some predictions were not fulfilled, and indeed produced results that were significantly against the hypothesis that police have a greater respect for law. Police were less inclined than non-police to believe that 'In the courts a poor man will receive as fair treatment as a millionaire', and they were less likely to believe that 'Violators of the law are nearly always detected and punished'. And along with others, they were also sceptical about the ability of juries to understand cases well enough to make a sensible decision. In other words, police respect for the moral principles embodied in law is tied to contempt for its practical operation. One reason for police scepticism may well be that juries frequently find not for the prosecution but for the defence in circumstances where the police are convinced of the suspect's guilt. Of course, police are frequently in possession of information not presented in court, e.g. previous convictions for similar offences, and information from criminal informants. Their scepticism extends also to views of the relative honesty of lawyers and policemen, police agreeing with the general public that 40 per cent of lawyers are generally dishonest, but rejecting such imputations against the police (3 per cent as against the public's 45 per cent!).

The nature of the goal relationship is a critical determinant of relations between groups. The police role in the adversarial system places them at the heart of a win-lose conflict that seems to generate antagonism towards their opponents in the system and to biases and misperceptions favouring the in-group in the course of their interactions with members of the public, whether victims or villains. Close observers of the police are not inclined to be altogether cynical about the excessive zeal which this conflict generates. Andrew Brown (1988) claims that the police concern with winning stems not mainly from competitive zeal but reflects a concern to ensure as far as possible that truth will out. On the basis of his observations of a group of London detectives for a number of weeks, he detected an essentially moral basis to police conduct: 'there remains a recognizable police style, which I think comes from their concern with truth: with what actually happens, rather than with what we might wish to happen'.

The experience of policing

One consequence of the police role in the adversarial system is what Lord Scarman (1986) called the 'dangerously low level of supervision of the processes of arrest, interrogation and charge'. Society leaves it largely to the police to determine what conduct in what circumstances shall be deemed criminal, and hence lead to arrest. We give discretion to the police to interrogate whom they will, and to investigate reported crime as they think fit. In other words, the police have an immense amount of discretion over what is defined as criminal behaviour, who should be arrested, how interrogation should be conducted, and so on. Not only is this true of the police in general, as an organized body on whom society depends for the fulfilment of this controlling role, it is true of individual policemen in their interactions with the public, away from the gaze and direct command of their superior officers.

Smith (1983), for example, found that many police officers (38 per cent) police sergeants (21 per cent), and even some inspectors (4 per cent) had never ever spoken to their Commanders. Perhaps more importantly, there was a strong correlation between judgements of the quality of supervision and estimates of frequency of interaction. Perhaps the most important point is that the behaviour of those who have the most contact with the public is not subject to detailed scrutiny. Indeed, senior officers generally make it clear that relatively superficial performance criteria are applicable to their subordinates, reflecting a concern with ends rather than means. Smith and Gray (1983) offer this answer as typical:

Q: How do you measure the performance of your Division?

Superintendent: I would tend to judge my Division by the stops, charges, PAS (persons at station). If they were low, it would suggest that morale had sagged or not enough work was being done. I would review those figures and compare them with the last three years. (p. 304)

Unsupervised police personnel are judged, it seems, by the number of persons they stop, arrest and charge, and they are disciplined for administrative rather than substantive offences against the code of conduct. Running out of petrol, for example, was treated more seriously than using unnecessary violence against a suspect (Smith and Gray, p. 315). That survey in London was followed by moves to improve supervision and to introduce a wider range of performance indicators, but it is likely that the emphasis on stop, arrest and charge remains the perceived core function of policing.

There is considerable variation in the response of officers to their role and circumstances, as might be expected from the lack of direct supervision. Evidence suggests that police are not so much stereotypically conservative and retributivist in their attitudes, as they are realists. Experience leads them to modify both the liberal views they are exposed to in training and the reactionary views of hardened colleagues they meet in their probationary days (Fielding and Fielding, 1991). They are less likely than the general public, for example, to think that relatively minor traffic offences have serious implications (Corbett and Simon, 1991), although they agree with the public on the blameworthiness of the more serious offences, and they agree on the rank ordering of offences. The reality is, of course, that the police cannot afford the time to take such offences as parking on double yellow lines and failing to use a direction indicator signal when the driver should as seriously as it appears the public imagine they do.

Not only does police experience create dilemmas for individual officers (Fielding and Fielding, 1991), but it creates considerable variation between officers. Stradling et al. (1990), for example, in an enlightening study of police attitudes to motorists whom they had stopped for speeding, showed that a majority was oriented towards prosecution and was less likely to be influenced one way or another by the offender's deferential attitude, whereas a minority was reluctant to prosecute but strongly influenced by an offender's failure to show appropriate deference. It would appear to be mistaken to take average attitudes of the police as reflecting the views of any one policeman in particular, a view reinforced by Reming's study of 'supercops' (1988). Supercops were defined by their exceptionally high productivity, as measured by their performance at or above the 90th percentile with respect to self-initiated felony arrests. Their tough-mindedness and authoritarianism were way in excess of those of the 'average' policeman, and highly akin to those of recidivist criminals. Similarly, LeDoux and Hazelwood (1985) report that a significant number of policemen are unsympathetic and antagonistic towards victims of rape in contrast to an 'average' view which is largely sympathetic and sensitive to the plight of rape victims.

Police-victim interaction

Although it is true that published crime figures are likely to underestimate the level of crime in a community, the discretion accorded police officers serves both to exaggerate and conceal the true level of crime. Complaints of burglary, for instance, may be discouraged by officers because supervisors are anxious to minimize the burglary count, or they may be exaggerated by officers not wishing to offend a complainant: 'You don't want to be the one who tells an irate citizen that they weren't burglarized. Citizens don't want to hear about [the burglary definition]. They know they were burglarized and if you try to tell them differently they'll think you're trying to downgrade the crime' (McCleary et al., 1982).

A number of studies suggest that particular categories of assault victim, for example children and women, are likely to be disbelieved or otherwise not taken seriously by the police, even to be blamed for their victimization (e.g. Morris, 1987, p. 185). Ferraro (1989) describes attempts in areas of the United States to implement a presumptive arrest policy in cases of woman battering in the context of family disputes. This policy states that arrests should always be made following a complaint if 'probable cause' (of an offence) exists, even if the victim has changed her mind and does not desire prosecution. Despite a policy of presumptive arrest, the predominant strategy of the police was conciliation – calming things and ensuring that immediate order was restored. Not only were arrests not made, but generally speaking no further action was taken to ensure that the trouble did not recur – such as putting the couple, or at least the woman, in touch with appropriate helping agencies. Situational factors prevailed strongly over policy conditions, and only if there was support for arrest in the situation – both disputants on the scene, willingness of victim to sign a complaint, current allegations of violence, male drunkenness and the like – would an arrest be deemed appropriate.

What this and other similar studies (e.g. Smith and Gray, 1983) make clear is that legal factors, concerned with establishing that a crime has been committed, are not necessarily the principal factors determining police response to victims' accusations, at least in cases of partner abuse. Police make an arrest when it is deemed appropriate so to do, and all kinds of extra-legal factors may determine judgements of appropriateness. One important extra-legal factor is the social status of the victim, a factor highlighted by Black (1976). A good illustration of this is a study by Smith et al. (1984) of the arrests made by police officers on 900 patrol shifts in 60 different residential neighbourhoods. When there was a complainant involved, there was a marked tendency – other things being equal – for police to be influenced by the race of the victim. Specifically, complaints by white females were more likely to lead to arrests then were complaints by black females.

The existence of bias reveals little about the way police actually reason their way to the decisions made. Rose and Randall (1982) indicate that officers investigating a complaint may view the demonstration that an offence (of rape, in this instance) has occurred as but the first step in the proof of the 'legitimacy' of a case, and that rapes will be viewed by investigating officers as lying on a continuum defined by 'real rapes' at one extreme to 'deals' at the other, a classification determined by judgements of victim credibility, consent, and offence seriousness as well as personal characteristics. Although the biases in this interpretative process have been documented especially in relation to the offence of rape, the evidence suggests that the number of complaints eventually pursued and prosecuted in the courts is relatively high for that offence. Galvin and Polk (1983), for instance, demonstrate that the attrition rate for rape is about the same as that for robbery and distinctly less than that for assault and burglary. With respect to the performance of the police, rape is second only to murder insofar as the rates for arrest and subsequent prosecution are concerned. Most rapes, however, are never reported to the police.

Williams and Farrell (1990) attempted to understand the reasoning behind police decision-making not by observation of the police response but by detailed analysis of the occasions on which arrests were made. They studied the response of police to accusations of child sexual abuse in day care. The stereotypical ('real') assault was by a male adult on a white female victim, and any departure from this (e.g. black victim, female perpetrator) reduced the chances of arrest and prosecution. In the absence of the stereotype, other 'aggravating' factors – e.g. oral sex, presence of physical force – would be needed before action was taken.

Criticism of police indifference to victims has been most prevalent in the case of wife battering, or abuse. Brown (1984) reported that whilst 49 per cent of victims found the police concerned and helpful, 13 per cent found them rude or hostile and blamed the woman, 16 per cent were more concerned with their own safety than that of the victim, and 22 per cent were concerned, but not helpful. The policy of arrest seems to be a key element in the controversy. Whereas most women would welcome an arrest policy – even if only because the husband can get treatment as well as or instead of punishment – the police do not see arrest as an appropriate policy, even though they generally view the behaviour as criminal and unacceptable (Saunders and Size, 1986). There is considerable disagreement about the effectiveness of arrest. Dunford et al. (1990) found that an experimental field study of the relative effectiveness of mediation, separation and arrest policies did not reveal any differences in subsequent recidivism, unlike earlier studies, although Jaffe et al. (1986) indicate that an arrest policy results in greater satisfaction on the part of victims, especially satisfaction with the police.

Police, suspects and citizens

There is little doubt that the decision to arrest a suspect is not guided solely by legal criteria, although some preoccupations that the public may have about police bias are not justified, as we shall see.

A recent controversy on racial biases in The Netherlands (see Junger, 1990) served to clarify the fact that a great deal of data now exists in Western countries that the police do not differentially arrest blacks and whites, despite considerable self-report evidence that suggests otherwise (e.g. Huizinga and Elliott, 1987). For example, Smith et al. (1984) show that an apparent racial bias is accounted for largely by the fact that 'all suspects in poorer neighbourhoods share a common fate – an increased probability of arrest'. An exception has to be made, however, for black females who in their study were not subject to the 'chivalry' extended to white women (see also Visher, 1983). A longitudinal birth cohort study of males also confirmed that police may, indeed, harass known offenders but do not 'question, chase or warn' blacks to any greater extent than they do whites (Erez, 1984).

There can, however, be little doubt that the attitudes of blacks towards the police reflects distrust and hostility to a greater extent than is evident in the views of majority groups. Erez (1984) reports that after contact with the police, whether or not it led to an arrest and regardless of type of offence, blacks were much more hostile to the police than were whites. This may be because different sub-cultural groups conceptualize police behaviour in different ways (Sullivan et al. 1987), as well as the fact that the response of police to suspects of different background may well vary in its provocativeness (Bull et al., 1983). Sullivan et al. (1987) report for example that the Police Demeanour factor loaded on different items for different groups, black teenagers, for example, responding badly to perceived 'rudeness' and 'lack of respect' more than black adults.

Certainly in London, different cultural groups differ in their attitudes towards the police in ways that reflect the quality of their perceived interaction with the police. Smith (1983) reports on attitudes towards stop and search, a policy which is believed to have been targeted against young blacks. Only 35 per cent of West Indians believe that the police only stop and search when one is acting suspiciously, a low figure compared with 58 per cent for whites, 66 per cent for Asians, and 68 per cent for other non-whites. Will street patrols by police officers, and friendly contact improve matters? The evidence suggests quite the opposite, Smith finding that there was a strong positive correlation between the amount of friendly contact with the police and extent of belief in seven types of police malpractice. Ben-Ari and Amir (1988) suggest that if contact is not to worsen relations between members of hostile groups, a number of conditions must be met (e.g. equal status contact, intimacy, common goals), conditions which are far from characterizing relations between the police and young West Indians living in London.

Detailed studies of the effects of police–citizen interaction on attitudes of citizens are scarce, but one recent study by Cox and White (1988) deserves mention for its attempt to differentiate between general attitudes to the police and more particular attitudes which may or may not be affected by specific encounters. The responses of 460 students who had received a traffic citation were compared with the responses of 373 who had not, on a number of different scales. Perceptions of the demeanour of the police were strongly influenced by interaction with them in adverse circumstances, but perceptions of competence (crime prevention effectiveness, confidence in police performance) and general perceptions of the police (e.g. 'Police officers are completely honest', 'Police officers are efficient in their work') were not affected. By demeanour, I mean perceptions of police brutality, and to a lesser extent police abusiveness and trust in the police; these were all influenced negatively. For example, students who had received traffic citations were more likely than those who had not to believe that police would practise certain forms of brutality – hitting people with batons and flashlights, 'rough up people who make them angry', 'harass groups and individuals whom they do not like' or be less likely to believe that 'if arrested, I feel confident that the police will provide for my personal safety'. It seems that interaction with the police breeds fear of the police in the minds of (minor) traffic offenders.

Pragmatism versus principles

It is neither practicable nor desirable for police to investigate all suspected criminal activity. For example, not all assaults can be investigated, and it is desirable that in some cases the complaint be negotiated away rather than formally recorded and processed. The police have a peace-keeping as well as a criminal investigating role, and the thoughtful application of discretion is surely justified. The pragmatic way in which discretion is handled is well illustrated in a study by D.A. Smith (1987) which examined in detail a sample of violent encounters between citizens where both parties were still present on the scene when the police arrived. Smith maintains that there are three main responses in terms of which the behaviour of police can be understood and reliably classified in such circumstances: they may mediate the dispute, attempting to reconcile the combatants; they may merely separate the antagonists, otherwise leaving them to their own devices. Or they may arrest one or another party to the dispute.

The first problem an officer faces may well be to determine who of the combatants might be deemed the victim. From the factors listed in table 7.1, we can see that victims helped determine their own status by requesting police action. In addition, the plight of a

Table 7.1 Factors affecting probability of arrest, in rank order of importance

---

Probability of arrest greater:
When formal action requested by victim
When whites rather than non-whites are involved
When there is antagonism shown towards the police
When the neighbourhood poverty level was high
When both disputants are male rather than a female victim
When there had been prior contact with police
When a weapon was used

Source: After Smith, 1987

white, male victim would more likely lead an officer to arrest the attacker than would that of a black or female victim. The suspect's behaviour was also important: if antagonistic, if similar events had occurred in the past, and if a weapon had been used, then arrest was more likely. Moreover, although crime level in the neighbourhood was not important, the neighbourhood's poverty level predisposed police to arrest the suspect.

Mediation, as opposed to mere separation, was used pragmatically in favourable circumstances, for example was more likely to take place in private rather than public locations, when formal action had been requested, when there had been no prior police contact and when the suspect had not been drinking: all highly *ad hoc* situational variables, not reflecting any systematic analysis of the characteristics of the case. The response, one can reasonably say, reflects pragmatic more than principled considerations.

The level of permitted discretion and the absence of clear principles to guide the exercise of discretion may create a vacuum which is filled by informal collective values amongst 'the men'. Holdaway (1983), in a study of English police officers, suggests that the lack of supervisory control generates a strong internal system of values and norms amongst the junior ranks which he characterizes as the locker-room culture. This culture supports malpractice by emphasizing the goals of fun, challenge, and action, goals which fictionally characterize police action, but whose fulfilment in practice has to be contrived. Hence, in this culture, discussions of 'the chase' are frequent and elaborate: 'Elaboration does not matter; memory is not central to the story. The important point is to heighten the sense of excitement and speed which is central to the occupational culture' (Holdaway, 1983, p. 57).

Police are inclined to escalate conflict by radioing for assistance rather than 'talking their way out of it'; by 'sailing close to the wind', intimidating suspects by threat of or actual violence. The locker-room culture, one fancies, is well understood, and is reckoned with at all levels. Holdaway, like Andrew Brown, acknowledges the positive side of the police's concern with subduing villainy. But unrealistic demands for results, combined with the inevitable frustrations arising from the adversary system, and the fact that police are largely reacting to circumstances rather than taking the initiative, all lead to practices which are of borderline morality and legality, but which lend excitement and fulfilment to an otherwise depressingly ineffectual occupational existence.

Jermier et al. (1989) have explored the meaning and consequences of physical danger for police officers, using standardized scales of occupational satisfaction. The results confirmed that police patrol officers as a group within the organization put great value on physical danger. Dangerous tasks were significantly associated with positive views of their jobs, with perceived task variety, significance and feedback. Partly, it seems, the physical danger validates the job as a worthwhile occupation, and the suggestion is made that the more dangerous work appeals to an officer's 'sense of duty'. Patrol officers and crime investigators are clearly sensitized to the physically dangerous aspects of their jobs, probably to an extent that is not justified by the (statistical) risks involved. Danger, for the police, is an important defining characteristic of the job, a fact which may prove problematic in the moves to professionalize the police, and to organize police work along more conventionally supervised and managerially controlled lines (e.g. Grant et al., 1982).

There is some evidence that the culture so vividly described by Holdaway has the effect of souring the relations between police and public in ways that will not easily be eradicated. There is the suggestion that by their provocative behaviour, unintentionally perhaps, police may, as Winkel et al. (1988) put it, 'create their own suspects'. An interesting example of this is provided by the study of Decker and Wagner (1982). These investigators examined how many officers and how many citizens were injured in citizens' encounters with police patrol units. The critical factor examined was whether or not officers patrolled singly or in pairs. The results showed quite clearly that the rate of police officers' injuries did not vary between one and two-officer patrols: single officers were no more likely to be attacked than were two officers. Two officers, however, were more likely to injure a citizen than was one officer. As the authors say: 'One-officer units were much less likely to escalate the level of confrontation of an already hostile situation' (Decker and Wagner, p. 381). Doubling up caused not only an increase in injuries to citizens but also a marked increase in the number of arrests made.

An experiment described by Grant et al. (1982) suggests that a determined effort to secure a commitment to ethical and professional standards of police conduct – an observance of suspect rights, stress on quality enforcement and attention to community relations and so on – can pay off in terms of a reduction of citizen–officer conflicts and complaints against the police. The principal aim, say the authors, should be to reduce the symbolic value to the police of arrests *per se*, to emphasize the 'quality' of an arrest, and to discourage styles of policing that encourage confrontational approaches and tactics. Such advice, of course, runs directly counter to the precepts of the locker-room culture.

Interrogation: verifying guilt

When a policeman has reason to believe that an individual has committed a criminal offence, that suspect should be cautioned, and any subsequent interview formally recorded. If carried out in a police station in the UK, any such interview would now normally be tape-recorded.

Police interrogation is essentially a question-and-answer interviewing process in much the same way as is a doctor–patient interview or a selection interview. Now that the mystique surrounding the interrogation of suspects is lifting, it is becoming clear that the skills involved are much the same as those required by interviewers in other contexts. Essentially, questions have to be asked which prompt the interviewee to recall relevant and accurate information, which is evaluated for relevance by the interviewer who continues interviewing until what has been elicited as far as possible conforms to what has been sought (see Dijkstra, 1987). Interviewing is essentially an information-gathering exercise and interviewing skill may be evaluated in terms of the interviewer's success in eliciting relevant and accurate information.

There are two main problems with this analysis which apply to interviewing in most contexts. First, consider the assumptions and motives of the interviewer. Many interviewers know in advance what they want their respondents to say. The doctor who has prejudged the diagnosis, the personnel officer who has already decided whom to appoint, and the police officer who believes in the guilt of a suspect, all will know what they would like their respondents to say. On the other side, patients may sometimes be strongly motivated to lie to their doctors about their symptoms or behaviour, perhaps not wishing to receive unwelcome advice. Candidates for a job may always have an incentive to be economical with the truth. And, of course, suspects in a police station will mostly wish to convince the police of the innocence of their actions. The information-gathering approach to police interviewing may therefore be undermined both by the interviewer who does not permit or even encourage the respondent to give an open, true account of their involvement or lack of involvement in a supposed crime, and by the respondent who may be exerting his or her imagination to the full in an attempt to produce a false but believable story; or they may remain silent and unco-operative. The prejudiced-police-officer problem may lead to the acceptance of false confessions, and the reluctant-respondent problem may thwart the investigative process. Let us examine these possibilities in turn.

Why suspects may falsely confess

There is probably an especial problem of false confessions in those countries where an adversarial system leads to the subordination of truth by the persuasiveness of advocacy and where the major role of the police is to construct the prosecution's case (Sanders, 1987). The voluntary false confession, in which a person confesses in the absence of external pressure, may issue from a variety of motives – protection of the real criminal, achievement of notoriety, punishment-seeking – and presumably will occur in many different societies and judicial systems.

Gudjonsson and MacKeith (1988), however, list two further types of false confession which may well reflect processes that are particularly salient under an adversarial system of justice. The 'coerced-compliant' (false) confession is knowingly false but given in the interests of a perceived advantage – being allowed to go home, to escape the threat of physical abuse, or to prevent the involvement of family or employer, for example. In 'coerced-internalized' (false) confessions, on the other hand, suspects begin to distrust their own memory and, at least temporarily, come to believe in their own guilt. Such was the reported experience of Carol Richardson, one of the Guildford Four who were wrongly convicted and imprisoned for 14 years for terrorist crimes. In her case, it was the alleged confession of a fellow-suspect that precipitated doubts about her own innocence. Whether or not the 'coerced-compliant' and 'coerced-internalized' cases can be so readily separated is a moot point, but instrumental motives are in principle distinguishable from changes of belief as factors underlying false confessions, whether operating separately or in combination. Let us look at some of the pressures that may lead to the coercion of suspects.

Interviewers' expectations

Gudjonsson and Hilton (1989) report an experiment in which the tendency to yield to false suggestions in a test of memory was shown to be influenced markedly by the experimental manipulation of the interviewer's perceived expectations. Those subjects who were given to understand that they 'should' be able to remember certain facts picked up false clues as to the nature of those facts much more readily than did those whose interviews were less demanding.

In a televised interview Carol Richardson mentioned the hatred her interrogators showed her, arising from their apparently unshakeable belief in her guilt. Eventually, her conformity to their beliefs was secured. There are many reasons why police interrogators may wish to believe in the guilt of those they interrogate. At its most prosaic, confessions save time that must otherwise be spent obtaining evidence by alternative and tedious means. Moreover, a majority of suspects do confess or make 'damaging statements' (Irving, 1980), and that in itself is incentive enough to attempt to secure a confession. Suspects who confess are much more likely to plead guilty (two and a half times more likely according to Baldwin and McConville, 1980), and many prosecutions where a confession was made (about 25 per cent according to Baldwin and McConville, 1980) would have been unlikely to succeed without the confession having been given in evidence.

Allied to the strategic importance of managing to secure a confession is the advantage of an interviewer's belief in the suspect's guilt as an aid to effective interrogation. When there is evidence enough against the suspect, justification for arrest and questioning is clear cut. When evidence is weak, the tendency to assume belief in the suspect's guilt regardless of evidence help allay public embarrassment of the interrogator (Stephenson and Moston, 1993).

Interviewing style

Morris (1980) concluded from her survey of the literature that in most cases the purpose of a police interrogation is to secure a confession, a finding substantiated in a recent survey of Metropolitan Police officers in London showing that securing a confession was the 'main aim' of interviewing in 80 per cent of cases (Stephenson and Moston, 1993). It is then not surprising that the predominant police styles of interrogation are geared to securing confessions rather than eliciting of evidence *per se* (Irving and Hilgendorf, 1980).

A recent study (Williamson, 1993) indicates that the major dimension in terms of which CID interrogators in London judge themselves may appropriately be called 'Perceived success'. Officers scoring high on this factor enjoy interrogation and view it as an important activity. They see themselves as being good at it, and securing a large number of truthful confessions. Their preferred styles are 'friendly' and 'counselling' (rather than 'business-like' or 'dominant'), and trickery is explicitly rejected as a technique. The interesting point about this factor is that although it shows an acceptance of the need to avoid unethical and coercive techniques in the new era of tape-recorded interviewing under the Police and Criminal Evidence Act and associated Codes of Practice (1985) (PACE 1984), the elevation of confession as the most important criterion of successfulness is apparent. Other factors (in total accounting for 50 per cent of the variance) were in decreasing order of importance: Dominance, characterized by a preference for quick questioning to keep up the pressure on suspects; Perceived Difficulty, characterized by fear of 'drying up' and recognition of the need for training; and finally, Persuasion, a factor in which interrogation is seen in somewhat Machiavellian terms: the weakness of many cases is recognized and the need to exploit interpersonal factors is recognized.

There is little evidence on the relative effects of different styles of interviewing, partly because of the difficulty of conducting experimental research in this area. Moston et al. (1992) report that interviewing style was related to strength of evidence, with more accusatorial styles being used when evidence was strong and information-gathering styles when evidence was weaker.

The coerciveness of the situation

Those who have observed police interrogation (e.g. Softley, 1980; Irving, 1980) agree that coercive tactics are not the reason most people confess. Sometimes they may appear to be, and in the 1970s when Irving and Softley conducted their investigations, a number of coercive tactics was practised in the majority of cases – in 74 per cent of cases according to Irving (1980). Police discretion may be promised – over the specific charge, releasing on bail – and implicit bargains made. The interviewing officer's expert knowledge, about the likely sentence, about the attitude of the courts, may be used as a potential reward to compliant suspects. The consequences of confessing or not confessing may be painted in exaggerated terms, to the distinct advantage of making a clean breast of it. The inevitability of conviction may be stressed given the (supposed) existence of hard forensic evidence already in police possession, including confession by accomplices. Promises of rewards – release on bail, food, cigarettes – and threats of punishment – removal of clothes for examination, delay of meals etc. – may be made.

As Farrington (1981) pointed out, the effectiveness of such tactics is not proved by their mere description. Indeed it appears from recent studies that the more stringent conditions under which interrogations are now carried out since the Police and Criminal Evidence Act was introduced in 1984 has not resulted in any reduction in the number of confessions. Irving and McKenzie (1988) report a dramatic decrease in the number of coercive tactics employed in interrogation since 1979, the time of the first Irving (1980) study – to 25 per cent of their 1979 level in 1986 – but with no evidence of a falling-off in 'admissions' or confessions (see also Maguire, 1988). Grant (1987) reports that in Canada the experimental introduction of video recording, which may be expected to all but eliminate the use of dubious tactics, has not led to a reduction in 'the high percentage of confessions and admissions' (p. 383), as it had been feared might happen. Similarly, Moston et al. (1992)

find that the percentage of confessions and admissions in London CID interviews under conditions of audio taping under PACE in 1988 is at a comparable level to that found by Irving in Brighton in 1979.

The review of psychological evidence on interrogation by Irving and Hilgendorf (1980) suggested that the circumstances of interrogation in a police station are inherently coercive, and do not require the additional use of coercive tactics to persuade many people that confession is an appropriate strategy or response in the oppressive situation in which they find themselves. One may say, that if false confessions are encouraged in such circumstances, then truthful confessions must be hard to resist making – for the average (and certainly new) criminal. Confession, it is said, serves to reduce the uncertainty associated with confinement, isolation and the implicit threat of physical harm this engenders especially in first-time suspects. Equally important, the shame, loss of control and stresses associated with confinement may combine to make one especially vulnerable to the suggestions of authority figures who, after all, have a right to interrogate you. Whilst confession is against one's interests and the suspect has a right to remain silent without adverse inferences being drawn, nonetheless, confessing seems to be an attractive option for many suspects.

There has as yet been no attempt to measure the perceived coerciveness of different interrogation settings and to relate such measures systematically to rates of confession. One might surmise, however, that if settings are important, there would be differences in confession and admission rates between them. It is interesting that the admission rate does vary markedly between police stations (Moston et al., 1992), and it is possible that these differences have a situational basis rather than reflecting differences in interviewer skill, or the character of suspects.

The perceived coerciveness of a confession is now an important issue in many criminal trials in England, because audio tape recordings of interrogations may be played in court for the benefit of the jury. There is now considerable support for the introduction of video recordings of police interrogations, which raises questions of how the recordings would first be made and subsequently presented in court which do not arise in the case of audio recordings. Lassiter and Irvine (1986) show that perceived coercion varies greatly with the camera focus – on the suspect or on the interviewer. If the focus is on the interviewer, then observers rate the detective's

Table 7.2 The impact of camera point of view on perceived interrogative coerciveness and attributional judgements of suspect's behaviour

	Camera Point of View		
	Suspect focus	*Equal focus*	*Detective focus*
Coercion	3.1	4.8	6.8
Confidence	6.9	6.9	6.6
Dispositional *minus* Situational Attribution	3.5	−2.4	−4.6

Source: After Lassiter and Irvine, 1986

coerciveness more than twice as great as when the focus is on the suspect, as table 7.2 demonstrates. An equal focus elicited ratings at a mid-way point. Confidence in the ratings was high throughout. Table 7.2 also shows that situational attributions for the suspect's behaviour assume increasing importance as one moves from 'suspect' through 'equal' to 'detective' focus. If such arbitrary, and exploitable, factors can, indeed, enter into estimates of coerciveness, it adds weight to the legal arguments for close scrutiny of the role of confession in the trial process.

Psychological attributes and states of the suspect

When listening to tape-recorded interrogations, I have sympathized with those suspects who become angry with officers who disbelieve and ridicule the accounts of innocent conduct given by the suspects. Whether the suspect be guilty or not, the interrogator by adopting a derisive tone and generally sarcastic manner may well evoke an angry reaction in the suspect that jeopardizes the prospect of any future co-operation. Gudjonsson (1989) describes three cases of individuals who not only in real interrogations but also in experimental tests of their suggestibility veered between an angry suspiciousness (and low suggestibility) to a ready and friendly attitude which was highly conducive to suggestibility. The cognitive set adopted by individuals has obvious implications for their willingness to resist or yield to the suggestions and wishes of the interrogator, whatever may be the basis of the attitude in evidence (see Gudjonsson and Clark, 1986).

Setting aside these transitional moods and states of mind, Gudjonsson (e.g. Gudjonsson, 1984b) believes that individuals vary consistently in their response to suggestions in interrogation. He devised a test which measured the extent to which subjects who have listened to a story of a mugging, yield to false suggestions in leading questions the experimenter puts to them. For example, one of the fifteen misleading questions asked 'Did the woman's screams frighten the assailants?', when no such event was mentioned in the story. Agreement with that item contributes 1 to the yield score. The 'yield' and allied 'shift' scores have been shown to be related in predictable ways to various other personality characteristics, like self-esteem (e.g. Gudjonsson and Lister, 1984) and, more importantly, to performance under real police interrogation. Gudjonsson (1984c) contrasted the results on his suggestibility scales of those who consistently denied their guilt with 'false confessors' who, despite having once confessed, subsequently withdrew their confession and pleaded not guilty. The false confessors had a measurably higher suggestibility score than did the 'deniers', although the scores of the false confessors fell within the normal range of scores on this test. What has to be explained is the remarkably low scores of the deniers most of whom, it also has to be said, were found guilty of the offences with which they were charged. The forensic relevance of this test is, therefore, unclear at the present, but a recent paper by Gudjonsson and Lebegue (1989) claims that the suggestibility score of a man who confessed 'believingly' to the murder of a close friend but was subsequently shown not to have committed the offence, was higher than average, and that his tendency towards compliance and his general eagerness to please was very marked.

Predicting confession as an outcome of police interrogation

The introduction of tape recording into many police stations since the introduction of PACE has considerably enlarged the scope of inquiries into the effectiveness of interrogation, and the factors which determine the decision to confess or to remain silent. In past research, a number of factors have been shown in isolation from other factors to be associated with the tendency to confess. Baldwin and McConville (1980), for example, suggested that age is a factor associated with the tendency to confess. In their study of Birmingham and London Crown Courts there was an apparently linear association with age, ranging from 60 per cent of those aged under 21 to only 34 per cent of those aged 40 or more who made either a full verbal or full written confession. Interestingly, however, first offenders were less likely to confess than those who had been previously convicted of an offence.

Studies of limited samples of this kind, employing just one or two predictor variables, throw little light on the motives for confession. Moston et al. (1992) conducted a survey of more than 1100 CID interrogations carried out consecutively within ten police stations in London. Three highly situational factors appear independently to influence strongly the tendency to admit offences: the strength of evidence in possession of the police, the advice of solicitors (invariably to remain silent), and the police station at which one is detained. Characteristics of the offence and of the offender were of no importance in comparison with these three situational variables. The two most important factors – of legal advice and strength of evidence – are readily interpretable. Suspects are in the one case bowing to the inevitable weight of hard evidence which incriminates them, and in the other are not unreasonably accepting the professional opinion of one from whom they have sought advice. The (lesser) situational influence of the police station may be related to differences between inner city and suburban practice. The moral for police officers would seem to be that extracting a confession in the absence of hard evidence is an uphill task, and that solicitors' advice does not work in their favour.

Securing a confession is one thing, but successfully prosecuting an offender is something else. What bearing does confession have on the decision of the police to charge a suspect with an offence, the first step in prosecuting an alleged offender? Moston et al. (1992) found that three factors independently determined the decision to charge: strength of evidence, the outcome of an interview, and sex of suspect. As might be expected, strength of evidence was the most important of these factors, followed by outcome of interview. Securing an admission is obviously a very important factor in determining whether or not a police officer proceeds with a case, independently of whether it will prove to be important in securing a conviction. Not confessing considerably reduces the chances of being charged and subsequently prosecuted for an offence, regardless of strength of evidence. The influence of sex of suspect on being subject to charge demonstrated that in this instance at least, all other things being equal, it is better to be female.

8

Stories in Court

Introduction: the character of courtroom interaction

The pomp, the imposed order, the antagonism and even the archaisms in a Crown Court trial in England convey the impression of adversarial justice according to the rule of law. A similar symbolic effect is conveyed in other courts – magistrates' courts, judicial inquiries, industrial tribunals – in which the verdict is not, however, left to the whim of untrained and available members of the public, but is in the hands of legal professionals or experienced laymen advised by professionals. In most courts admission of those members of the public who wish to attend is added testimony to the propriety of the proceedings, which can normally be freely reported.

Courtroom dramas on television, film and radio and in books are highly popular forms of entertainment. They are so because, as in real trials, they deal not in dry legal debates – in real trials, these are hived off into separate and unpublicized discussions between judge and lawyers – but because of the dramatic tensions, uncertainties, conflicts and mysteries inherent in what Beach (1985) calls the 'storifying' that characterizes courtroom interactions.

The dramatic tensions and uncertainties can be sustained in part because the all-important ending to the story – the verdict – is in the balance, and we know from real cases that the vagaries of jury decision-making are such that the outcome may remain highly uncertain even after weeks or months of wrangling in court. But more interestingly the dramatic interest is there because, in a well-fought court case, the evidence that is proved in court is given different and conflicting interpretations by the opposed sides, and the observer has to search for those vital clues which point to the 'truth' of one or other version. In the best stage courtroom dramas,

of course, a key element always makes its appearance in the clos-
ing minutes just before the jury retires to give its verdict, and the
judge mercifully permits its disclosure to the court.

Stories are the stuff of courtroom interaction as they are the stuff
of everyday conversation, so it is not difficult for untrained lay
persons to enter into the spirit of the occasion and the task of
judgement (see Bennett and Feldman, 1981). Indeed, judges seem
to have the utmost faith in the ability of the average jury person
to know a true story when they hear it. The stories that are told,
however, are by-and-large told by the lawyers not by the witnesses,
and certainly not by witnesses as they would tell them in everyday
social contexts. So-called 'conversational analysis' of courtroom
interaction reveals a domination by one party – the lawyer – that
is quite uncharacteristic of the ebb and flow of natural discourse
(Atkinson and Drew, 1979). Examination and cross-examination in
court are principally designed to elicit from witnesses the elements
of evidence that are central to the construction of one or other
side's story. Holstein (1988), for example, shows that in the examination and cross-examination of persons whom the authorities are
seeking to commit to mental hospital, 'crazy talk', or not as the
case may be, is induced by the form of questioning: it is a consequence of an interactional process that is determined primarily
by the examiner. More generally, Penman (1990) demonstrates a
very strong relationship between the actor's role in court – barrister
or witness – and the implications of what was said for the relationship. Crudely, what the barristers say has more effect on the esteem
or 'face' of the witness than vice versa, with barristers trying predominantly to boost the morale of their own witnesses and to
embarrass witnesses from the opposition. Rarely are witnesses
permitted to fight back, or, of course, ever to ask a question.

In the remainder of this chapter, I want to show how the manner
in which the proceedings are conducted influences the way in which
stories are presented and received in court. The studies I shall
describe have for the most part been concerned to establish whether
or not the formal relationships, linguistic conventions, and language
of the court assist or hinder the presentation of a defendant's or
witness's version of events. The approach is essentially pragmatic,
whilst bearing in mind the possibility raised by Atkinson and Drew
(1979) that improving the 'interactional comfort' of participants
will not necessarily increase the effectiveness of their performance.
Indeed, there is evidence (Webb, 1990) that in less formal settings,

like the industrial tribunal, the ability of rhetorically unskilled participants to put across their point of view may be even more undermined than it is in established courts of law.

What makes a story convincing?

This is an important question addressed by Lance Bennett and Martha Feldman in their provocative and exciting book, *Reconstructing Reality in the Courtroom* (Bennett and Feldman, 1981). These authors accept that telling competing stories is the essence of courtroom interaction, but they emphasize that a story's truth does not guarantee its emergence as a plausible candidate for belief and acceptance. Essentially this is because stories in court are a technique for ordering and presenting evidence, an activity that can be performed more or less skilfully, and which is dependent for its success on the quality of available evidence, something over which the story-teller (defence or prosecution lawyer) may have little control. In addition, the hearers of the story may be overly impressed by who tells the story and how, rather than its effectiveness in accounting for the available evidence.

The importance of story structure to its acceptance by hearers was demonstrated in an experimental study by Bennett and Feldman in which student subjects were asked to tell true or false stories to the group of students. The listeners were asked to vote privately on the status of the stories as 'true' or 'false', and it was discovered that these judgements were totally unrelated to the actual truth value of the stories; a true story was as likely to receive a 'false' as a 'true' vote, and vice versa. Story length in words, and the number of actions it contained – straightforward measures of complexity – were also unrelated to truth judgements, as were number and length of pauses – a measure of uncertainty. The important feature of the story to which listeners appeared to respond was the coherence of the story, as assessed by a measure that Bennett and Feldman termed 'structural ambiguity'. To be coherent, a story should have a central action to which the various characters, objects and events ('elements') in the story should be clearly connected, either directly, or indirectly by virtue of their clear relation to other elements. The key feature here is the clarity of the relationships between elements and their linking to the central action. Bennett and Feldman found that the larger the proportion of ambiguous links in the story, the less likely it was to be believed. Structural ambiguity was the only measure which successfully predicted how listeners would vote: the less ambiguous a story, the more believers it would attract.

The relevance of this study to courtroom interaction is clear. Judges and juries will be impressed by, and tend to believe, that version of events and explanation of evidence whose elements are the more unambiguously related one to another and to the 'central action' which accounts for the known or alleged harm that has been done. In the adversarial system, it is in each side's interests so to distort its presentation of the evidence that its own story or version of events has the greater clarity and is therefore to be believed. Of course, structural ambiguity may be perceived in stories that are true, leading those whose stories may lack clarity through no fault of their own to become embittered and angry. Members of minority groups, for example, may find that their accounts of events are ill-received because the conventions of their social group which serve to clarify the actions in a story are not shared by the minority who sit in judgement upon them. In England, newsworthy incomprehension is not infrequently betrayed by judges who ask for definitions of words and phrases that are perfectly comprehensible and common-place to those who circulate in a less exalted social sphere. However, and perhaps even more importantly, the key role of stories in courtroom interaction explains why it is that, despite the formality of language and complexity of issues raised, lay participants are capable of participating intelligently in the proceedings and even rendering sensible verdicts. As Bennett and Feldman say:

> The story is an everyday form of communication that enables a diverse cast of courtroom characters to follow the development of a case and reason about the issues in it. Despite the image of legal jargon, lawyers' mysterious tactics, and obscure court procedures, any criminal case can be reduced to the simple form of a story. Through the use of broadly shared techniques of telling and interpreting stories, the actors in a trial present, organise, and analyse the evidence that bears on the alleged illegal activity. (Bennett and Feldman, 1981, p. 4)

Beach (1985) notes that in a lengthy trial the complexity of the task of integrating different witnesses' accounts of events is problematic, and that an individual witness may even have difficulty integrating their own evidence in response to lawyers who may shift rapidly from one date to another. One principal reason for the persuasiveness of the well-structured story is the welcome simplicity and coherence it brings to a mass of assured but conflicting, sometimes wavering and shifting accounts of witnesses. The past, as Beach puts it, is 'dense' and the jury will seize gratefully on that reconstruction which yields the greatest clarity.

Tensions between the perceived and factual status of reconstructed events

Trials focus on the past and its reconstruction. In a courtroom transcript of a murder trial, Beach reports that of a total of 9500 utterances, 8640 or 91 per cent were concerned with past events, only 7 per cent with what was going on in the present, and a mere 2 per cent with future interaction. Table 8.1 summarizes the functions of utterances broken down by temporal reference. Future and present utterances are concerned with regulation of courtroom behaviour, whereas past utterances are concerned exclusively with reconstruction of events.

Consistent with the adversarial form of courtroom interaction, the distinction between factual and perceived past events emerged as crucial to understanding the form of debate. In the following passage, for example, the defence lawyer, in order to verify a psychiatric diagnosis of the accused, is trying to establish that the defendant was acting 'unusually':

Q: He just said, just made the single statement, I'm going to stop taking medication?

A: No, I can't say that's all he said, but that's all that I can remember him saying. It seemed like an unusual thing to say.

Q: And he was acting unusual that day?

A: Well, it's hard for me to say that, because that's the first time I saw him; as I said, this is kind of an unusual thing for a person to say, and that's why I remember it.

Q: You said it's hard for you to say whether he was acting usual or unusual that day?

A: No, no I said I really didn't observe him before that, and when I said the word unusual, I said that seemed like a rather unusual thing to say, and I remember it, but, no, I wouldn't say that there was anything unusual about his behavior other than it

Table 8.1 Function of time-related utterances

Temporal Reference	Communicative Functions	Language Devices
1. Future (2% = 186 utterances)	a. Procedural/ Instructive b. Performance of an Action c. Delusions	a. Lawyers' opening statements b. Requests c. Projections/Fantasies
2. Present (7% = 674 utterances)	a. Monitoring and Maintenance Formulations	a. Lawyers' objections Bench discussions Judges' instructions to lawyers, witnesses and jury members
3. Past (91% = 8640 utterances)	a. Reconstruction	a. Yes–No, 'Wh' (Who, What, When, Where, Why, How) and clarification questions. Fragmented/Narrative answers

Source: Beach, 1985, 12

seemed that there was something worrying him (from Beach, 1985, p. 14)

Here the lawyer is attempting to influence the witness's misty perceptions to obtain an unambiguous factual statement. In other cases a lawyer may wish to turn an unambiguous factual statement into something less certain, less assured, in order to be able to create doubt in the minds of the jury about the truth of one story or another. Much courtroom interaction is dominated by the tensions between the factual and perceived status of reconstructed events.

When only one story is told

The magistrates' courts in England are a good instance of what may happen when one side in the court debate is less able to tell its story than the other. McBarnet (1981) points out that in the lower, magistrates' courts, where justice is mostly dispensed by lay magistrates advised by the Clerk of the Court, only 19 per cent of defendants obtain legal representation, whereas 99 per cent have legal representation in the higher courts. Many defendants just do not know how to proceed according to the rules of the court. For example, the first opportunity to speak, to tell one's story, may come when the defendant is permitted to cross-examine a witness. Instead of cross-examining the witness, a defendant will frequently proceed to make a statement, to give their account of what happened the night the police called, or the fight started, or whatever. This leads to instant rebuke and may lead to loss of the opportunity to challenge a witness. For example:

Magistrate:	Would you like to ask any questions?
Accused:	All I said was, 'what's happening?'
Magistrate to Policeman:	Are you in any doubt that this man was committing the offence?
Policeman:	No
Accused:	I never opened my mouth except to ask what was happening.
Magistrate:	You can't deliver a peroration at this point. Have you (moving on to 2nd accused) any questions?' (McBarnet, 1981, p. 184)

Although the magistrate should in theory assist defendants in cross-examination, in practice, according to McBarnet, this rarely occurs in an effective way, the assistance being limited usually to the statement that questions should be addressed to the witness. This bleak exchange is apparently typical:

Accused to Magistrate:	All I can say is ...
Magistrate:	It's him you ask the questions
Accused:	No questions then. (McBarnet, 1981, p. 185)

This structural imbalance in the lower courts is well illustrated by Carlen (1974). The incompetence of the normally unrepresented defendant renders any challenge to the fairness or appropriateness of the proceedings 'as being either out of place, out of time, out of mind or out of order' (Carlen, 1974, p. 104). Magistrates are able in the absence of an effective representation of the accused to define and control the situation in the interests of the court and the pro-secution rather than justice. And they may exercise that power. A probation officer who attempts to represent his client's interests gets short shrift in this extract from a case in which a boy has been taking drugs:

Probation Officer: But he is not an addict
Magistrate: Yet he's a drug-taker. You make fine distinctions [Magistrate laughs] A drug-taker may become an addict (Carlen, 1974, p. 111)

The layman's story is laughingly rejected in that example, and blithely ignored in the next, where the defendant, on a drunk charge, has complained that although he had informed the police that he needed to take medicine every four hours, he had not been permitted to see a doctor whilst in custody:

Magistrate: You must take this up with your MP
Defendant: But I am not at this moment interested in my MP, Sir, I am interested in explaining to you why I must appear a bit strange at this moment . . . because I haven't had any pills.
Magistrate: Yes, I quite understand. Three pounds fine.' (p. 106)

The respective attitudes of defendants and magistrates, as portrayed in Carlen's work, is rather aptly summed up in this brief exchange between a defendant told by the magistrate he can say 'anything he wants' before being sentenced for drunkenness.

Defendant: I don't think I've anything to say that you would want to hear.
Magistrate: Very well then. Pay one pound.

These common routines in magistrates' courts reflect structural differences in power deriving largely but not entirely from knowledge of appropriate procedures and conventional routines. However, courtroom exchanges in higher courts where defendants are adequately represented by counsel may nonetheless appear intimidating enough to witnesses and defendants. Penman (1987) outlines nineteen 'rules' derived from an analysis of rebukes in courtroom discourse. For example, judges will rebuke lawyers for asking 'double-barrelled' questions, because the witness will not know which to answer. A lawyer will rebuke a witness for not being precise.

Lawyer: Where exactly were you standing?
Witness: In Mart Street
Lawyer: Yes, but where *exactly* in Mart Street?

Although such rules – as avoidance of double-barrelled questions, or being precise, or not giving more information than requested – may be seen to be in the interests of mutual comprehension, they may nonetheless appear to be coercive and humiliating to a witness. And, in fact, such questions are often deliberately coercive and humiliating. The lawyer's job is to establish the truth of his client's story and to destroy the credibility of the other side's story. The demand for precision is one technique whereby the ambiguity of a story may be exposed. The conclusion that the witness 'did not know where he was standing' may become a part of the fabric of evidence and will be exploited when the lawyer subsequently, and probably sarcastically, reconstructs the opposing side's story of the events that took place. Moreover, as Valdés (1986) perceptively points out, 'co-operation' in the required question and answer sequences coerces witnesses into acceptance of the conclusions of one's interrogator.

In the following passage, the second phase of the cross-examination of a witness in an American courtroom, Valdés claims that the lawyer's purpose is to establish that the defendant became angry towards the officers – no more, and no less.

Attorney: Now, when you got there – ah-you say that – the officer – asked you to do a field sobriety test and they asked to look at your arms. Isn't that right?
Witness: Well – the lady cop asked me if I was drinking, and then she gave me a sobriety test – After I passed it, the cop asked for me to re..roll up my sleeves. I ignored him. He told me – either you're gonna DO as I say, or you're gonna spend one easy night in JAIL.
Attorney: That made you mad didn't it . . .
Witness: Whoa, whoa. Let me finish up your question. Then – he turned around – went for the side baton. I rolled my sleeves up – by the time he got back – took his fighting stance, my sleeves were already rolled up.
Attorney: Alright.
Witness: He wasn't interested in my arms or my sleeves any more.
Attorney: This made you mad, didn't it – when he asked to look at your sleeves?
Witness: Well

Attorney: Yes or no? This made you mad?
Witness: Well, it was – it you know, kind of ... Let me put the
              question to you. Wouldn't it a made *you* mad?
Attorney: Just give me an answer, yes or no?
Witness: Yeah it made me mad. (Valdés, pp. 298–9)

Such coercive proceedings are not confined to the context of criminal justice. In the different legal context of industrial arbitrations, Morley et al. (1988) describe how appeals by individuals on grounds of fairness were managed (or negotiated) by the court 'applying a technical set of rules. Those who understood the rules were more likely to be successful than those who did not' (p. 130).

Combat between equals?

Coerciveness is built into the rules for 'co-operative' dialogue in a way which threatens especially the unrepresented defendant. But let us assume for the moment that the defendant is represented, and that the adversarial system is on full display as the respective barristers lead their sides into combat. We may then ask whether or not the rules of the game, and the way these rules are interpreted by the judge, operate fairly. Or is one side or the other given the advantage? Does one side's story rather than the other tend to emerge more clearly? Lind (1982) suggests that the order in which the respective stories are presented (prosecution or defence first) does not impinge strongly on their acceptability to juries, so the general context of the adversarial system would not seem to confer any strong advantage either way. It is possible to ask another question, however, concerning how effectively adversarial the respective parties are. Is the degree of combativeness evenly distributed when defendants are represented? Under the adversary system, are defence and prosecution lawyers equally combative? And if there is an imbalance, should we hope that it would be in the interests of the defence, and that the defence lawyer would be especially vigilant?

Danet and Bogoch (1980) measured the combativeness of lawyers in two rape, two murder and two assault trials. For example, the coerciveness of questions was examined. Declarative questions, like 'You did it, didn't you?' were deemed to be more coercive than Interrogation Yes/No questions, like 'Did you do it?'. The latter are in turn said to be more coercive than Interrogative – who questions (who? what? where? when? why? questions) which in their own turn are more combative than Requestions, which merely invite the witness to answer a 'wh' question (e.g. could you tell us what happened last night?). By counting the number of questions in these different categories and using a number of additional indices of combativeness – like the number of objections to one's opponent's line of questioning – combativeness was measured and its use examined in relation to three independent variables: (a) the attorney's role – for the prosecution or for the defence; (b) type of examination – direct or cross-examination; and (c) seriousness of offence.

In total numbers of questions, the ratio of questions in cross- and direct examination, focus on the defendant's actions, and objections to opponent's line of questioning, prosecution lawyers appear to be more combative than defence lawyers. This did not apply to the coerciveness of question form. If anything, defence lawyers appeared to be more coercive than their prosecution colleagues. There was, however, a consistent effect of seriousness of offence in the case of question form, such that defence lawyers were apparently more coercive than prosecution lawyers in the less serious cases of assault and rape, but on a par with their prosecution partners in the case of murder. Put another way, it seems that prosecuting lawyers are more combative in serious than in less serious cases, whereas defence lawyers are more equally combative throughout (see figure 8.1).

Danet and Bogoch conclude that these judges in the United States generally distribute their responses to objections even-handedly between defence and prosecution. The exception to this is an apparent partiality in cases of rape, where the prosecuting lawyer's objections are twice as likely to be overruled as are those of the defence lawyer (see figure 8.2). The absolute number of objections on which the percentage figures are based is of interest. There were too few objections in assault cases for reliable statistical analysis (18 in total), more in rape cases (67) but many more in murder cases (230). Clearly, lawyers are most zealous (and legitimately so in more than half the cases, according to the judges who upheld a majority of the objections) the more serious the offence. This effect is independent of the difference in overall number of questions in murder, rape, and assault trials.

Dunstan (1980) takes issue with Danet and Bogoch on the

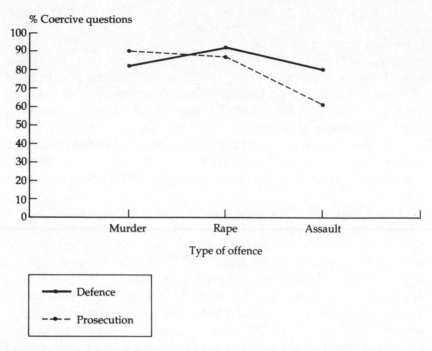

Figure 8.1   Coerciveness of question form in cross-examination by type of offence, and representation
Source: Danet and Bogoch, 1980

interpretation of their findings in terms of combativeness. There is no single relation between linguistic form and coerciveness, according to Dunstan. Of course it is true that the context of each and every question is missing in Danet and Bogoch's analysis, and the latter should no doubt have validated their measures of coerciveness by securing ratings of sections of the transcript by unbiased judges. The number of cases examined is also small, and the possibility that lawyers seek to create impressions (of thoroughness, tolerance or whatever) that have strategic value is not considered. Possibly it is too naïve to think that to do an effective adversarial job, the lawyers must be necessarily overtly combative. Nevertheless, the analyses of Danet and Bogoch establish the possibility that criticisms and evaluations of the fairness, impartiality and thoroughness of the participants may be critically examined using content analysis of this kind. There is a need for more research to build on the lead they have given.

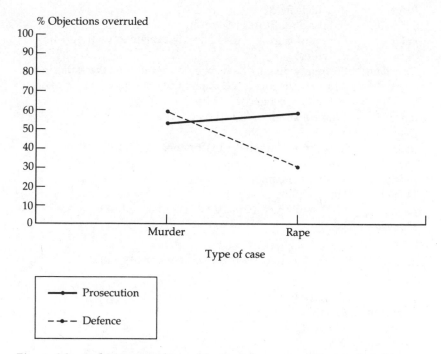

% Objections overruled

Figure 8.2 Judges overriding objections by prosecution and defence counsel in murder and rape cases*
* Too few cases of objections by prosecution in assault cases for reliable analyses to be conducted
Source: After Danet and Bogoch, 1980

Demeanour in court

Telling a good story depends as much on the expectations of the listeners as on the skills of the story-teller. Wodak (1980) makes the point that, at least in the inquisitorial context of an Austrian courtroom, the expectations of the judge based on the social class of the defendant play a major role in determining whose story will be believed. In the following case – one of 16 trials for motoring offences analysed by Wodak – the middle-class defendant gets off to a cracking good start:

Judge: G.F.?
Defendant: Yes, good morning
Judge: You are a Doctor of Philosophy
Defendant: Yes

Judge:	In which field?
Defendant:	Philosophy. Pure Philosophy
Judge:	Pure philosophy? How does that relate to your sporting activities?
Defendant:	For many years I have been a member of the Austrian Alpine Club. I have led expeditions and have undertaken arduous ascents.
Judge:	You are single? You live at . . .?
Defendant:	Yes
Judge:	You are a University instructor?
Defendant:	Yes
Judge:	Average income?
Defendant:	6000 schillings
Judge:	6000 schillings. No capital, no financial obligations?
Defendant:	No.

Compare that with another example, of a working-class defendant.

Judge:	Religion?
Defendant:	Catholic
Judge:	Married?
Defendant:	Yes
Judge:	Have a household?
Defendant:	Yes
Judge:	And you live?
Defendant:	In the . . .
Judge:	So, and then we need your education
Defendant:	Primary and secondary school
Judge:	Each for four years?
Defendant:	Yes

In the first, the judge goes out of his way to put the defendant at ease and to treat him respectfully, in contrast to the routine, terse and impersonal tone of the second. The second continues in a way which confirms the impression you might have gained of the judge's hostility to this defendant and his story:

Judge:	Yes, and what else?
Defendant:	Well, I was near the crossing, suddenly the car came from the right, I saw it, but I couldn't manage to brake anymore. So –
Judge:	You couldn't brake, couldn't you try to swerve somehow?

Defendant:	No
Judge:	Do you know what this is?
Defendant:	No
Judge:	No again. You can't answer this question either?
Defendant:	Yes – to steer somewhere else, did you mean? Or?
Judge:	Yes – every vehicle has a steering wheel. If one turns it around, the direction changes, doesn't it? If it's not broken. If one turns this thing, it is called swerving – to put it briefly. Understood? Yes?

The judge's continuing interview with the Doctor of Philosophy, by contrast, displays sympathy and consideration:

Judge:	No previous convictions. Do you plead guilty or not guilty?
Defendant:	I plead guilty to having overlooked the woman, even though I was paying full attention.
Judge:	Flötzersteig, near the Wilhelmine Hospital. Now what happened?

In reply to this apparently sympathetic request to give an explanation of how this gentleman had come to find himself as a defendant in court, the young lecturer gave the following helpful version of events:

Defendant:	Well, I was in the center lane, because there were cars parked on the right side and about the place where the accident later occurred, the row of parked cars ended on the right side, and therefore, I wanted to change lanes because the right lane was then clear and also I looked into the mirror and suddenly I see in front of me, or rather, left of me, a figure and my first thought was that it's completely impossible and I was really shocked that this could be possible at all, that now in front of me something to my left, a human being appears, and before I could start braking, the collision happened and somehow I had also realized that the vehicle behind me skidded. With this I had realized that the woman was thrown towards the curb and there this was my first thought: no further accidents, if behind me cars crash into me and therefore – eh – I went to the left. After this, upon later consideration, this had to be explained that due to the deformation of the fender on

the right side, braking occurred. I already wanted to steer the car to the right in order to stop it in this way against the curb, therefore I had the impression that the car was going to the left. I then could orient myself and braked and stopped right at the curb.

The long, detailed and self-serving account of his knocking over the woman given by the defendant is listened to patiently by the judge, and they part company after the following amicable exchange:

Defendant:	Yes, I wish to thank you for the conduct of the trial and especially for the mild sentence, and I accept the sentence.
Judge:	Hopefully, it will go all right in June. Then you will become a professor?
Defendant:	This can be applied for, after a certain time, the professorship, after the habilitation, after 3 years it can be applied for – it is difficult.
Judge:	Will you earn more then?
Defendant:	Professorship? Yes, one can live on that quite well.
Judge:	More than now?
Defendant:	I think the starting salary is about 10,000 shillings, the starting salary.
Judge:	O.K. Thank you.

The lecturer interacted skilfully with the judge, establishing a common educational background, and conversing in the elaborated middle-class code of drawing-room conversation. The story he provided is elaborated, detailed, consistent and essentially plausible. The accident is objectified as a misfortune which the defendant did his utmost to deal with in an effective way, before he dutifully accepts responsibility with a guilty plea.

As for working-class defendants, the example given, according to Wodak, is typical of the genre. Little or no empathy is apparent, and the judge's attitude is unsympathetic and patronizing. The working-class defendants were apparently consistently ill-at-ease, frequently switching linguistic styles in an anxious effort to please the judge. Middle-class defendants were more consistently relaxed, adopting easy, flowing narrative styles – which they share with the judge – throughout the interaction. Their plausible stories were generally believed, and they received sympathetic treatment.

O'Barr (1982) reinforces the view that establishing an easy, em-pathic rapport with the court is of critical importance to the per-ception of the story which the defendant has to tell. He talks of demeanour evidence which may enhance or may detract from the persuasiveness of the content of the evidence given in an adversarial context. Evidence may be proved legally, but its impact varies according to the interaction style of the defendant. Juries, claims O'Barr, are permitted, 'to assess style, paralinguistic cues, and non-verbal behaviour to determine trustworthiness, credibility and so on, using the same evaluative criteria used in everyday life' (O'Barr, 1982, p. 46).

Lind and O'Barr (1979) suggest that the impact of speech style is related to gender. Women, it is said, tend to adopt a 'powerless' speech style, which incorporates both linguistic and paralinguistic features. For example, intensifiers are employed like 'so', 'very' and 'too', which are combined with emphasis and other non-verbal signs ('I like him *so* much'); empty adjectives are used ('divine', 'charming', 'cute'), together with polite forms; hedges ('well', 'you know', 'I guess'); and rising, more varied intonation. Those who employ this speech style are said to be perceived as being more feminine but less convincing. The authors' research in which male and female actors each adopted the two speech styles in presentation of witness evidence from actual court cases supported that view. Interestingly, the effects of speech style were very similar for both gender conditions, although there was a trend for men to be the more favourably perceived in the powerful, and women in the powerless condition.

The work of Lind et al. (1978) confirms that a narrative style in which witnesses give long or extended answers to questions elicits different reactions from a fragmented speech style in which terse, broken answers are given. However, the data were based on subjects' estimates of how lawyers would perceive the evidence, and there were marked differences between the estimates of law students, and non-law undergraduates. Law students, it seems, thought that lawyers would be impressed by women who adopted an elaborated style, whereas non-law students thought that men would be better received when they adopted such a style. Apart from indicating that style of speech does influence judgements, it is very difficult to draw any general conclusions from this study: the precise character of narrative testimony is not clear (we know only that it is longer), and the usefulness of the dependent variable is unclear. The ambiguities in the experimental evidence suggest the need for further exploration of this important issue.

It will be seen that there are many obstacles to the adequate presentation of stories in court by defendants who are not versed in middle-class arts of self-presentation, or are unwilling to accommodate to the interactional demands placed upon them. The need for adequate representation in court under our adversarial system, including magistrates courts, and increasingly in industrial and other tribunals, is generally recognized, but assistance is not generally provided. Wodak's research indicates that an inquisitorial system may not be an improvement, at least in those relatively trivial cases where the judge dispenses justice speedily, having first failed or not, as the case may be, to establish a sympathetic rapport with the defendant. The task of developing procedures which impinge fairly on all classes and sections of society is a requirement of all judicial systems, and is one which would especially benefit from comparative studies, both between different types of court within our own country, and between countries.

Accommodation in court

There is growing evidence that lawyers and judges accommodate linguistically to different defendants, sometimes functionally, sometimes not. Philips (1985) found remarkable similarity in the way different judges helpfully simplified and expanded the constitutional language when explaining their rights to defendants who had pleaded guilty. Aronsson et al. (1987) show that lawyers and defendants effectively achieve a middle-ground of speech formality, lawyers becoming less formal in the interactive phases of a trial, defendants becoming more formal than in non-courtroom discourse. The lawyers' avoidance of technical expressions and the lowered 'information diversity' of their interactive speech is appreciated by defendants, who then do not resent the complexity of language in other parts of the trial.

Specific groups of defendants do not consistently fare so well. For example, Goldyn (1981) reports that gay litigants in cases of appeal are frequently the target of gratuitous asides. Smith (1985) reports that there was little relationship between the legal terms that juveniles actually understood and the terms that judges, lawyers and other key personnel viewed as needing to be understood. Pearson (1976) suggests that women are spoken to in terms that imply a different criminal motivation and a different disposal or outcome: 'we see a reinforcement of popular notions about women: that they are not fully responsible for what they do, that their problems are not social but individual and so require attention from helping agencies, and that when they do take deliberate action (commit crimes), such behaviour is an irrational manifestation of "crime disturbance"' (Pearson, 1976, p. 273). The husband may even be called in to 'say something which might help your wife', or 'something which might explain why she behaved this way', and questions like 'Has your wife been her normal self lately?' being asked. In addition psychiatric reports may be requested, even though there is no reason to suspect mental disturbance. With women, courts are less likely to accept 'rational' explanations for crime (e.g. 'I was broke') than they are for men, an observation confirmed in Allen's (1987) analysis of why it is that women defendants are far more likely to be dealt with by psychiatric than by penal means. 'We are very sorry to see you here' is a sympathetic response which men rarely hear from the court, but which women will be treated to as an indication that it is especially inappropriate for them to be breaking the law.

Bennett and Feldman's experimental work was used by them to suggest that coherence of the stories that emerge in the trial – and in particular the two main stories developed by the defence and prosecution respectively – is what determines their acceptance by juries. We shall examine what juries do with stories in a subsequent chapter, but at this point some problems with this viewpoint should be clarified. First, it is apparent that the internal coherence of the story by itself cannot be the sole criterion of its truth, because the essence of a good story within the context of the trial is that it should be seen to be consistent with the evidence, i.e. those facts that have been established about the harmful events that took place outside the courtroom, and that brought the trial into being. In other words, what Bennett and Feldman mean by the coherence of the story comprises both its structure and its relation to the evidence as established in court. Coherence cannot be assessed simply in terms of story structure.

We have also seen in this chapter that the way in which stories are told and who tells them are of considerable importance to their acceptance. Lawyers from the 'wrong' social background learn to shift from one speech style to another when they appear in court (Garner and Rubin, 1986), and briefing lawyers learn to 'tell their tales' to barristers using linguistic devices which are persuasive independently of the coherence of the case (Kurzon, 1985). Jackson (1990) makes the important point that juries have to make sense not only of the stories *in* the trial (i.e. the stories of the crime) but the story *of* the trial. As he states:

> There is a conflict between the champions: the professional com-
> petition of the advocates. There is the combat of the parties to the
> dispute, manifest very often by their location in spatially opposed
> places in the courtroom. And there may also be a different form of
> professional combat between the judges and the advocates. Judge
> and jury also relate to each other within a narrative framework . . .
> messages from the judge to the jury that they ought to take a certain
> view of what they have seen; a final message from the jury to the
> judge that they regard the accused as guilty or not. We have, then,
> a plurality of narrative discourses at work in the trial. (Jackson,
> 1990, p. 16)

A verdict of 'guilty' or 'not guilty' may stem from the unfolding of the story of the trial as much as from the relative coherence of the stories in the trial. The analysis of how these stories develop and interact to inform the jury's or other decision-makers' verdict has hardly begun, but a remarkably powerful impetus has been given to that needed programme of research by Bennett and Feldman's pioneering analyses.

9

Testifying in Court

Introduction: psychology out of court?

The enthusiasm which psychologists have shown for research on eyewitness testimony has been matched by lawyers' and legal scepticism about the usefulness of psychologists' insights (King, 1986). Eyewitness testimony is a topic which lends itself readily to experimental and laboratory techniques of inquiry, and this makes it an easy target for those who would accuse psychologists of artificiality. More tellingly, however, psychologists have been accused of addressing the wrong questions: psychologists have sought to act as consultants, advising on how to improve the performance of eyewitnesses. Instead they should have paid more attention to the role that testimony plays in the criminal justice system (Twining, 1983). There is, for example, a huge literature on identification evidence – much of which stresses its unreliability and some of which suggests how it might be improved. There are, however, few studies of the circumstances in which police actually conduct parades, and of the use to which the results of such parades are put. Maybe, as Twining claims, parades serve such a variety of purposes that evaluating them in the laboratory strictly as a visual identification technique may be missing the point of their all-purpose value e.g. to eliminate suspects, gain time, frighten into confession and so on. The 'law in action' is what we should be studying, not an idealized abstraction which Twining refers to as 'the standard case'. Twining draws a parallel between the experimental psychologist and the 'expository lawyer', for both of whom theoretical analysis of 'the standard case' detracts from an understanding of the 'law in action'.

Twining's analysis deserves attention because it may point the way to a more clearly focussed research strategy in future. Table 9.1 contrasts the standard case of the legal textbooks (and laboratory psychological research) with common variations found in the context of real cases. The contrast between the two highlights the danger that conclusions based upon the study of convenient laboratory stereotypes – e.g. eyewitness identification of the invariably male assailant – may be inappropriately generalized. Twining argues strongly in favour of psychologists moving to a contextual and away from an expository approach to the study of the justice system. He notes that in certain instances, the movement is already under way, for example, in the study of 'ear-witness' testimony and of 'cross-race' identification.

It is implicit in Twining's criticism that psychologists have not taken witnesses into their confidence. There is almost nothing published from the perspective of witnesses themselves, with the single and recent exception of child witnesses. It might be assumed that coercion by relatives, pressure from lawyers, prejudice from court personnel, threats from other protagonists, and who knows what else will affect the candour and quality of testimony by witnesses. One would not imagine this from the work of psychologists, which has invariably assumed what memory researchers always do assume, that subjects in their experiments will answer questions to the best of their ability. Maybe that can be assumed in the laboratory. It certainly cannot be assumed of witnesses in the police station or in court.

Whilst what has come to be known as the ecological validity of research into eyewitness testimony may be questioned, it should not be overlooked that one incentive for the laboratory studies has been gross miscarriages of justice in which eyewitness identification evidence helped to condemn an innocent subject to arrest, trial and imprisonment. Psychology has rightly pointed to the unreliability of eyewitness identification. An article in the *Independent* (Jenkins, 1990) mentions a number of recent cases which have gone to appeal, successfully, because eyewitness identifications, in some cases several years after the event, have been the principal evidence against the accused and the jury were not given sufficient instructions as to its unreliability. It is to the good that the results of psychological investigations helped convince the legal establishment in the UK that normally eyewitness identification should be supported by substantial other evidence before a conviction should be permitted by the judge. In support of the applicability of psychological research, a recent case study of expert testimony concerning eyewitness identification lists more than 50 procedural rules that research suggests should be observed by those criminal investigators seeking to use eyewitness identification evidence (Wagenaar, 1988a).

There is also no doubt that knowledge about factors affecting the accuracy of testimony is being sought by lawyers, both prosecuting and defending, with a view to advancing their clients' interests. Psychologists are increasingly called upon – especially in the United States – to give expert testimony. A survey (Kassin et al., 1989) of 63 leading researchers in the area of eyewitness testimony reports that 54 per cent had testified on the subject of eyewitness testimony at least once, with an average of 7.6 occasions. As many requests (most of which came from defence lawyers) were turned down as were accepted, and in practice the experts gave evidence equally for the prosecution as for the defence, and betrayed a preference for civil rather than criminal cases. Whether from concern for justice, or for the advancement of clients' interests, expert knowledge of eyewitness testimony will be increasingly demanded and, it seems, willingly provided.

Why are psychologists and a growing number of lawyers and judges showing increased tolerance for the results of scientific research on eyewitness testimony? One reason is that there is now a substantial body of reliable findings that are applicable to the assessment of factors determining the validity of eyewitness testimony generally, and eyewitness identification in particular (see Deffenbacher, 1991 for a recent review). Given the existence of this body of scientific knowledge, it is proper that it should be (judiciously) used.

Whilst psychologists may have information that will help decision-makers render an appropriate verdict, Wagenaar (1988b) makes the point that it is not for experts to usurp the court's role in evaluating the validity of evidence and assessing the guilt of a suspect in a particular case. The expert's role is to provide information that may be used in forming that opinion. In Wagenaar's view, expert evidence on eyewitness testimony should be confined to estimates of the likelihood of obtaining evidence of a particular kind in the conflicting circumstances as outlined by prosecution and defence. Experts should not be tempted into giving an opinion about the truth of the evidence in question. For example, if I claim to have seen a man driving the get-away car (as the prosecution

Table 9.1 Ideal type or standard case of misidentification and possible variants

Standard case	Some possible variants
A *witness* (W) of indeterminate age, sex, class, race, and occupation	W was middle-aged, male, myopic, middle class, white, bank clerk or immigration officer
sees	contact was by telephone or involved a combination of visual, aural, and other impressions
an *incident*	W alleges that O was present in a particular vicinity, e.g. a theatre, a bar, a bed
of *short duration*	over a period of hours or longer
which becomes the subject of *criminal* proceedings	the issue of identification arose in a civil proceeding or a tribunal hearing or a non-legal proceeding, such as a university disciplinary hearing
in a *contested* case	the case was not contested, for example, O pleaded guilty or the case was settled out of court or proceedings were dropped
tried before a *jury*	the (contested) hearing took place before a bench of magistrates or a professional judge or a court martial or other tribunal
in which W *willingly*	W was coerced or bribed or compelled to testify
gives *evidence*	the information given by W was used for purposes other than forensic evidence, e.g. as information leading to suspicion or investigation, or to neglect or elimination of a line of enquiry
of the *identity*	it was sufficient for the purposes of the inquiry that O was placed within a certain class of people rather than was identified as a unique individual

Table 9.1   (Cont.)

Standard case	*Some possible variants*
of the *accused* (O)	the object of identification was a *thing* (e.g. a car, a typewriter or a gun) or an *animal*
a person of *indeterminate* age, sex, class, race, and occupation	O was a black, male youth or a one-legged elderly woman
who was a *stranger* (i.e. previously unknown to W)	the subject was well known to W
W's evidence is unsupported by other evidence of identification	W's evidence was corroborated or denied by other testimonial or circumstantial evidence
and is *unreliable*	several factors in the particular situation enhanced the probability that the identification was reliable – e.g. W was an experienced or trained observer, the period of observation was substantial, O was already known to W, and so on
but *results*	the information or evidence of W was not believed by the jury or other relevant participant(s)
in the *conviction* of O	the *mischief* of the alleged misidentification was not that the subject was wrongly convicted or acquitted, but that he or she suffered *vexation* and/or *expense* and/or *delay* (with consequential injury through being suspected or arrested or interrogated or charged or sued, or suffered some *other* serious damage, such as injury to reputation or loss of a job

Source: Twining, 1983

also claim), what is the likelihood that I was mistaken and that (as the defence claims), it was a woman driving the car? That likelihood can be estimated from results of relevant experiments, and is information to be taken into account by those whose job it is to express an opinion about the validity of my claim to have seen a man. Courts frequently try to put the expert witness in the invidious position of expressing an opinion about the case in question, a temptation that it is both appropriate and possible for witnesses to resist. However, it appears that insisting on the correct presentation of expert testimony is not always rewarded by comprehension. Wagenaar (1988b) reports a case in which he carried out an experiment (using 210 witnesses) to discover the likelihood that in essentially similar circumstances to the case in question, a policeman might wrongly identify a woman driver as a man. One hundred and sixteen subjects (55 per cent) reported seeing a man, leading the judge to the unshakeable conviction that there was a 55 per cent chance that the woman in the case in question had, indeed, been the driver of the car! That, however, is inappropriately to convert facts about the likelihood of mistaken identification directly into opinions about the guilt of an individual suspect. The psychologist's job as expert witness is to provide relevant facts based on experimental or other observations for the benefit of those whose job it is to decide on the truth of the matter.

The problem of overgeneralization

Some of the hostility to the application of psychology in the courtroom comes from the tendency for results of experiments to be overgeneralized. The oft-quoted (by psychologists) lack of relationship between confidence and accuracy of testimony is a good example. Most studies of confidence and accuracy have been carried out in relation to the visual identification of suspected criminals in an identification parade, whether live or using mugshots. Such identifications are extremely unreliable, and the confidence with which an individual selects one from the others is little guide to the accuracy of that selection. That said, there is little justification for the common assertion as a general principle that the confidence of a witness is no guide to the accuracy of what is reported, as for example V.L. Smith et al. (1989) say in their concluding paragraph: 'Common-sense and the Supreme Court notwithstanding, confidence is not a useful indicator of the accuracy of a particular witness or of the accuracy of particular statements made by the same witness' (p. 358).

Confidence is highly predictive of accuracy in some circumstances. Stephenson (1984) demonstrated that more confident witnesses were, indeed, more generally correct about their recall of what had been said in an interrogation subjects had listened to: earwitness testimony, in other words, is an exception to the 'rule' (see also Bull and Clifford, 1984). Sanders and Chiu (1988) report again a frequent finding that the recall of actions may be extremely reliable, in contrast to the recall of what people look like, and other perceptual detail. Although Wells and Murray (1984) make the conventional claim that 'eyewitness confidence is not useful as a prediction of eyewitness accuracy in actual criminal cases' (p. 169), that statement is based largely on the results of studies of visual identification of people, and not from memory of events. Moreover, virtually all studies have concentrated on the validity of comparisons between individuals whose confidence varies. Individuals may rightly feel that within themselves, the events they recall confidently are more likely to be correct than those they are doubtful about (Stephenson, 1984; but see also V.L. Smith et al., 1989). Moreover, Cutler and Penrod (1989) report good support for the optimality hypothesis (Deffenbacher, 1980), which states that even in the specific case of person identification, the better the viewing conditions, the stronger the confidence – accuracy relation.

Frequently in defiance of commonsense, psychologists are somewhat too ready to extrapolate from one finding or set of findings obtained in controlled experimental studies to guidelines for judges and juries. For example, Yarmey (1984) suggests we should treat testimony by old people (and children) with the utmost caution. The suggestion that we might disregard the testimony of an elderly person merely because they are elderly is not justified by findings that memory deteriorates in old age, as in many respects it undoubtedly does. All testimony, by people of whatever age, should be carefully scrutinized for its plausibility, consistency and likely reliability. Age in itself does not make observers any more or less useful to the courts, nor more or less susceptible to the many other influences that determine the accuracy of testimony (see, for example, O'Rourke, et al., 1989). Jurors may equally well assess the weight to be given an elderly person's as a young adult's testimony. There are instances where the elderly person's testimony may, other things being equal, be given greater credence than the young adult's, where for example the elderly person had relevant interests, experience and background knowledge that the younger person lacked.

Estimator and system variables in testimony

A distinction first made by Wells (1978) between 'estimator' and 'system' variables will now be employed, because it is an important distinction for the criminal justice system. System variables are those that can in principle be changed in the interests of 'improving' the system. System variables can in many instances be controlled and indeed, are systematically influenced, for example in the rule regarding use of leading questions in cross-examination. Estimator variables, on the other hand, refer to the conditions of observation and these obviously cannot be changed. They are still of interest to the forensic psychologist and the court, because knowledge of their effects provides information that can be used by the courts in determining the weight to be given to a particular item of testimony. The distinction between estimator and system variables can be clarified by the following examples taken from a 'test' of eyewitness knowledge (Deffenbacher and Loftus, 1982).

These two questions differ in that the first is concerned with the conditions of observation (an estimator variable), and the second with the circumstances of recall (a system variable).

1. 'When a person experiences extreme stress as the victim of a crime, there will be:
   (a) generally a greater than normal ability to perceive and recall the details of the crime.
   (b) generally the same ability to perceive and recall the details of the crime as under normal conditions.
   (c) a majority of people will become better at perceiving and recalling crime details whereas others become worse at it.
   (d) generally a reduced ability to perceive and recall the details. (p. 27)
2. Suppose a house were burgled and the resident got a glimpse of the burglar through the window. At a later lineup the resident attempts to make an identification. Assume there is a 10 per cent chance that the resident will be mistaken. Now in addition to

the above facts, assume that the resident was first shown photographs by the police, but recognized none of the people in the photos. Assume further that the person the resident later picked in the lineup was shown in one of the photos that had earlier been viewed. The chance of an incorrect identification in this latter situation would then:

(a)   remain about 10 per cent
(b)   decrease below 10 per cent
(c)   increase above 10 per cent
(d)   decrease below 10 per cent for women and increase above 10 per cent for men. (p. 29)

In the test you are asked to choose one, best answer. The evidence is that most people will indeed choose the 'best' answer i.e. the answer that best summarizes the relevant scientific experimental evidence, which in these two instances is (d) and (c) respectively.

The disruptive effect of extreme stress on the ability to perceive and recall events is generally recognized to be a factor of some practical importance. It is, however, a factor that affects directly the ability to perceive and store events as they are witnessed, and hence indirectly determines the subsequent quality of recall. By way of contrast, the effects on recall of showing photographs of the suspect to witnesses who subsequently identify that suspect in a live identification parade is a procedural strategy employed directly at the time of recall. It is a characteristic of procedure which is quite separate from the circumstances of the initial viewing of events. The ability to control such variables seemed paramount to Wells (1978): system-variable research investigates factors amenable to control in actual criminal cases, for example, the use of mugshots, or the size of the identification parade; and estimator-variable research, investigates factors (like the age of the suspect) which are beyond the control of the criminal justice system and whose effects can therefore merely be estimated. There are grey areas. (Where, for example, does work on the effects of post-event information fit in?). It is useful however to highlight the distinction between work which might have immediate relevance to reform of the system (system-variable research) as opposed to work whose main effect is to inform the experts.

Lest it be thought that commonsense always coincides with what the scientific evidence implies, consider the following example (again taken from Deffenbacher and Loftus (1982)), which few people answer 'correctly':

Concerning the effects of the amount of training or experience a person has had in making eyewitness identification, which of the following statements seems most reasonable to you?

(a) Police officers in general are better than civilians at recalling details of another person encountered for only a few seconds.

(b) When asked to watch a busy street for incidents of an illegal nature, civilians report more 'possible' thefts than do police.

(c) It appears to be quite difficult to train people to become better at recognizing faces seen previously.

(d) Only police officers with 20 years or more experience possess greater ability than civilians to recognize faces seen previously. (p. 28)

Less than 20 per cent of respondents endorse the 'best' answer (c), the most popular response being (a), a commonly held view for which there continues to be no hard evidence, despite many attempts to test the hypothesis that police are especially good observers.

Estimator variables: individual and situational effects

Individual differences

There are few studies of the extent to which individuals are consistently good or bad eyewitnesses, although Boice et al. (1982) show that accuracy of eyewitness recall of a purse-snatching is positively correlated with performance on a range of other tests of observational skill.

The ability to recall accurately is a task which continues to be employed in tests of general intelligence and which is strongly associated with other measures of intellectual performance. Hence, it is no surprise to find that ability to observe and recall accurately is related to age, a broad generalization being that children improve steadily up to the age of about 14, and that people deteriorate steadily from late middle age onwards. We may, therefore, expect an individual to perform best in young and middle adulthood: not as a child, and not as an old person. To say that, however, is not to say very much, for individual differences are not so great as to make it impossible to say that the testimony of this particular little girl or that particular old man, should not be believed because she is so young, or because he is so old. There will always be

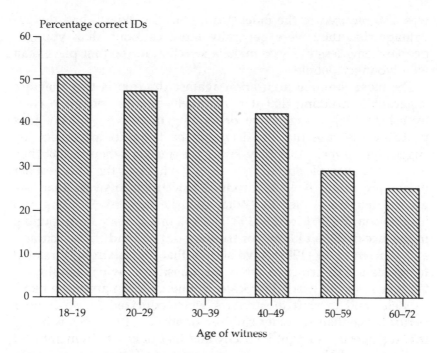

Figure 9.1 Percentage of correct identifications by persons of different age
Source: O'Rourke et al., 1989

circumstances in which the testimony of almost any individual may be invaluable. Nonetheless, findings such as those portrayed in figure 9.1, showing that the number of people correctly identifying a (filmed) robber reduces from 51 per cent in 18–19-year- olds to 25 per cent in 60–72-year-olds, may in some circumstances be the kind of information which juries should be informed about.

The young probably perform less well in eyewitness testimony research as much because of their inexperience as of their lesser capacity: the old, on the other hand, are to some extent victims of their long experience. Because of their greater experience, older persons are more likely to rely on (probably useful) stereotypes, and unconscious transference of experience from past situations. Yarmey (1984) shows, for example, that older people are more likely than young adults to misidentify an innocent bystander at the scene of an assault when that bystander was 'criminal-looking' rather than 'inoffensive-looking'. Overall ability to pick out the culprit was also reduced in the older group, but the elderly had the advantage that they were generally more cautious than younger people, being less likely to make a selection in the first place than were younger people.

The most common accusation against children is that they are suggestible, meaning that it is relatively easy to confuse a child by asking highly suggestive or leading questions. Indeed, it is probably the case that children can be led into inaccuracy by suggesting to them that they know the answer when in fact they do not. For example specific questions ('What was the colour of her hair?') are more likely to produce inaccurate answers than are general questions such as 'What did she look like?' (Dent and Stephenson, 1979). Moston (1987) shows that repeated questioning in the face of 'Don't know' (or true) replies will induce inaccuracy, and Warren et al. (1991) have shown that age is strongly related to resistance to criticism from the questioner when employing Gudjonsson's Suggestibility Scale. Young children are more likely to yield, and to shift their views when criticized for their poor performance than are older children or adults, although a warning that the questions might be tricky and that only well remembered material should be included in answers was effective across all age groups.

The implication of this research is that we should strive to improve techniques of interviewing, rather than disallow children's testimony. The potential accuracy of children's testimony is well documented experimentally (Moston, 1987) and clinically (e.g. Jones, 1987), the latter documenting the remarkable case of a three-year old girl who was able to give surprisingly accurate descriptions of the man who kidnapped, assaulted and attempted to murder her, and of the detailed circumstances of the incident.

Very young children can, in appropriate circumstances, give valuable evidence, as all reviews of the relevant literature, from psychological and legal perspectives, indicate (e.g. Loftus and Davies, 1984; Ceci et al., 1987; Naylor, 1989). The question is whether the adversarial courtroom is ever the appropriate venue for interviewing children. We shall return to that question.

When gender differences have been found, which is not often, they favour women rather then men (Ellis, 1984). It is clear that attitudes and expectations associated with gender may in the complex everyday environment interact with characteristics of the victim and nature of the crime to produce differences in what is perceived and accurately recalled, but there seems little reason to believe that gender is of significant importance in this respect. Penrod et al. (1982) note that women seem to differ from men in their memory for stressful events, but that the results are conflicting and need further study.

Do members of one race perceive greater similarity in the faces of other races than they do in members of their own race? The issue of cross-race identification occupies an increasing amount of space in the literature, although the likelihood is that a considerable variety of individual differences and situational factors influence the extent to which the superiority of own race identification is demonstrated. The effect has been frequently studied with respect to blacks and whites in the United States, and the review by Lindsay and Wells (1983) indicates that a number of studies demonstrate a more or less equal superiority of own race identifications in the two races. Nevertheless it appears that the effect is much better substantiated for white subjects than it is for black or other races in the United States.

An interesting slant is provided by Brigham and Ready (1985). In an identification parade or line-up, the suspect is placed amidst a number of 'foils', i.e. persons who are generally similar in physical appearance and dress to the suspect, and so chosen that the suspect does not stand out in any obvious way as different from all the others. Subjects in their experiment were asked to select photographic foils for an identification line-up. Five foils, similar in general appearance to a suspect, had to be selected from a pile of photographs. One important measure of performance was the number of photographs selected as 'similar' to the suspect. It was assumed that the more photographs a subject deemed to be similar to the suspect, the less distinctive the individual suspect was seen to be. As predicted (see figure 9.2) there was an interaction between race of subject and race of photographic foil, but there was a much greater difference between the subject groups in selection of blacks than of whites; cross-race confusion was greater for blacks than for whites. Lindsay and Wells (1983) interestingly suggest that cross-race identifications have greater diagnostic value in practice than own-race identification. Same-race witnesses are more likely to have the confidence to select from the line-up, thus increasing the number of innocent as well as guilty suspects that are likely to be selected. The greater caution of cross-race identification increases the ratio of guilty to innocent suspects being picked out.

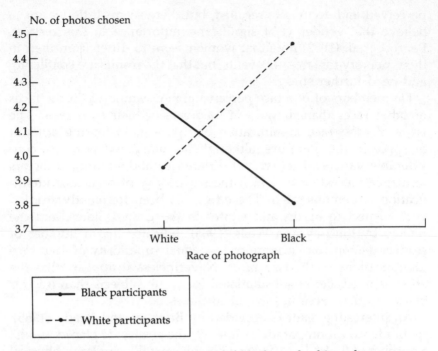

Figure 9.2 Number of photographs of blacks and whites chosen as similar to target photo by black and white participants
Source: Brigham and Ready, 1985

Witnessing factors

The general view is that extremely arousing events lead to poorer testimony for the events in question. The theoretical justification for this expectation is found in the Yerkes-Dodson Law, which postulates that up to a certain level arousal may facilitate per-formance, but that increases beyond that level are detrimental. There is much experimental evidence which supports this view (e.g. Penrod et al., 1982). However, a remarkable case of a real-life murder with many first-hand witnesses subsequently interviewed by both police and psychological researchers (Yuille and Cutshall, 1986; see also Stephenson, 1984) indicates that a violent event need not in itself impair the accuracy of testimony. Events and details were still recalled accurately months after the event, and the accuracy of recall was as great for information that had not been recalled during earlier questioning as it was for that which had been given in response to questioning shortly after the event. Maybe this real-life event occurred without a stressful build-up over time so that detrimental levels of stress did not affect perception of the event. Yuille and Cutshall's demonstration of the accuracy of so many of their witnesses, even many months after the event, casts doubt on the validity of general statements about the detrimental effect of highly arousing circumstances on the recall of events, and it contributes to the continuing controversy about the precise effects of seriousness of crime.

One recent experimental demonstration indicated that violence may normally have a distracting effect by causing witnesses to focus on one salient aspect of the situation to the detriment of more general observation. Loftus et al. (1987) show that subjects viewing a film will focus on a gun held by a customer in a restaurant, rather than (in the alternative version of the film) on a cheque in his hand. Identification of the suspect in a line-up, and the answers to a number of specific questions, were more accurate in the 'cheque' than in the 'gun' condition. In an ingenious and realistic simulation of the 'weapon effect', Maass and Köhnken (1989) enrolled students to participate in an experiment on sport-related activity and psychological well-being. The investigators demonstrated that having been approached by a white-coated female experimenter with a syringe, who then talked to them for 20 seconds before leaving, a student subject was very much more likely to misidentify foils in a live identification parade than when the similarly white-coated female had approached them with a pen in her hand. The distraction caused by the syringe is similar, the authors suggest, to the distraction that witnesses to a crime may experience by the weapon in the hand of the assailant.

Various other attitudinal factors – like the frequency and length of exposure to the events or people, familiarity with the background, the novelty and interest of the events, and the level of processing required – have all been shown to affect eyewitness testimony in ways that are predictable from their effects on memory generally (Penrod et al., 1982). All these factors may either compel or permit greater attention to be paid to the perpetrator of a crime and hence facilitate subsequent recognition in, say, an identification parade. The frequency and length of exposure facilitates greater attention to detail; lack of familiarity with the background encourages attention to be paid elsewhere than to the perpetrator; and novelty and interest generally heightens attention including attention paid to the perpetrator. Level of processing refers to the degree of intellectual work that has to be done to accomplish a given task. It would, for example, be predicted that if your only interest in observing the person was to identify the sex of the individual, the level of processing required would normally be less than if the age or character of the individual had to be assessed.

Post-witnessing factors

It is a general commonsense understanding that the longer the delay between witnessing and recalling an event, the poorer will be the testimony. This is incorporated into the rule that written notes or accounts of an event must be made as soon after the event as is reasonably possible if they are to be used to refresh the memory in court (Stephenson, 1990). There are large differences in the rate at which performance deteriorates depending on the mode of recall (e.g. free recall or recognition) and the stimulus domain (e.g. verbal or visual). However, there is normally a substantial early loss of detail followed by a more gradual decline in performance, although this decline is minimized when subjects know they are to be tested later (Egan et al., 1977).

Just as important as time is the finding that new information may seriously interfere with remembering. Loftus and Ketcham (1983) refer aptly to the malleability of eyewitness accounts, showing that adults as well as children are thoroughly suggestible when, for example, a questioner refers in passing to the existence of an object that does not exist, e.g., 'How fast was the white sports car going when it passed the barn while travelling along the country road?' The barn does not exist but more than a week later 17 per cent of subjects referred to it when giving an account of the journey.

There is some controversy in the literature as to whether such changes in memory are permanent, or whether such new or 'distorted' recollections merely exist alongside the original memory (e.g. Bowers and Bekerian, 1984). Gibling and Davies (1988) indicate that the detrimental effects of showing misleading pictures between observation and test may subsequently be offset by appropriate techniques of interviewing. Unconscious transference, a process by which familiar faces are wrongly categorized, may also lead to false identification, as with the railway clerk held up at gunpoint who later identified a sailor on a line-up as the robber. The sailor was not the robber, but had a familiar face because he had occasionally purchased tickets from the clerk (see Ellis, 1984).

How does discussion and recall with a fellow witness affect one's memory for an event? The evidence suggests that the completeness and accuracy of a single account is improved where two or more witnesses get together to compose it (Clark et al., 1986). This is because members of a group may correct one another's errors of fact, and because more observations are made in total than when a lone individual gives an account of a witnessed event. Moreover, individual recall subsequently benefits from the experience of collaborative recall. Nevertheless, there are drawbacks to collaborative testimony (Stephenson, 1990). Certain categories of observations are omitted from group accounts; they are less likely than are individual accounts to comment on personal reactions and motivations (Stephenson et al., 1986). In addition, groups do not capitalize fully on all the information that individuals possess; much is lost in the process of amalgamating the accounts. Even more importantly groups are influenced by one another's confidence, especially confidence in those plausible but not strictly correct inferences about what must have occurred. Finally, groups with a vested interest in what they recall – as when two police officers recall the content of an interrogation – may be more inclined to fill in the gaps by inferring the details, and they may profess confidence in demonstrably false recall. (Stephenson et al., 1991.)

System variables

Most of the work on factors that are controllable – in particular within the control of the criminal justice system – has been conducted in relation to issues of identification evidence, but there is a tradition which emphasizes the importance of techniques of interviewing for the accuracy and comprehensiveness of testimony in general. Despite promising results initially, subsequent work has discredited the use of hypnosis as a technique for improving testimony, largely because, it seems, hypnotized people will try too hard to oblige the hypnotist by producing memories which fulfil the hypnotist's expectations (Orne et al., 1984). A review of experimental studies comparing interviewing under hypnosis with normal interviewing (Mingay, 1987) found no evidence that hypnosis improved memory for realistically portrayed crimes and incidents. Despite the largely negative findings of controlled studies, the debate continues. Watkins (1989) has argued cogently that the question of the forensic value of hypnosis is not yet decided. Experimental evidence, he argues, does not detract from the view that hypnosis may greatly aid the relationship with the interviewer when a victim or client is attempting to recall perhaps painful, stressful events and that this improvement in itself may facilitate recall.

The technique of context reinstatement has apparently been more successful than hypnosis in providing evidence that memories can be enhanced. Following Geiselman et al.'s (1985) lead, Cutler et al. (1986, 1987) have used snapshot reviews of the scene of crime and cognitive interview techniques (e.g. mental reinstatement of the context surrounding an incident, rehearsal of events in different orders and from different perceptual perspectives) to help enhance the comprehensiveness and accuracy of recall and eyewitness identifications. The attempts have met with moderate success, with respect both to eyewitness identification and amount of material recalled. This is an important development for it has been consistently found in the past that attempting to improve comprehensiveness by asking more specific questions merely encourages the introduction of error (Dent and Stephenson, 1979). These techniques seem to hold out the possibility that free recall becomes not only accurate but comprehensive without the accompanying introduction of errors that specific questions, and hypnosis, seem to encourage.

Fisher et al. (1989) have found that training police officers to use cognitive interview techniques increases by about 40–50 per cent the amount of apparently accurate and useful information obtained from suspects and witnesses, but no figures are available for the improvement to be expected from training using more conventional interviewing techniques. Nonetheless, this study is important in its demonstration of the usefulness of the technique in practical settings. A recent evaluation of the technique using children suggests that the technique is more effective with adults (Geiselman and Padilla, 1988) but the general usefulness of the technique is confirmed in a study of the recall of car licence plates – an important forensic skill – by McKinnon et al. (1990) who in two experiments produced 20 per cent or so improvement in recall using the cognitive interview techniques in conjunction with a simulation device for manipulating

Table 9.2 The logic of photo identity parade

	Suspect is not the perpetrator	Suspect is the perpetrator
Eyewitness has perfect memory	Refusal to select any picture	Selection of target picture
Eyewitness has imperfect memory	Refusal to select any picture, or chance selection of pictures	Refusal to select any picture, or chance selection of pictures

Source: Wagenaar, 1988a

the position of numbers and letters. Memon and Bull (1991) conclude from an extensive review of the literature, that the techniques should become an established part of the repertoire of interviewing skills of police officers and others whose job it is to facilitate recall of events by witnesses.

The identification parade

When is an identification parade fair and its results to be trusted? This question is vitally important in the (relatively few) cases in which identification evidence is either the sole or the determining factor in assessing guilt. Wagenaar (1988a) portrayed the 'logic' of the ID parade as in table 9.2. There are four possible situations defined by whether or not the eyewitness has perfect memory, and whether or not the suspect is guilty. In only one situation will the choice definitely lead to correct identification – when the suspect is guilty and the eyewitness has perfect memory. When the eye-witness's memory is less than perfect, we rely on the fairness of the line-up to ensure that only by chance will the suspect be picked out by the eye-witness. Wagenaar lists no less than 50 rules that must be followed in order to ensure fairness. The most important of these come under four headings as follows:

1 *Absence of extraneous bases for recognition of suspect* It is clear that an eyewitness must not know the suspect in advance, for that in itself would be a basis for recognition. For the same reason, those who have been exposed to the suspect by photograph should

not be allowed to make subsequent ID, and no witness should be asked to identify the same suspect more than once. Witnesses should also not be allowed to talk to one another, as this will provide another inappropriate basis of recognition of the suspect.

2   *Appropriate instructions*   The task is to identify the *one* person whom witnesses recall having seen, and this should be emphasizd in the instructions. IDs based on 'likeness' should not be encouraged. It should always be emphasized that the wanted person is possibly not in the line-up at all.

3   *Composition of the parade*   This is of critical importance, because appropriate selection of foils (non-suspects) can ensure that if the witness's memory is not perfect, only chance will govern the ID of one member of the parade rather than another. It has been argued that similarity of members of the line-up to one another is an essential feature of fairness, an argument which taken to its conclusion could suggest that all foils should be clones of the suspect. Luus and Wells (1991) on the other hand, argue strongly, and correctly, that line-up foils should resemble not so much the suspect as the witnesses' descriptions of the criminal. Foils may well then legitimately differ from one another in respect of characteristics not mentioned in the description given by the witness.

Chance will not determine the outcome if more than one suspect is included in the parade, or if witnesses are permitted to point to more than one person, or if the parade consists of less than about 6 people, or if *all* foils do not fit the prior descriptions obtained from witnesses, or if all foils are policemen and the suspect just happens to be a tramp! One way of determining fairness of composition is to have mock witnesses attempt to identify the suspect from prior witness descriptions. Ideally, mock witnesses should spread their IDs across *all* members of the parade. Malpass and Devine (1983) refer to the importance of maximizing the *functional* size of the line-up, which is the number of persons in the line-up who would be likely to be selected by non-witnesses attempting an ID merely on the basis of descriptions of the suspect: the larger that number of persons, or the nearer the functional to the numerical size, the fairer the line-up is to the suspect situated within it.

4   *Unconscious suggestion*   The most effective way of ensuring that police officers do not unconsciously suggest who is the suspect is to have police officers conduct the parade who do not know the suspect's identity. In addition, the proceedings should be recorded

and observed by neutral parties to ensure fairness and to permit later evaluation of fairness. The ease with which an investigator may quite unconsciously convey expectations and attitudes to subjects in an experiment has long been known. Stephenson and Kniveton (1991) inadvertently proved the appositeness of research on the experimenter effect to the very issue of the fairness of line-up procedures. The first 41 subjects in an experiment on confidence of selection and rejection of line-up members had been tested before it was decided to improve the conditions of the experiment by eliminating the possibility that the experimenter's knowledge of who the subject had selected might have produced an experimenter effect. Results from the subsequent 30 subjects flatly contradicted the highly significant effect yielded by the first 41 subjects, much to the amazement of the experimenter concerned. Confidence in both the selected and rejected members of the line-up was strongly determined, it seems, by the totally unconscious communication by the experimenter to the witness of knowledge of the accuracy of the witness's selection.

Children in evidence

In acknowledging the right of children to be heard in court, our adversarial system of justice has created a dilemma. Children are, indeed, more readily intimidated than are adults, more anxious to please, and their identities more easily threatened. Nonetheless in the right circumstances it is acknowledged that their truthful evidence can and should be heard. But the adversarial system does not provide these circumstances. Far from it. The system of examination and cross-examination in open court many months after the events in question took place could have been specially designed to make it impossible for all but the most remarkably robust of children to excel. A prosecution of a group of adults for sexual abuse collapsed at the Old Bailey in London when the prosecution offered no further evidence following the breakdown during cross-examination of one of the principal child witnesses (Mills and O'Sullivan, 1991). This highly publicized trial of five people accused variously of rape, buggery, and other offences came to an end when the 10-year-old girl concerned was in the fourth day of giving evidence. The case raised many issues which psychological research has addressed, one of which is the long-term consequences not only of the ordeal itself, but also of confirming in a child's mind the prediction of abusers that they would not be believed if and when they tell others about the abuse. Jaffe et al. (1987) show how confusion and breakdown of the child are a natural outcome of a situation which demands public betrayal of their abusive protectors, but that the courts may perceive such confusion as lying, the child's uncertainty even in some instances amounting to contempt of court for leading the court astray.

The clinical needs of the abused child are, of course, hopelessly at odds with the requirements of prosecution. Pynoos and Spencer (1986) describe a format for interviewing children who have witnessed violent incidents. The therapeutic aims seriously undermine the precise determination of what happened, and if fulfilled would undermine the child's willingness and ability to give evidence about the event in court.

Wakefield and Underwager (1989) point out that children's accusations of abuse frequently arise in the context of divorce and custody cases, and that the acrimonious conditions prevailing in such cases may well put pressure on the child to construct partisan accounts of what occurred. From a sample of 110 divorce or custody cases, 85 (77 per cent) were instances where the court found no abuse had occurred, a significantly higher figure than obtained in other categories (day care, friend or neighbour, stepfather/relative, own child) where the conviction rate was in all cases more than twice as high. In custody and divorce cases, the relentless opposition in the child's mind between parents' (themselves conflicting) and authorities' constructions of the child's reality is especially fierce, and, as Maddock (1988) puts it in an excellent descriptive account, 'the stage is set for uncertainty, self-contradiction, and lack of reliability' (p. 201).

Children can, indeed, testify reliably. Recent studies have confirmed even the moral competence of very young children, who, for example, at the age of seven know that lying is wrong even when condoned by a parent (Haugaard et al., 1991) and whose testimony at the age of five or six is reasonably reliable following the re-telling in repeated interviews (Tucker et al., 1990). Nonetheless, the fact remains that the conditions under which children have to testify are totally inappropriate. Goodman et al. (1991) report on the need to protect child witnesses from the rigours of the adversarial system. It may well be that in due course the speed, impartiality, skill and care shown in interviewing children and conveying the results of those interviews to the court will drastically improve. If it does, we may well have seen the beginning of the end of the gladiatorial approach to obtaining evidence from witnesses as practised in adversarial courts. The respect given children may sometime thereafter be shown to other witnesses.

10

Twelve Available People: How Juries Decide

I wish, actually, there were more evidence for and against this 12-person system. It was tried extensively in the New Testament, but unfortunately Jesus was such a strong personality that his 12-disciple panel cannot really be called an impartial set of witnesses.

I wish above all that somebody had done a scientific analysis of this random 12 people system. Would it not be possible to keep a count of jury cases as they go along? All one has to do is go to the defendant after the trial and say: 'Well, the jury has reached its verdict and it can't be changed now, so just for the unofficial record can you tell us whether they were right or wrong?' You would build up a picture fairly soon of how well it was working.

But I suppose that if you think the best way of deciding the facts is by random opinion, you wouldn't put much trust in scientific analysis to decide the virtues of that system. The only thing you could do would be to ask 12 people at random if the jury system worked.

As soon as my first case starts, I'll ask them. Ask the jury what they think about juries. Should be interesting. Unfortunately, I won't be able to tell you, as I have promised not to talk about my jury experiences. Pity. Could have decided the facts for once and for all. (Miles Kington, on being called for jury service, *The Independent*, 31 March 1987)

Miles Kington's ironic observations may remind us that to sit on a jury in England, no qualifications are required other than age and the right to vote in elections; furthermore, juries deliberate in secret and are accountable to no one, and their verdicts are delivered by foremen who, being human, may sometimes render verdicts that surprise even their fellow members of the jury, and frequently surprise judge, police, lawyers and public alike by their apparent perversity, or at least eccentricity.

The jury system is nonetheless admired by scholars, practitioners and public alike. Legal opinion in particular looks favourably upon the jury as an institution which may protect the rights of the individual against the power of the state and malicious prosecution. Just as in the United States the jury was employed to resist the power and authority of the British Crown, so in our own day it is applauded for thwarting the state's attempts to punish citizens who expose the government's chicanery. Somewhat more controversially, by involving citizens in judicial decision-making the jury system is said to secure the commitment of the people to their country's legal system. Most controversially of all, it is claimed that jury deliberation is a reliable way of establishing the truth of a contentious matter. Even the recommendation of the Roskill Commission in 1986 that in complex fraud trials juries should be replaced by a panel of assessors with financial expertise seems not to have dented that fundamental belief in the efficiency of amateur group decision-making. Is this faith in the jury system justified? Or as Baldwin and McConville (1979) somewhat mischievously suggest, does it really matter how efficient jury decision-making is, when only about 15 per cent of serious offences reach the stage of trial by jury? Let me begin to answer this question by examining work which has probed the validity and reliability of jury decisions.

Do juries make valid and reliable decisions?

The evidence appears to indicate that juries set about their task conscientiously (McCabe and Purves, 1974), and the judges approve of their decisions in a majority of cases (Kalven and Zeisel, 1966). However, there are those, for example the police, who would dissent from the first proposition, claiming that many professional criminals are perversely acquitted by juries. We shall also discover that the fact that a majority of decisions is approved by judges is not conclusive of the jury's efficacy. We should also bear in mind that almost none of the research has observed real juries at work, and that in England since 1981 it has not been possible even to question jurors about their experiences of having been on a jury.

Table 10.1 Number of jury convictions, acquittals, and hung juries in relation to judges' views of what the verdict should have been

		Jury Verdict			
		Acquit	Convict	Hung	%
Judge would have:	Acquitted	479	79	39	16.7
		(13.4%)	(2.2%)	(1.1%)	
	Convicted	604	2217	158	83.3
		(16.9%)	(62.0%)	(4.4%)	
		30.3%	64.2%	5.5%	100

Source: Kalven and Zeisel, 1966

One of the largest and most influential studies of juries ever conducted (Kalven and Zeisel, 1966) examined the verdicts of 3576 trials in the USA. In that study, the judge's view of the evidence and of what the verdict should have been was compared systematically with what the jury decided. The authors concluded that 'as a fact-finder it [the jury] is not in any interesting way different from the judge'.

That conclusion has been generally accepted by scholars but in my view, the comparison between judges and juries shows some very interesting differences indeed. Consider the results set out in table 10.1. In 64.2 per cent of the cases, juries voted to convict, and in the vast majority of those cases (96 per cent) the judges agreed that a Guilty verdict was appropriate. However, this degree of overlap is less surprising in view of the fact that judges would have returned a Guilty verdict on 83.3 per cent of all defendants. By chance alone, the judges would have agreed with the convictions on 83 per cent of occasions. Agreement on acquittals, however, is correspondingly appalling, with judges voting to convict 604 (57 per cent) of the 1083 persons that juries would have acquitted. The degree to which judges' views predict what juries actually decided and vice versa can be estimated, using a statistic (Goodman and Kruskal's lambda, or λ) that varies – like a correlation coefficient – between 0 and 1 (Goodman and Kruskal, 1954; Leach, 1979, p. 278). λ in this case is .21, indicating only a 21 per cent improvement in predictive power over guesswork informed only by knowledge of the relative proportions of accused persons that juries or judges found guilty or not guilty.

The value of λ incorporates predictions from judge to jury and from jury to judge, but to illustrate, let us focus on jury decisions. We know that the majority of prosecutions in Kalven and Zeisel's sample ended in conviction. We might reasonably guess that – in the absence of other information – any one case drawn randomly from the 3576 cases would be a successful prosecution. We would be wrong in many cases, but our prediction would be improved only to the tune of 21 per cent (λ = .21) if we knew the judge's verdict in that case. In effect, Kalven and Zeisel's work suggests that if the judges' views are taken to be the criterion against which the validity of jury decision-making is evaluated, then juries are very poor performers, and vice versa. Judges and juries agree that a majority of defendants is guilty. Unfortunately they do not agree on whom to find Not Guilty.

No-one knows for sure why the juries disagreed with judges so markedly. However, the judges themselves attributed the disagreement between themselves and the juries they instructed, to the following factors:

	per cent
Sentiments on the law (equity)	29
Sentiments on the defendant	11
Issues of evidence	54
Facts only the judge knew	2
Disparity of counsels' abilities	4
	100

(Kalven and Zeisel, 1966, p. 115)

Although these figures represent only the judges' informed guesswork, let's take the figures seriously. If we applaud juries for disputing the law's appropriateness (29 per cent), and forgive them for not knowing facts known only to the judge (2 per cent) or being swayed unusually by one counsel's superior abilities (4 per cent), that leaves 54 per cent of cases of disagreement between judge and jury, in which juries misinterpreted the evidence, and 11 per cent in which jurors let their private feelings about the defendant influence their decision. It is apparent that the police are probably right to assume that strictly speaking many defendants are fortunate to have been tried by jury and not by a more legally informed tribunal.

The λ value of .21 may well exaggerate the real extent of agreement between judges and juries. After all, the judges made their 'decisions' by questionnaire, after the trial had been conducted, i.e. after the juries had delivered their verdicts. Their judgements, in other words, were not independent of the juries' decisions. Given the judges' generally favourable attitudes towards juries then in marginal cases they may well have been inclined after all to agree with the juries' verdict.

There is a further important point to be made about these figures. Most commentaries on Kalven and Zeisel highlight the 2.2 per cent of the total number of cases where juries found for guilt, and judges would have acquitted. This figure is said to be very low, and 2.2 per cent is, indeed, a relatively small number as a proportion of all cases (although the 79 or more persons involved may have been less than ecstatic about the verdicts). Those 79 cases, however, are a comparatively sizeable proportion (13.2 per cent) of all those whom the judges would have acquitted. The judges were much less inclined to acquit than were juries, so that figure of 13.2 per cent indicates that juries are unlikely to be convicting for sound reasons. The figure rises to nearly 20 per cent when the 39 'hung' juries are added to the total of failures to acquit.

The judges' analyses of why juries' verdicts so contradicted the judges' own views did not suggest that a very coherent alternative strategy to the judges' own was being followed by the juries. Other studies have confirmed this conclusion about the apparent waywardness of juries. Baldwin and McConville (1979) also found in a study of jury performance in nearly 1000 cases in the Birmingham (England) and London Crown Courts, that perverse convictions and acquittals were a sorry feature of jury decision making. As in Kalven and Zeisel's study perverse acquittals were very frequent, 36 per cent of acquittals being doubted by at least two parties – judge, police, prosecuting barrister, defence barrister – in the case. Serious doubts about acquittals were expressed by the police in 44 per cent, and by the judge in 32 per cent of the cases, but even the defence solicitor expressed serious doubt in 10 per cent of the cases. Unlike Kalven and Zeisel, they found scant evidence of legitimate extra-legal or equity factors in the acquittals, nearly all of which flew in the face of the evidence.

Of the equally perverse convictions, 10 per cent of which were doubted by at least two from amongst the judge, police, defence and prosecution, even the police were sometimes at a loss to understand how their case had proved convincing to a jury, and judges were dismayed that their virtual instructions to acquit had apparently not been comprehended by the jury. Of course, as it was not possible to interview jurors or listen to their deliberations, it was not possible to know why they 'went wrong' so frequently. It was, however, the case that black defendants were significantly more likely to feature in the perverse convictions than in the perverse acquittals.

The reliability of any measuring instrument refers to its consistency when used on different occasions, and it is an essential prerequisite of validity. If it could be shown that the jury was a reliable instrument for determining guilt of the defendant, that could indicate the existence at least of a consistent basis for disagreement with the judges. The reason for the number of their acquittals might, for example, reflect their consistently more exacting application of the standard of proof, to include elements of 'unreasonable' doubt that it would not have occurred to the judges to entertain.

One measure of the reliability of any measuring instrument is the ability of two identically constructed versions of the instrument – a ruler, for example, in the case of physical measurement, or an IQ test in the case of intelligence – to give the same results when applied in the same circumstances. In the case of juries, we may ask whether or not two juries, formed using the same selection procedure, are likely to produce the same verdicts. Will one jury do the same as another?

The study by McCabe and Purves (1974) of shadow juries constituted a stringent but limited test of the reliability of jury decision-making. In that remarkable study, for each of 30 Oxford Crown Court cases, shadow juries were established composed of prospective jurors selected from the electoral register in the same fashion as the regular jurors. They attended court and deliberated at the same times as the real juries and delivered verdicts (to the experimenter) in the same way. If 'the jury' is a reliable instrument for measuring guilt, then there should be substantial agreement between the 'real' and 'shadow' juries. Table 10.2 shows the results that were obtained.

Whilst there is a statistically significant association between the verdicts of the two sets of juries, there are clear discrepancies which might alarm, or more frequently console, prospective defendants. You would not be consoled by the prospects of being one of the

Table 10.2 Verdicts by real and shadow juries in Oxford Crown Court
trials

		Shadow Juries			
		Guilty	Hung	Not Guilty	Total
Real Juries	Guilty	11	–	2	13
	Hung	–	–	1	1
	Not Guilty	5	1	10	16
	Total	16	1	13	30

Source: McCabe and Purves, 1974

three (23 per cent) whom shadow juries would have set free (or
'hung' on), out of 13 that the real juries found guilty. On the other
hand six (38 per cent) of the 16 found guilty by shadow juries were
exonerated by the real juries. Lambda (λ) this time yields a figure
of .43, indicating a 43 per cent improvement on guesswork when
predicting results from one type of jury to the other. A figure of .43
falls far short of perfection, although it is appreciably higher than
the .21 found for judge–jury agreement. It has to be said that this
shadow jury study alone does not testify to the soundness of the
jury as a reliable, consistent measure of the guilt of defendants.

To the extent that there is consistency in juries' performances,
the results of Kalven and Zeisel suggests that they are exercising
a bias towards leniency. Indeed, experimental evidence indicates
that factions in favour of acquittal are consistently more effective
than factions in favour of prosecution. Moreover, this is especially
likely to occur when the standard of proof is that of reasonable
doubt rather than the preponderance of evidence (MacCoun and
Kerr, 1988). The instruction to observe the reasonable doubt
standard of proof does, it appears, have the general effect of
increasing the influence of acquittal-prone individuals on juries.

Members of the shadow juries in the McCabe and Purves' research
were interviewed after the trials were over, and many expressed
astonishment at the results of the real juries in cases where there
was a conflict. Some of their comments reveal clearly why they
think the jury might be unreliable. One highlights the elusive
character of instructions to the jury to have the case proved 'beyond
reasonable doubt':

The instructions to the jury are very meagre. Guilt must be proven beyond reasonable doubt. That this is too vague for a collection of amateurs is demonstrated by the astonishing fact that the real jury found this defendant guilty, unanimously. I would recommend the presence in the jury room of a knowledgeable official with a short-hand record of the proceedings. (p. 76)

Another reflects on the contrast between the apparent objectivity of the law and its evidential rules, on the one hand, and the human capriciousness of courtroom proceedings:

The machinery of the law seems to aim at total, dispassionate objectivity, and yet the final verdict arises from an informal, very human group situation ... I am worried by this discrepancy. How far can one tell people to 'put things out of their minds'? Trials pretend to get 'facts' but these are always muddied by human elements; yet these elements are supposedly to be discounted. Rational judgements are expected; yet the skill-in-trade of counsel is innuendo, and inference is relied on. At some points the proceedings resemble an elaborate game. (p. 72)

Yet another opines that it all comes down to relative skills of defence and prosecution lawyers, given the weakness of the case:

Very bad prosecution lawyer, very poor and flimsy evidence, very poor defence lawyers. I maintain that if the prosecutor was good this trial would not have taken half the time it did. I also maintain that if there had been two good defence lawyers the two accused would have been acquitted. (p. 77)

So, jurors are not certain what their task is, they are aware of being swayed by all-too-human factors in the courtroom drama, and they are sometimes amazed by the one-sidedness of the proceedings. Whilst experiencing astonishment in certain cases that real juries did not agree with them, the shadow jurors' reflections on their experiences make the diagnosis of unreliability quite understandable. Of course, this formal evidence of unreliability comes merely from only one study in one English Crown Court. The shadow jury technique offers scope for more systematic studies of reliability. In the meantime, we can examine the plethora of (mainly laboratory experimental) research on juries and jurors for more clues as to the sources of its unreliable and invalid decision-making.

The jury's task: not for a jury

The jury does not do a good legal job, and whatever it does do, it does not do it very consistently. One cannot, however, blame individual jurors for this unhappy state of affairs. It is probably true that jurors for the most part tackle the job they have to do conscientiously enough. The problem lies in the mechanism of the jury itself, not in the attitudes or even the competence of its members.

There are many tasks which a group of 12 people might be expected to perform better than individuals: for example, tasks which can be subdivided, like solving a large crossword puzzle; or tasks in which quantity of production is important, like recalling *Times* headlines of the previous year; and tasks in which the contributions of different members are simply added together, as in discovering errors in a proof-reading task (cf. Steiner, 1972). However, deciding whether or not a defendant is a murderer, or a fraudster, or a rapist, according to law in the light of the evidence presented in a trial, is neither subdivisible, quantifiable, or additive.

To begin with, the task cannot sensibly be subdivided: say, by juror 1 listening on the first day, juror 2 the second, and so on, whilst the others take the day off. The task, on the contrary, demands that the verdict be based on a judgement of the evidence taken as a whole. Neither is the task quantitative, demanding speed or mass production. Indeed the pace at which the task is performed is quite beyond the control of members of the jury until the time comes for their deliberation. The task is what Steiner calls an optimizing task, not maximizing, calling for a single appropriate judgement. The task is also what Steiner would call disjunctive: not everyone can be right, and the task is to prefer one person's verdict to that of another, not to add together the contributions of each and every body. Let us consider in more detail the nature of the jury task in the light of these important aspects of group decision-making, as a basis for evaluating studies of the various influences on jury decision making.

Jury decision-making is a unitary task: but who will do the work?

Informal observation of juries during the course of a trial leads me to suspect that many jurors intuitively grasp the inappropriateness of deciding facts in criminal trials by taking a randomly selected group of 12 adults and requiring them to endure the contradictory arguments of prosecuting and defence counsel, and listen to the rehearsed testimony of witnesses for days on end. Prompt attention in the opening minutes of the first morning session soon deteriorates into inattention, doodling and awareness of considerable physical discomfort as the day wears on – unless the case is of truly compelling interest or importance: Most are not.

Social loafing – relying on others to do the work – is a well-documented group phenomenon (Latané et al., 1979), and may be expected to flourish in the jury, especially in long trials where there are many delays and presentation of complex material which cannot be retained for subsequent study. Yet jurors do not have to qualify – by passing a comprehension or memory test – in order finally to contribute to the deliberations which determine the verdict. There is no guarantee whatsoever that the most appropriate people will either be motivated to listen attentively to all the evidence in order to be a position to render an intelligent verdict or if they are motivated to listen, will do so with a view to rendering a verdict impartially. Few commentators have criticized juries in scandalous cases – like those of the Guildford Four, and the Birmingham Six terrorist trials in England – where seriously flawed prosecutions were not spotted by the juries concerned. Jurors, as much if not more than those without the burden of responsibility, will respond to the evident consensus of opinion amongst judge, prosecutors and public alike that the most appropriate outcome is a successful conviction. For such juries to render an impartial verdict in the circumstances of such trials would have required not only insight into the deficiencies of the case that had escaped the notice of police, lawyers, newspapers, friends and the judge himself, but an heroic determination to defy public opinion.

Jury decision-making is an optimising task: but what are the appropriate criteria?

Juries should begin their examination of the evidence when starting their discussions at the end of the trial, in order to bring in a verdict which the evidence demands. Normally, jurors have taken no notes and must rely on recalling all matters of substance without any assistance from other human or mechanical aids. Of course, in practice, juries do not systematically examine the evidence because the difficulties of doing that collectively are almost insurmountable. Jurors will have formed more or less tentative views about what the verdict should be before they formally come together to consider their verdict. The task they collectively face is one of securing a consensus. If a consensus exists and is revealed at the start of deliberations by a straw vote, then the jury, indeed, may decide it has little work to do as a group. More typically, discussion soon reveals the need to negotiate what issues are important, and what evidence is relevant. Jurors must reconcile those decisions of victims, witnesses, police and prosecutors which have brought the accused to court with the well-rehearsed and plausible evidence which the defence has presented. Most commonly, deliberations soon reveal a range of views, not always with a clear majority in favour of one verdict or another. Before bringing in a verdict of Guilty juries seem anxious to achieve something like a two-thirds majority in favour of conviction: otherwise, Not Guilty is the preferred verdict (Davis, 1989), with theoretically different consequences in juries of different size (Davis et al., 1975). The question is 'By what means are two-thirds majorities achieved?'

The film featuring Henry Fonda, *Twelve Angry Men*, demonstrated two inconsistent majorities at different stages of their deliberations, reflecting two major influence processes: majority influence and minority influence. A clear majority of jurors initially believed in the defendant's guilt, and this would normally have been sufficient to persuade the minority fairly rapidly to agree to a conviction. Indeed, Saks (1977) showed that the correlation between time taken to the first vote and total deliberation time was .48. Once a majority is perceived to exist, the jury's task becomes one of focusing upon, and eliminating, the areas of disagreement which cause the minority to dissent. An early vote greatly accelerates that task. However, in *Twelve Angry Men*, one man consistently and energetically argued that the required standard of proof – beyond reasonable doubt – had not been achieved, and his views, at very long last, finally prevailed.

The essential ambiguity of the criterion 'beyond reasonable doubt' (see Connolly, 1987) leaves it open for determined minorities to thwart the wishes of the majority in any but the most clear-cut of cases. Much research has shown that when the validity of arguments is standardized, then the style of argument, the consistency of viewpoint, and unyielding confident response to expressions of alternative views can be highly effective in overturning a majority (Nemeth, 1986). Whether for reasons of prejudice, malice or sincere conviction, it is possible for a minority, rightly or wrongly, to ensure that the interpretation of the defined standard of proof is exploited to its advantage. Social processes of influence, persuasion and even bargaining may be the predominant factors in the achievement of consensus when a large group is inappropriately given the optimizing task of applying the defined standard of proof to the ill-recorded and variously recalled preceding days of evidence.

An important study of real jury decisions by Reskin and Visher (1986) illustrates how irrelevant factors may influence the outcome. The investigators examined the results of 38 sexual assault trials, evaluating strength and type of evidence both during the trials and according to the press at the close of the trial. The results showed that where there was evidence of assault in the form of so-called hard evidence, e.g. injury to the raped woman and possession of a weapon by the rapist, then a verdict of Guilty tended to prevail. In the absence of such hard evidence, various subjective responses to the woman's character, whether or not she worked, her attractiveness, her 'carelessness' on the occasion in question, and so on, all determined very strongly the verdict that was rendered. Juries, the authors conclude, judge it appropriate to bring such factors into play when 'liberated' by the lack of conclusively hard evidence. Whilst such factors are, of course, strictly irrelevant to the optimizing task of applying the standard of proof, they are factors which a fact-finding mechanism consisting of a group of 12 assorted strangers will find it all too tempting to latch on to as an aid to facilitating not 'truth', but agreement.

Jury decision-making is a disjunctive task: but will the best person win?

Conflicting views cancel out one another, and cannot be added together. One person or another must be heeded, but not all; one verdict must be returned, not a diversity of views, however well expressed and however valid the points they make.

Arbitrary and undue influence goes to some members of groups, by virtue of their status, experience, gender or other visible sign of rank and influence. Reflecting on the fact that behaviour patterns in the outside world impinge on deliberations within the jury room,

Saks and Hastie (1978) summarize findings on the selection of the jury foreman by observing that 'the person most likely to be chosen foreman is a high socio-economic status male who sits at the end of the table and initiates the discussion' (p. 92). Unfortunately, such a person is not necessarily the one whose views should most be heeded.

An interesting experimental study has suggested that the moral values and attitudes of members of a jury may also play a disproportionate role in determining who has the most influence (Lupfer et al. 1987). The investigators found that individuals whose moral reasoning emphasized the importance of universal principles and acting according to principles of individual conscience were more likely to vote consistently for acquittal. Further, such people were more likely to have their views respected, to be deemed influential, and to be recommended as appropriate candidates for the job of foreman of the jury. Whilst it is possible to speculate about why high-level moral reasoners command such consistent influence and respect, this study more importantly points to the fact that group decisions reflect the values and persuasiveness of their members as much as they do the objective merits of the case.

Ideally, the jury should pay particular attention to that person or to that subset of people having the most acute appreciation of the nature of the task, who have most assiduously attended to, comprehended and remembered the evidence, and who are least likely to be prejudiced in favour of or against the defendant. In fact, juries do not deliberately seek out the views of the best qualified and give them precedence; rather, as we have seen, they embark on a search for agreement, and a variety of social processes operate to bring about the victory of one faction over another. It is, unfortunately, almost inevitable that the process (coming to agreement) by which the task (choosing the appropriate verdict) is accomplished, becomes an end in itself.

The jury's task: what's really expected?

It is doubtful whether judges and lawyers really expect juries to do a sound *legal* job; if they did, the jury system would long ago have been abolished. Rather, they expect juries to decide which of two competing theories give the better account of the harm that has been done, and for which the defendant is being held responsible. Whatever the merits of the prosecution or of the defence, equal opportunity and encouragement is given by the judge to each side to develop their positions to the full, thereby creating in the observer's mind the notion that the two theories are equal competitors for attention and possible approval.

Theories, of course, are stories, and stories can be told by and comprehended by jurors, judges, defendants and prosecutors alike. The fact that the adversarial trial is constructed out of competing stories is probably what enables jurors to tolerate and ultimately bring a criminal trial to its conclusion by simply approving one or other narrative. But stories have also the function of enabling jurors to cope reasonably effectively with the task of deciding what are the salient facts in a case, ordering them and remembering them. Always in a detective story, and frequently in murder trials, the question of motive emerges as a critical issue. This is because a plausible motive may serve to make salient and integrate an array of otherwise unconnected and in themselves meaningless actions. By way of illustration read the following story, taken from Thorndyke (1977) and used by Linz and Penrod (1984). The story consists of 35 propositions:

> (1) There was once an old farmer (2) who owned a very stubborn donkey. (3) *One evening the farmer was trying to put his donkey into its shed.* (4) First, the farmer pulled the donkey, (5) but the donkey wouldn't move. (6) Then the farmer pushed the donkey, (7) but still the donkey wouldn't move. (8) Finally, the farmer asked his dog (9) to bark loudly at the donkey (10) and thereby frighten him into the shed. (11) But the dog refused. (12) So then, the farmer asked his cat (13) to scratch the dog (14) so the dog would bark loudly (15) and thereby frighten the donkey into the shed. (16) But the cat replied, 'I would gladly scratch the dog (17) if only you would get me some milk.' (18) So the farmer went to his cow (19) and asked for some milk (20) to give to the cat. (21) But the cow replied, (22) 'I would gladly give you some milk (23) if only you would give me some hay.' (24) Thus, the farmer went to the haystack (25) and got some hay. (26) As soon as he gave the hay to the cow, (27) the cow gave the farmer some milk. (28) Then the farmer went to the cat (29) and gave the milk to the cat. (30) As soon as the cat got the milk, (31) it began to scratch the dog. (32) As soon as the cat scratched the dog, (33) the dog began to bark loudly. (34) The barking so frightened the donkey (35) that it jumped immediately into its shed. (Linz and Penrod, 1984, pp. 4–5)

Table 10.3 Distribution of 69 jury verdicts in a simulation study of a murder trial

First degree murder	6
Second degree murder	39
Manslaughter	20
Not Guilty	0
Hung	4
	69

Source: Hastiè et al., 1983

In his experiment Thorndyke studied the effect on memory of leaving out the third proposition, which tells us what the old farmer was attempting to do, and which if known makes sense of all the sub-goals and activities described in the text. Subjects remembered many more propositions when the critical third proposition was included than when it was absent from the text. Bennett and Feldman, it will be recalled, emphasized the importance of a good story structure as a basis for belief in the truth of the story. The implication of Thorndyke's work, and that of many other cognitive psychologists (see Jackson, 1988) is that a coherent story structure is important for basic comprehension and recall of relevant facts.

The detailed analyses of jury decision-making processes by Hastie et al. (1983) indicate that invalid deviant verdicts are associated with poor comprehension and poor memory for the salient facts of the case. They had 69 different juries assess the same case, presented by actors on video in three one-hour long segments. This simulated murder trial was based on a real trial, but naturally the selection of salient facts for presentation on video would have the effect of standardizing jurors' understanding, knowledge and recall of the material of the trial. Five verdicts were open to the jurors, and table 10.3 shows the distribution of jury verdicts across the five possibilities. In the actual trial, second degree murder was the verdict and according to experts, only that verdict was possible. Alternative verdicts were, however, provided by 38 per cent of the juries. The contingency coefficient of .43 between predicted and actual results is statistically significant, but its relatively low size prompted the authors to compare the comprehension of and memory for testimony, and for the judges instructions, of those juries who got it 'right' (second degree murder) and those who got it 'wrong' (first degree murder and manslaughter). For the most part, the erroneous verdicts – first degree murder, and manslaughter – were associated with errors of comprehension and memory, for example in recalling legal definitions of the crimes in question, as well as details of individuals' testimony.

An imaginative and productive experimental study by Aronsson and Nilholm (1990) demonstrated powerfully the salience of story structure as a validating force in the reconstruction of events. They gave 'lay judges' unique pieces of information about a custody case that if comprehended and recalled would lead them to side with the father or mother of the daughter whose custody was in dispute. The discussions indicated how persons of like mind would unwittingly collaborate in the fabrication of new material confirming their jointly held position. Moreover, the same facts would be incorporated into opposing interpretations – for example the child's wish to live with the mother showed either her dislike of the father, or the mother's undue influence on the child, according to your point of view. It was also noted that members who had been supplied with divergent and conflicting items of information, who had conflicting views and interpretations, who had fabricated distorted information in the interests of the consistency and plausibility of conflicting narrative accounts, nonetheless behaved as if all members shared a common understanding of the facts of the case: 'No-one expressed any distrust with respect to the authenticity of the opposing parties' factual background . . . Divergent stories were typically explained in terms of memory deficits, never in terms of divergent premises or in terms of opponents' interpretation of events' (Aronsson and Nilholm, 1990, p. 311).

A story model of juror decision making

The story framework provides a means whereby jurors comprehend, recall, use, bend and create factual material in criminal trials. But in the end, a verdict has to be given that at least purports to be consistent with definition of criminal categories. How is this consistency delivered? Pennington and Hastie (1986) develop the idea that the story model provides a mechanism both for the comprehension of evidence and for its interpretation in terms of verdict categories.

Any story has three main episodes, emphasizing in turn (a)

initiating events (The Beginning); (b) psychological states, physical states, goals and actions (The Development) and (c) consequences (The Ending).

In interviews with 26 subjects who had seen the three-hour video-taped trial of a man called Johnson for murder, described above (Hastie et al., 1983), it was found that jurors told very different stories of the evidence. The narratives provided by the 26 jurors had very little in common, conveying only the fact that Johnson and Clemens had been in a bar, Caldwell had hit Johnson, and that Johnson had subsequently stabbed Caldwell: a bald framework of a story which omits all the interesting detail regarding psychological states, goals and consequences, details which make the story both comprehensible as an account of the actions of real people, and most importantly which make it possible to categorize the killing of Caldwell as an act of first degree murder, second degree murder, manslaughter, or none of these.

Although having been given identical information in the three hours of taped evidence, jurors differed greatly in their rendering of the meat of the story (The Development), and their accounts differed systematically according to the verdicts they had rendered. The following story is the one that emerged from the accounts given by those who favoured a first-degree murder verdict:

> In the afternoon Johnson and Caldwell were in Gleason's Bar when a woman named Sandra Lee asked Johnson to give her a ride somewhere the next day. Caldwell became enraged because Sandra Lee was his girlfriend. So, Caldwell pulled a razor on Johnson and threatened him. Johnson did not have a weapon on him and went home. Johnson [angry or humiliated] decided to confront Caldwell and show him once and for all who was boss, by killing him if it came to that. Later Johnson's friend Clemens came over and agreed to back him up. Johnson got his knife and Clemens and Johnson went back to the bar to find Caldwell. They went into the bar and after a while, Johnson and Caldwell decided to go outside and have it out. Caldwell hit Johnson, renewing Johnson's vow to get Caldwell once and for all. He pulled his knife, raising it up, and thrust it into Caldwell. A policeman saw the stabbing and rushed over but Caldwell died almost immediately from a massive chest wound.

In this story, the essential requirements of a first-degree murder verdict are established: intention to kill followed by purposeful resolution to carry out the intention. There is no doubt concerning the appropriate mental state. The circumstances indicate little excuse for forming this intention, at least by way of immediate provocation, and the resolve to kill was maintained over a long period of time. The killing itself was carried out in fulfilment of the resolution, Johnson's return to the bar having provoked Caldwell merely to hit Johnson.

By way of contrast, the common elements of the manslaughter narrative establish a motive of self-defence in the context of a well-intentioned discussion initiated by Johnson:

> In Gleason's Bar in the afternoon, Caldwell threatened to kill Johnson so he left the bar. Then later that night, Johnson went back to the bar. After a while he and Caldwell went outside to talk over their differences, so Johnson thought, having had a history of arguments with each other and a longstanding jealousy between them. Outside, Caldwell punched Johnson, alarming him as he remembered Caldwell's earlier threat. Johnson pulled a fishing knife that he was carrying, intending to prevent Caldwell from harming him with a razor as he had previously threatened. In the confusion of the fight he stabbed Caldwell, but later, Caldwell's razor was found in his back pocket.

One may wonder how it is that such contrasting accounts can emerge from the same evidence. Indeed some jurors arrived at a Not Guilty verdict, their common narrative stressing the violence of Caldwell's attack and the necessity of Johnson's defensive but essentially accidental killing. The explanation of the differences lie in the necessity for jurors to reconstruct reality in response to the alternative and conflicting demands of the court. The logical order of influence between Evidence, Verdict and Story would suggest the following progression from:

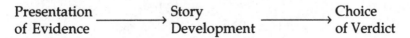

Presentation   →   Story   →   Choice
of Evidence   Development   of Verdict

In practice we know that a preferred verdict will influence understanding and memory of the evidence, and that stories are likely to be constructed that will justify the preferred verdict. Stories themselves will modify the impact of evidence, and the evidence itself may greatly constrain choice of verdict. In practice, the relation between Evidence, Story and Verdict is more realistically portrayed as follows:

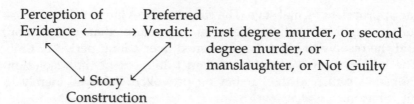

In other words, all three reciprocally influence one another.

The verdicts juries give may sometimes seem wilfully perverse. That may be an illusion. Seemingly perverse verdicts may emerge naturally enough from the creative narrative construction required by legal definitions of criminal acts. Stories provide answers to the pressing questions of identity, mental state, actions and circumstances that are required to establish blame. There is a story behind every verdict.

Too many stories

We should not be misled into thinking that prosecution and defence counsel necessarily each does a brilliant job of creating a single alternative story of the crime which the jury will compare and contrast with the opposition's before deciding which it prefers. Matters are frequently more confused than that, both because the advocates are not always as skilled or well-prepared as they should be, and because there are frequently more alternatives than that of being merely Guilty or Not Guilty of one specified offence. In the Pennington and Hastie example, for instance, four verdicts were possible, each with quite different implications for sentencing.

If many different criminal narratives contend for supremacy in the early moments of a jury's deliberations then, other things being equal, it is likely that that jury will spend longer determining which version should serve as their model for determining blameworthiness than when there are few alternatives. Holstein (1985) investigated this possibility, but found that matters were more complex than he had initially supposed.

Holstein (1985) had 48 mock juries view a video tape of a mock trial in which the defendant was accused of theft of bricks from a disused property. The defendant denied intent to steal, claiming that the property in question had been abandoned. The testimony of three witnesses and the defendant was shown, and the judge

Table 10.4 The resolution of jury deliberations with different numbers of schematic interpretations articulated in them

Is the deliberation resolved?	Number of schematic interpretations articulated in a deliberation			
	1	2	3 or more	Total
Yes: Unanimous verdict	12	13	5	30
	(100%)	(72%)	(28%)	(62%)
No: Hung jury	0	5	13	18
		(28%)	(72%)	(38%)
	12	18	18	48
	(100%)	(100%)	(100%)	(100%)

Source: Holstein, 1985

explained how the law should be applied. The juries (of five or six people) deliberated to a verdict.

Juries predominantly discussed 'what really happened', and came up with as many as five different stories or 'schematic interpretations' of events. Whilst there were two basic stories – 'knowingly taking other's property' versus 'removing worthless property' – other interpretations emerged, for example, in defence of the accused: 'I don't think he could be guilty. *He didn't think there was an owner*. Just abandoned bricks. He figured he could put them to good use so he took them' (p. 95).

The analysis of results did, indeed, show that the more stories that were put forward in the early stages of deliberation the longer the deliberations continued. More importantly, however, the greater the number of stories put forward, the less likely was there to be a unanimous verdict. Table 10.4 shows the distribution of unanimous verdicts and hung juries according to the number of schematic interpretations. Of particular interest is that when three interpretations emerged in the deliberations, the indications were that the verdict with two interpretations in its support was less likely to be accepted than the singly-supported verdict.

This finding is not surprising when it is realized that alternative defences may well be contradictory. For instance, one juror in favour of the defendant suggested early on that the defendant took the property under the impression that it had no owner: 'Sure, he went on the property, and took them when he saw them just laying there . . . but see, in his mind, he says, you know, he didn't feel that they belonged to anybody, even though he saw the sign. Apparently he didn't feel that they belonged, so he took them' (p. 95). Also supporting the defendant, another juror opined that: 'He probably did the State of Michigan a favour by taking them . . . They were just laying around in a mess, an eyesore for the neighbourhood . . . Well this guy sort of went in and helped them out' (p. 94).

Unfortunately, the second story contradicts the notion, expressed in the first story, that the bricks had no owner. Two alternative (and inconsistent) versions of innocence are less convincing than one.

Fitting the crime to the script: effects of juror, defendant and situational characteristics on narrative construction

Different jurors may have a preference for different 'scripts', and there is a considerable industry in the US devoted to ensuring that as far as possible only appropriate jurors are selected: those whose attitudes will not constrain their narrative construction to the detriment of one verdict or another. The scientific basis of 'scientific jury selection is a matter of considerable debate, but the search for a rational basis for appropriately matching jurors to cases goes on apace. The question is of more interest to the legal profession in the US, where there is much greater scope for influencing the selection of jurors by individual challenge than exists in the UK.

The belief is certainly prevalent that jury composition is an important variable influencing their decisions. Hans and Vidmar's review (1982) suggests that men are less likely to convict accused rapists than are women, and that younger people are generally less conviction prone. Little consistent effects of race in the USA have been demonstrated. The better educated are more likely to convict, but the effect of personality variables is inconsistent, with authoritarians being more punitive once conviction is secured, but probably not more likely to convict in the first place. Interestingly the work of Nemeth and her colleagues (Nemeth, 1983) suggests that although men on juries may be perceived as being more influential, there is no evidence for their views being more influential or indeed for their proposed verdicts to be any different from those of women.

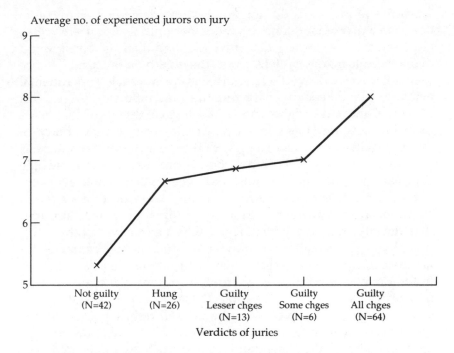

Figure 10.1 Juror experience and verdict
Source: After Dillehay and Nietzel, 1985

There is now some evidence that the link between juror composition and verdicts is mediated by differences in narrative preferences which then 'prescribe' different verdicts. Fulero and Penrod (1990) report that in an unpublished experiment in which 48 mock jurors were interviewed about a rape trial they had seen on video, none of the many attitude and personality measures were related directly to verdicts. They were, however, linked directly to stories, which in turn were related to verdicts.

Dillehay and Nietzel (1985) introduce good evidence from studies of real jurors that increased experience of trial narratives may induce a tendency to convict. The greater the number of experienced jurors there are on a jury, the more likely is the jury to convict, as figure 10.1 indicates. Although the range of experience on most juries was high, the average experience seemed to exert a remarkably consistent effect, indicating perhaps that feedback from previous trials (e.g. number of previous convictions of a defendant) prejudiced jurors in favour of a trial narrative culminating in guilt.

Studies of real trials do not suggest that defendant characteristics have a marked influence on outcomes of trials (e.g. Kerr, 1982), although it has to be said that the social and financial background of defendants markedly determines the quality of the legal defence they will receive. Nevertheless, there is considerable experimental evidence that defendant characteristics may influence judgements of guilt. Dane and Wrightsman (1982) suggest that these biases are probably best explained in terms of the relative plausibility of different narratives. They suggest that in courtroom trials there is an unwritten, but widely understood script which determines the expectations of the participants. We expect villains and evildoers to be unattractive, of low socio-economic status, of dubious moral character, from a powerless minority group, and to have attitudes that deviate from the norm. Thus, when attractive, high status, majority-group members of previously good moral character (to list the principal characteristics deemed to influence jurors) appear in the dock accused of, say, attempted murder, the temptation to find reasons for acquittal is strong. Or so the experimental studies seem to suggest. However, as Le Van (1984) rightly points out, the quality and extent of research on the effect of such factors as physical attractiveness of the defendant leaves much to be desired. For example, studies which indicate the supposed disadvantage that unattractive female defendants face have normally used male 'jurors', leaving the disadvantage of being an unattractive male at the mercy of female 'jurors' an unexplored issue.

Situational effects on the trial narrative

The jury's role is to conclude the trial with the pronouncement of a verdict, and newspapers frequently report high profile trials in terms which suggest that the jury verdict will inexorably reflect the outcome of the dramatic contest that has taken place in court. There is, in other words, a narrative of the trial (Jackson, 1988) that influences their preferences for one verdict or another, and thereby constrains perception of the evidence and construction of their story narrative.

Many extraneous factors may influence the trial narrative. Recently in England a self-confessed Irish terrorist was found Not Guilty in a trial at the Old Bailey, and it was widely assumed by press commentators that the jury's leniency was linked to revelations of police misconduct in previous well-publicized Irish terrorist convictions. Greene and Loftus (1984) produced experimental evidence that a highly-publicized case of mistaken identification strongly influenced the views of students judging the guilt of a defendant accused of robbery who had been positively identified in a line-up by the shop assistant.

Jurors do not shed their background knowledge and experience on entering the courtroom. Pre-trial publicity surrounding the case on which a juror sits is remarkably difficult for jurors to ignore, as a recent study by Kramer et al. (1990) has indicated. Generally, this publicity is detrimental to the interests of the accused, whose image and supposed crimes may have been exposed to the jurors for a considerable time prior to the start of the trial. It seems that instructions to ignore prior exposure have little effect.

A rather more subtle form of adverse publicity comes when a defendant is charged with and tried for two or more offences in the same trial. Can the jury really evaluate the evidence independently for each separate offence? They seem not to be able to do that. Such joined offences are more likely to result in a guilty verdict (Bordens and Horowitz, 1985; Tanford et al. 1985), and, again, judicial instructions did nothing to mitigate the detrimental effect of 'joinder' (Greene and Loftus, 1985). It seems that the defendant in a joined trial is viewed more negatively, and that this leads to narrative construction consistent with the less flattering assessment of the individual's character.

The trial narrative is of considerable importance to the evaluation of witness evidence and thence to the role that their evidence may play in the construction of the criminal narrative. Encouraging witnesses to provide trivial or even irrelevant detail enhances their credibility, as recent experimental studies by Bell and Loftus (1989) have demonstrated. Illegitimately casting doubt on the competence of an expert witness is detrimental to the evaluation of that expert's evidence: mud sticks (Kassin et al., 1990). Improving the confidence with which a witness gives evidence seems guaranteed to increase its influence on jurors, as yet another recent study indicates (Cutler et al., 1990). More interestingly, and contrary to simplistic understanding of the literature, there are advantages accruing from child and elderly witnesses. Identical evidence given by 8-year-old, 21-year-old and 74-year-old witnesses is least well regarded when given by the young adults, possibly indicating that articulate, confidently conveyed evidence from young children and elderly people impresses precisely because it confounds expectations (Ross et al., 1990). Defence lawyers should note that even absent witnesses may be more influential than their physically present counterparts, but only when the witness concerned is peripheral to the case for the prosecution (Webster et al., 1991).

Concluding note

Would *you* choose to be tried by jury rather than by a tribunal of professional judges? If you are guilty, of course you would, assuming that the conclusions of Kalven and Zeisel (1966) still hold; and that juries are less prone to convict than are judges. If you are innocent, however, and there is an absence of convincing evidence against you, then you might care to trust that the judges are less likely to deliver a perverse verdict than is the jury. Distasteful though the conclusion may be, it is nonetheless true that in jury trials, determining the truth of the matter is not the prime objective. The court is established, and its rules so framed, as to give both sides an equal chance to compel acceptance of their recommended verdict. Almost certainly, in such circumstances, the guilty are more likely to go free, and the innocent to be convicted than would be the case if the facts of the matter were sought in a non-adversarial forum. It has traditionally been thought that the adversarial and jury system protects the innocent from wrongful convictions. Recent well-publicized cases in the UK have confounded that hope. It is, perhaps, ironic that a few well-publicized cases of wrongful conviction have prompted suggestions for radical reforms of the system which the police have been seeking in the interests of convicting more of the guilty.

11

Punishing the Offender: Sentencing in Practice

Introduction: justifying sentencing research

Blamed successively by the victim, the police and jury, our accused awaits sentence. He or she at that moment may well marvel at the fateful series of decisions leading to this moment. The convict may now also ponder by what principles the judge will determine and justify the sentence that is so soon to fall.

Should the charge be criminal damage, it will be of some comfort if our United Kingdom criminal lives in Powys where the chance of a convicted defendant receiving a custodial sentence is a mere 4.2 per cent. Woe betide the guilty one who lives in South Yorkshire (19.5 per cent), and especially Kent (25.3 per cent) (quoted by Mills, 1990). Such apparent inconsistencies have prompted much of the research into sentencing by social scientists. Systematic variations may also occur between different judges on the same circuit, or different magistrates on the same bench, and, of course, individual sentencers may themselves be inconsistent from one 'identical' case to another (see McFatter, 1986, for an interesting experimental demonstration of this point).

Another compelling motive for research into sentencing is the sense of dismay occasioned by our continuing failure to reform an overcrowded prison system. This becomes tragically evident in the numbers of young people given custodial sentences. Tutt and Giller (1989) point out that the prison is generally accepted as being inappropriate for young people, and that closer co-operation between the police, courts, social services and the probation services can lead to dramatic reductions in the number of young people requiring a custodial sentence. Of course, if prison does young people little good, it probably has little value for adults either. Tutt and Giller's (1989) arguments that 'agreed targets' should determine the managed flow of convicted young people to appropriate disposals – prison being reserved for those few for whom there is genuinely no alternative – can easily enough be applied to convicted adults. As it is, the plight of young people in prison, and the attempt to eliminate it for that group, make us uneasy about a sentencing system that leaves judges to punish convicts (within a prescribed range of options for any given offence) according to whichever purposes of punishment seem to them appropriate.

A third compelling motive for good and detailed research into sentencing lies in the social injustice of a prison population weighted so heavily against the poor and the socially disadvantaged (Home Office Report, quoted in Cohen, 1991) – the unemployed, uneducated, homeless and mentally ill. Of course, this state of affairs reflects not only sentencing practice, but also the process whereby cases are sifted by successive decision-makers, and the lack of perceived alternatives to penal custody.

Guidelines and aims

There have been attempts to adopt a quasi-scientific approach to sentencing, establishing guidelines based on existing judicial practice, or on the modelling of what appears to be judicial practice, and by attempts to operationalize one or other theory of sentencing. There are persistent differences in this country between the behaviour of magistrates in rural, metropolitan and urban areas, and this has led to the promulgation of national guidelines or tariffs, based upon standard or average practice. Tariff sentences are applied routinely in the case of motoring offences. Gibb (1989) reports what amounts to a rank order of offence seriousness for relatively minor offences, with guideline fines for English magistrates ranging from £500 ('grievous bodily harm') to £50 ('Drunk and disorderly') with 'handling stolen goods' in the mid-range at £250.

Simester and Simester (1990) describe a more complex approach to sentencing of sex offenders, and demonstrate that the behaviour of judges in the aggregate can be modelled fairly successfully, at least with respect to those who sit in the New Zealand Court of Appeal. They studied 67 sexual-offence sentencing decisions handed down by that Court of Appeal, and found that of 23 variables included in their model, 18 were predictive of length of prison sentence, explaining 76 per cent of the variance in sentence length. Interestingly, aggravating and mitigating factors in the circumstances of the offence itself were more influential than the factors related to the character of the offender. Age of victim was important, relationship of the victim to the attacker, sex of the victim and the use of violence – all of these were of greater importance than the existence of previous convictions, or the offender's expression of remorse. The authors conclude that a 'model of consistent sentencing' can be extracted from the practice of the Appeal Court, based on the analysis of the mitigating and aggravating factors present in each case.

Of course, Appeal Court judges are obliged to set consistent standards as well as they can, and their behaviour is not necessarily typical of general practice in the ordinary courts. There is no reason why their judgements should not be used, as in this instance, to develop sentencing guidelines for judges, if standardization of sentencing is, indeed, thought to be an appropriate goal. Andrews et al. (1987) also indicate that in principle, judges asked to comment in an experimental setting will tend to agree on which mitigating and aggravating factors are important. Information in real trials, however is not presented in such an abstract and schematic form as it comes to judges in the Appeal Court, or the psychology laboratory. More complex models of sentencing are required if even the basic question of type of sentence is to be addressed (Sebba and Nathan, 1984).

In addition to the seriousness of the offence, and the normal range of mitigating and aggravating circumstances, the risk of further offending and the consequences of being mistaken about the degree of risk (see Gottfredson et al., 1989), are important factors to consider in the decision to imprison. Naturally, different judges in practice take these factors into consideration in different ways. Only by appealing to the primacy of one of many different sentencing aims (e.g. rehabilitation, general deterrence, incapacitation and retribution) is it possible to become confidently prescriptive. That is exactly the policy adopted by von Hirsch (1985) who espouses a 'Just Deserts' philosophy and bases his guidelines on assessment of the seriousness of offence, and past history of offending of the current offender. He suggests that to treat the offender as anything but a fully responsible agent who deserves punishment scaled according to his or her offence is to act disrespectfully towards that individual. But if it is inappropriate to give the offender less than what is deserved by their behaviour, it is equally wrong to be more severe than is justified, whether because of a desire to protect society, deter others or even to rehabilitate the individual concerned. Standardization of punishments according to deserts would make discrepancies such as between one killer receiving two years' probation for strangling her brutal husband, and another receiving life imprisonment for stabbing and killing her husband in similar mitigating circumstances, less likely to occur (Marks, 1991).

It is argued that uniformity could stifle legitimate and continuing debate. As Marks points out in her report, the sentence of two years' probation may well have been prompted by the outcry in an earlier well-publicized case of one woman who was jailed for life, and lost her appeal to be cleared of murder on grounds of provocation. Nevertheless, von Hirsch and Jareborg (1989) reported that Sweden has now enacted laws which endorse the 'proportionality' principle. Amongst other things, the new statute will ensure that 'Imprisonment is . . . invoked chiefly in two situations: where the penal value (seriousness) of the conduct is high; and [also] when the penal value is in the upper-middle range, and the offender has a significant criminal record' (p. 275).

Arbitrarily selecting one penal philosophy (retribution in the case of Sweden) is inappropriate because there is a continuing and perfectly legitimate conflict between competing philosophies. It is a conflict which is highlighted by the proposal to abolish imprisonment as a punishment for most juvenile crime. For juveniles, the goal of rehabilitation is no doubt more appropriate than it is for adults, but, of course, there is no age at which rehabilitation becomes an irrelevant aim and retribution all at once of paramount importance. And that is to leave out of account deterrence and incapacitation, both of which seem on occasions to be highly desirable aims, which no society is likely altogether to ignore.

In contrast to the results yielded by Appeal Court judges, and by simulation of sentencing behaviour, Douglas (1989) reports considerable systematic variations between magistrates in use both of type and severity of punishments. There were no overall differences in leniency because different magistrates, even in the same court, come down hard on different kinds of crime. Far from denigrating this state of affairs, Douglas suggests that predictable sentences handed out according to a formula would not be seen as 'just'. It is likely, he suggests, 'that an end to disparity would result in condemnation of a system which could be perceived as overly rigid and as characterised by a refusal to recognise the distinctive features of each crime and each defendant' (p. 51). The courts would then be perceived to be proceeding in an inappropriately mechanical way.

Psychological research on sentencing has looked mainly at the judges, their attitudes and behaviour, searching both for consistent variations, and evidence of biased and illegitimate use of strictly irrelevant factors, like the race or sex of the defendant. We shall now critically examine that research, emphasizing those studies that have tried to tease out the sentencing strategies of judges, and of others like probation officers, who influence the judges' decisions. We shall pay particular attention also to gender bias in sentencing, and we shall describe work which critically examines the public's much-vaunted draconian views on sentencing.

Judges and judging

English judges are a conservative and conformist people whose attitudes are not easy to change. English magistrates, mostly amateur judges drawn from a range of occupations, seem to be chosen to resemble judges who have risen to the heights of their legal professional practice: they are relatively old, they are of high social standing, and they vote Conservative (Kapardis and Farrington, 1981). More importantly, those who sentence criminals tend to have a similar set of attitudes about political and social life more generally, as well as distinctive views about crime and the role of punishment in society.

Judicial attitudes and behaviour

In 1971 Hogarth reported a study of Canadian magistrates, in which a comparison was made between the views of magistrates and other groups in relation to their standing on a number of attitudinal dimensions derived from a survey of a large number of respondents. The results are shown in figure 11.1, and indicate that magistrates are second only to police officers in their belief in retribution (labelled Justice), their belief that individual deterrence works

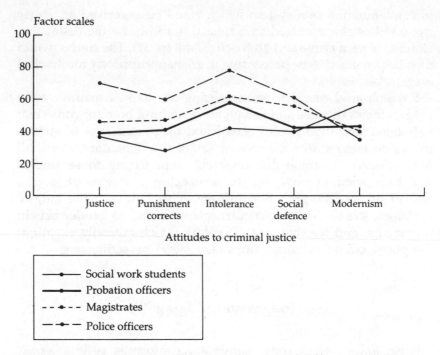

Figure 11.1 Attitudes towards criminal justice of different groups
Source: After Hogarth, 1971

(Punishment corrects), their authoritarianism (Intolerance), their beliefs in general deterrence (Social defence) and their distrust of rehabilitative practice (Modernism).

Did their attitudes affect their behaviour? On the whole there was little indication that attitudes were associated with the type of sentences that were handed out. A distinction can be made between institutional sentences, fines and suspended sentences or probation. Institutional sentences tended to be used when there were previous criminal convictions, and a demonstrably high level of culpability in the present offence. Fines were imposed predominantly when there were no previous convictions but a high level of culpability, and suspended sentences were imposed when there were no previous convictions and low culpability. Clearly, some form of standardized prescriptions ensure that, for the most part, first offenders, for example, will not be imprisoned, and financially hard-pressed first-time shoplifters committing trivial offences are not further burdened by being heavily fined. Attitudinal variables, however, were associated with the severity of sentencing within categories of sentence. Magistrates high on Social Defence, who believed that, for example, 'the main objective in the sentencing of offenders should be to deter potential offenders from committing a crime' were likely to give longer prison sentences than were those who scored less highly on that particular dimension.

Hogarth found that three main orientations to sentencing existed, as judged by scores on his attitudinal dimensions. The orientations reflected three traditionally accepted aims of sentencing: Retribution, Rehabilitation and General Deterrence. There was some evidence that in the case of relatively minor offences, those who favoured Rehabilitation gave longer sentences, whereas for serious offences, belief in Retribution and General Deterrence led to the imposition of longer sentences.

McFatter (1978) found essentially similar results in an experimental study of students, who, in a sentencing exercise, were told to adopt one or another orientation towards sentencing. Those instructed to adopt the Rehabilitative orientation were less punitive in terms of recommended length of prison sentences only in respect of serious crimes. For less serious offences their sentencing was quite as rigorous as those bent on Deterrence or Retribution. Interestingly, an orientation to Rehabilitation led the mock sentencers to attribute more blame to the victims of crimes, as if to justify the sentencers' consideration for the well-being of offenders. Conversely, Oswald (1990) showed that judges (in West Germany) who took the victim's perspective, were more inclined to attribute blame to the offender.

Social constraints on sentencing behaviour

When a judge does something like sending a pregnant woman to gaol for refusing to testify against her partner (as happened recently in England), the subsequent outcry indicates the strength of the normative constraints that operate in sentencing. Konečni and Ebbeson (1979, 1982) conducted archival studies of the factors determining judges' sentencing decisions. They examined the relationship between all the information available to the judge before sentence, and the nature of the sentence given, using the multiple regression technique of log linear analysis. Of the many factors coded in each case, one factor stood out as a crucial determinant

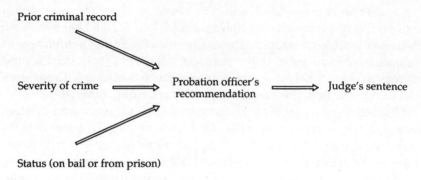

Figure 11.2 Factors affecting sentencing
Source: After Konečni and Ebbeson, 1982

of the judges' decisions: the probation officer's recommendation given at the conclusion of the officer's pre-sentence report. There were, indeed, other important factors that were associated with the judges' sentence, predominantly legal factors, like the prior criminal record of the offender, the severity of the crime and whether or not the offender had been released on bail before sentence. These three factors, however, were precisely the ones that determined the probation officers' recommendations. Other factors that supposedly are taken into account, and that form a major part of the probation officer's justifications of their recommendations (see Spencer, 1988) – like family situation, employment record and status – have little or no effect on the probation officer's recommendations, and the judges' actual sentences. The clear picture which emerged from their study was as portrayed in figure 11.2.

The method employed and the results obtained in these studies of sentencing have been replicated in studies of bail setting, and the disposal of mentally disordered offenders (e.g. Konečni et al., 1980). Interestingly, in a quite different setting – the juvenile court in England – Stafford and Hill (1987), in apparent ignorance of Konečni and Ebbeson's work, showed that the inclusion of the Social Inquiry [Probation Officer's] Report, increased the explained variance in the magistrates' sentencing severity from 29 per cent to 63 per cent, with prior criminal record, and severity of current offence being the other principal predictors. As they say, such findings have clear implications for how social workers and probation officers present information in court.

This and other work all point to the strong influence of the probation officer's or social worker's advice on the behaviour of sentencers. After all, as Spencer (1988) points out, the probation officer knows somewhat more about the defendant than does the judge, and as a professional is 'uniquely qualified to make decisions regarding the proper disposition of the case' (p. 76). The enterprising work of Rush and Robertson (1987) confirmed that judges are, indeed, 'deferential' to the recommendation of probation officers. They conducted a study of the influence of probation officers' reports by asking judges to give their provisional judgements at different stages of the officers' reports, and also to indicate which facts of the report they found most influential. They found that judges agreed with probation officers in 77 per cent of the cases, of which about half were cases in which judges deferred to the probation officer. Judgement in the remaining 23 per cent for the most part represented a compromise between the officer's views and those of the judge.

Judges are not necessarily acting in a mechanical way, blindly accepting the advice of the appropriate professional, or accepting unthinkingly the importance of standard criteria like indices of the seriousness of the offence or the presence of past convictions. A good pointer to judges' attitudes is provided in Maynard's (1982) account of the negotiations he observed in plea bargaining that determined the sentencing outcome in cases of relatively minor offences. Plea bargaining is a process of settlement designed to keep cases out of the formal process of courtroom trial, whereby the respective lawyers agree with the judge as to the appropriate disposal of a case. Frequently, it was observed that an appropriate sentence for the particular offender was decided upon, followed by a search for an offence that would warrant that sentence. Descriptions of the person are apparently crucial in this process, as in this case of a young student who had admittedly stolen a $40 car permit and used it:

> Defence counsel: 'He's a young guy, a student out there, and the court's file would have a letter from the dean of students asking for any possible courtesy in this case. I think that the dean of students' position is that the guy should not have a criminal record.' (Maynard, 1982, p. 351)

The favourable description of the student was used to justify a non-criminal charge such that the prosecutor agreed eventually that the defendant should plead guilty to a vehicle code infraction instead of theft. As the defence counsel later said:

> My logic is that I don't think the young man considered himself a thief, and that one of the things we punish is, you know, somebody that takes something out of a store bloody well knows it's stealing, and bloody well knows who he is and what he's done. (Maynard, 1982, p. 352)

Such instances of plea bargaining make explicit some of the assumptions of sentencing in criminal trials, and betray also the essence of the strategies employed by probation officers to convince the judge of the appropriateness of one sentence or another. Drass and Spencer's (1987) penetrating analysis of probation officers' written recommendations illustrate graphically how information is used selectively to build a portrait either of essential criminality – deserving of a more severe sentence – or of essential normality in an uncharacteristic mode – and hence justifying leniency. Regression analyses indicated that prior record, seriousness of offence, negative attitudes towards the consequences of the offence, positive attitudes towards the future were all related to reported risk for probation. An analysis of the patterning of cases indicated that the convict's reported attitudes, and especially the reported absence of positive attitudes were critical in the portrayal of 'high risk' cases, and critically responsive to the impact of factors like gender, race and age. For example, neither race nor gender were strongly related to the recommendations independently, but being a black male in conjunction with prior arrests and no mention of positive attitudes was distinctly detrimental.

In a subsequent report, Spencer (1988) analysed many probation officers' reports and recommendations and demonstrated that the highly standardized form in which they are presented – summary of offence and defendant characteristics followed by the recommendation – conceals a process whereby the background information is selectively drawn upon to justify the recommendation that will be made. The extra-legal information, like employment status, remorse, ambitions and so on, rationalizes the recommendation, but does not prescribe it. As he says: 'Officers construct and interpret the summary as a *warrant* for the recommendation which follows; the information contained in the summary renders the recommendation reasonable, rational, and in accordance with various bureaucratic protocols' (Spencer, 1988, p. 65).

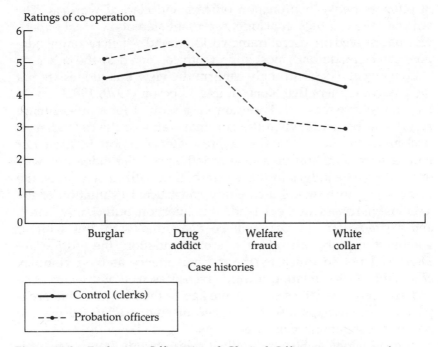

Figure 11.3   Probation Officers' and Clerical Officers' prognosis for cases of different criminal schemata
Source: After Lurigio and Carroll, 1985

Probation officers seem to have highly developed notions of what constitutes a case for severe or lenient sentencing. Legal criteria are critical, but attitudinal information – on which they are professional experts – is crucial to the final determination of true criminality, and subtly and effectively used, as Spencer states, to 'warrant' a recommendation. Lurigio and Carroll (1985) demonstrate that experienced probation officers have well-developed schemas (or stereotypes) of different criminal types – the burglar, the drug addict, the welfare fraud and the white collar criminal, for example – that strongly influence their recommendations, at least in simulated studies. Figure 11.3 shows that probation officers differentiate strongly in their evaluations of the prospects for the burglar and the drug addict on the one hand, and the welfare fraud and the white collar criminal on the other. Clerical workers in the probation department made no such differentiation. On the other hand, 'mixed' schematic presentations elicited no such consistent differences of offences between probation officers and clerical workers. The schema, one can only conclude, represent stereotypes that experience has proved are useful frameworks around which recommendations can be made, and, most importantly, accepted by the judiciary.

Cohen et al. (1985) strongly confirm the view that judges are not the passive ciphers that Konečni and Ebbeson (1979, 1982) would have us believe they are. For example, a request for a pre-sentence report will be made when the criminal status of the defendant is unclear to the judge. Neither a pre-sentence report in itself nor indeed representation by a lawyer influenced the judge one way or another. The judges in this study individualized sentences, the authors say, in terms of a carefully constructed evaluation of the 'criminal hardness' of the defendant in question. Sufficiently 'hard', and a pre-sentence report will be dispensed with, but with or without the probation officer's recommendation, the judges 'are impressed not so much by the current offence as by a complex criminality factor relating to prior record as well as to subjective and ascriptive variables such as the age of the offender, his occupation, and perhaps also his degree of co-operation during the police investigation' (Cohen et al., 1985, p. 114).

Unfortunately, as Stewart's (1980) research indicates, many arbitrary factors may enter into the construction of criminal hardness including the physical attractiveness of the defendant. However, Macrae and Shepherd (1989) have conducted experimental work in which the effects of physical attractiveness and closeness to the criminal stereotype of faces were systematically evaluated. Findings of guilt or innocence were closely related to the criminal stereotype but unrelated to attractiveness.

Is sentencing discriminatory?

It can be convincingly argued (e.g. Carlen and Cook, 1989) that a 'just deserts' sentencing policy has manifestly more adverse consequences the more socially disadvantaged you are to begin with, and that the intrinsic unfairness of sentencing has been exacerbated by the high levels of unemployment and widening gap between rich and poor which has occurred in England over the past decade or so. In addition a number of contributors to Carlen and Cook (1989) argue that norms and 'tariffs' are frequently subverted by the courts to the systematic disadvantage of blacks and to the

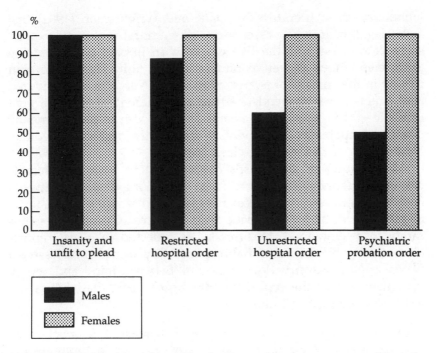

Figure 11.4 Male rate of psychiatric disposal as a percentage of female rate, by type of disposal, 1980–84
Source: Allen, 1987

advantage of white collar offenders. The position with regard to women is more complex, with evidence for both greater leniency in some cases where 'mental illness' may excuse the (respectable) offender committing a serious crime, and greater punitiveness when less 'respectable' women may receive quite severe punishment for relatively minor crimes (Allen, 1989). Allen (1987) documents the greater tendency for female offenders to be 'psychiatrized' at the lowest level of psychiatric involvement (see figure 11.4), this being due largely to the way in which male crime is construed unsympathetically as decisive, planned action, and women's crimes sympathetically as an understandable response to social and psychological problems.

It would be surprising, indeed, if stereotypes and anxieties that typify the general population did not affect judges and magistrates. American jury research has dealt with sentencing decisions by jurors. It is apparent from the review of this largely experimental laboratory-based literature by Dane and Wrightsman (1982) that 'extra-legal' factors like race, social class, moral character, expressions of remorse and the like do have an impact on sentencing recommendations as well as on findings of guilt. They place their review in the context of 'script processing'. Verdicts are delivered and sentences recommended which are coherent in terms of generally accepted sequences of events. So that, for example, the mental disorder script better fits the violent crime of the respectable woman than it does of the working-class man.

Allen's study of the court's construction of male and female criminality abundantly demonstrates the striking disparity between males who are seen to behave criminally and females whose inner psychic worlds apparently belie their 'offences'. Criminality seems rarely to be 'intended' by women, as reflected in social reports about them, and their criminal responsibility seems to be lessened by the apparent destruction of the link between mind and action. As Allen says of the report on one woman who had killed her lodger by setting fire to him:

> The woman does not act of her own volition: she is a puppet of others who 'set the stage for her tragedy'. She does not *make* relationships, but merely 'finds herself' in them, exploited, put upon and victimized. And even the killing is not presented as an act that she herself has done, but simply as a 'retaliation' that 'takes place' (causing her terrible distress in the process). The activity of the woman is allowed to vanish; what she 'does' is effortlessly assimilated to what 'happens'. (Allen, 1987, p. 41)

The most striking aspect of these sympathetic observations about female killers is their absence in the descriptions of the male killer who is universally:

> a subject of *action*: his individuality is marked out by what he *does*, where he *participates*, how he *acts* in the world. The reporter finds all that needs to be said about him in the domains of the active and external: his occupation, his finances, his habits, his sexual activities, his crimes and so on. This treatment is characteristic of the documentation of male cases. (Allen, 1987, p. 40)

This construction of male criminality provides one good reason for the high proportion of mentally-ill male offenders to be found in the prison system.

The 'criminality' script does not, however, work consistently in favour of one category of offender or another, as Allen (1989) clearly suggests. Willemsen and van Schie (1989) also report that girls may well be judged more severely than boys and be seen to require more severe sanctions than boys for committing status offences like truancy or absconding. Boys, on the other hand, are more severely judged for typically delinquent behaviour like violence against people and property. The authors suggest that where behaviour is stereotypical – as violence is in the case of boys – it is more likely to be judged in terms of stable internal characteristics that require correction. As Lurigio and Carroll (1985) indicate, stereotypes for different offences are quite detailed, and their operation in contradictory ways in different cases at the stage of sentencing may account for the failure to obtain strong general association with demographic variables like class, race and gender. The association of masculinity with criminality does seem, however, to lead to an overall bias in favour of women (see Orsagh, 1985), and it may well be true that different jurisdictions in different places hold different stereotypes which lead to variations in sentencing bias from one place to another. For example, Kempf and Austin (1986) found more evidence of racial discrimination against blacks in (white-dominated) Pennsylvanian suburbs than in more densely urbanized areas.

Evidence that sentencing may be influenced by group processes now comes from a number of studies. Walker and Main (1973) compared the performance of judges sitting singly and in groups of three with respect to civil rights cases, and concluded that the bench of judges showed greater leniency, i.e. a pro-libertarian bias. Evidence that a bench of two or three lay magistrates may be more lenient than a single professional has been provided by Diamond (1990). Stipendiaries are paid professionals – normally ex-barristers – who deliver judgements sitting alone. Lay magistrates deliberate in groups of two or more usually, three. Diamond (1990) found that lay magistrates were more lenient than stipendiaries, and she concluded that this is due to their greater identification with defendants as accused members of the public and their lesser concern with the goal of protection of society than was the case with the stipendiaries. The possibility of a group decision effect cannot, however, be ruled out, given the absence of conditions in which a lay magistrate sits alone, or the stipendiaries in groups. For whatever reason, lenient views may carry more weight than punitive views in magistrates' discussions and decision-making.

The circumstances in which judges arrive at their sentencing decision should also be examined more closely with a view to understanding how discriminatory sentences – one way or another – may arise. For example, Croyle (1983), in a unique study, demonstrated that consistent racial biases – both pro- and anti-black – could be discerned over the long term in the judgements of different judges, and the recommendation of different prosecuting and defence attorneys in St Louis County Courts in the USA. He showed that different three person group combinations of pro- and anti-black attorneys (prosecution and defence) and judge consistently arrive at either pro- or anti-black decisions. The judge's prejudices are highly influential when the attorneys are neutral, in both pro- and anti-black directions. However, the judge's pro-black prejudices count for little when both prosecution and defence attorneys have a record of anti-black recommendations. In that instance, racial bias is strongly expressed, although not as strongly as when all three have anti-black records.

Croyle's study is of considerable interest and importance. It demonstrates well how judicial biases may become salient in some circumstances but not in others, and it demonstrates a strong organizational work group effect on sentencing (see Eisenstein and Jacob, 1977). It also demonstrates, as does much of the most interesting work on sentencing, how effectively archival material in the form of reports, transcripts and recorded decisions, may be employed in research.

What the public wants: retribution?

Public opinion polls and experimental studies in different countries invariably seem to discover that the public finds sentences too lenient, and is seemingly hell-bent on retribution, and a 'just deserts' policy in sentencing (Gebotys and Roberts, 1987). However, in recent research there are a number of pointers to the conclusion that many of the surveys and experiments that convey this image of public demand for a retributive approach have engineered their own conclusions by too severely limiting both the amount of information on which judgements might be based and the response alternatives available to subjects, thereby failing to take adequate account of individual differences in the views of people.

An important experimental survey study by Rossi et al. (1985) used 'vignettes' which differed on as many as 20 different dimensions, each dimension having from between 3 and 57 levels of the variable in question. Individual and corporate crimes were covered, as were length of sentence awarded and a whole range of offender and victim characteristics. Vignettes were generated randomly by computer and each respondent in the survey responded to a randomly constituted selection of 50 vignettes. An 'area probability' sample of 774 citizens of Boston, and various other samples of convenience ensured that over 53,000 vignettes were responded to. A typical computer-generated vignette read as follows:

> 'Frank F., 20, a black, an employed parking lot attendant was convicted of stealing merchandise from a Department store counter worth around $1000. In the last five years, the offender has been arrested once, but not convicted. The offender has offered to make up for the crime by paying damages. Frank F. was sentenced to 7 years in prison
>
> The sentence given was. . . .
>
> Much too low   Low   About Right   High   Much too high

Only 16 per cent of the variance in ratings was determined by the measure of crime seriousness. What else determined ratings of severity? Age, race and socio-economic status had limited effect on severity ratings of property crimes, being rated less severely for blacks, young people and higher status people. Crimes by females, however, were generally rated as more deserving of leniency than crimes by males. Prior offending, especially more than once, merited greater severity, disconfirming the key element of the 'just deserts' approach to sentencing. Offences against females and strangers elicited harsher judgements, as did first offences against property rather than persons. There was also strong evidence that different types of crime (property and person versus white-collar versus victimless crime) evoked different criteria and scaling mechanisms.

Consequences to the victim were a very powerful modifier of the seriousness of a crime, especially in the difference between crimes of violence resulting in death from those in which a lesser degree of injury was sustained. This confirms a finding of Hoffman and Hardyman (1986) that harm done is more important than 'culpability' in determining crime seriousness. Contrition failed to convince anybody, although a willingness to pay compensation was beneficial. Being under the influence of drugs and alcohol invariably aggravated the severity of punishment.

Individual differences in the raters were important determinants of severity ratings. Overall, the consistency of individual judgements was high, indicating that principles of rating had some idiosyncratic features: the sentencing principles of individuals were more consistent than the principles that emerged overall from the public at large. Females were consistently more severe than males, and crime seriousness was a more important factor for them, seriousness also being given greater importance by those higher on the social class scale.

Those who believed in the essential 'differentness' of criminals, who feared being victimized (not who had been victimized) and who had recently experienced negative life events, were all harsher in their severity judgements. In addition, those who believed in a 'just deserts' theory of punishment and viewed punishment as an effective deterrent were also, predictably enough, harsher in their judgements.

There appears to be much less uniformity in the views of the public about crime and how to control it than is implied by the generalizations that often emerge in discussion of public opinion polls of views on sentencing. The systematic approach adopted by Rossi et al. has added especially to our understanding of the importance of individual difference variables in views about sentencing. A number of novel findings – different approaches to scaling of offences for different types of crime, the role of life events on sentencing views, importance of general societal views, and the indication that individual implicit theories of sentencing are important factors in judgement – should be explored further.

Nevertheless, the findings of Rossi et al. (1985) support the results of a number of other studies. The relationship between sentencing severity and attitudes towards punishment was the subject of an inquiry by Carroll et al. (1987). In two studies they found strong evidence for two broad orientations towards sentencing: Punitive and Rehabilitative. These involved different chains of reasoning which are influenced by various personality and attitudinal variables (see table 11.1). Those with a Punitive orientation believe that criminals choose their careers and must be dealt with by repressive measures designed to incapacitate or to dissuade by fear. The liberal line of reasoning, on the other hand, stresses our

Table 11.1   Orientations to sentencing

	Conservative and Moralistic	Liberal
Sentencing	Punitive	Rehabilitation
Attribution of Criminal Causality	Belief in individual causality	Economic and societal attributions
Personality	Authoritarian Dogmatic Internal locus of control Low moral stage	High moral stage
Political Outlook	Conservative: no change	Social change by government action

Source: After Carroll et al., 1987

obligation to change the social conditions that cause crime and to rehabilitate the offender in society.

The research of Rossi et al. notwithstanding, are judges being too lenient for the public's taste? There is evidence that members of the public generally underestimate the severity of the courts. Hough et al. (1987) show that the general public's recommended sentences for a variety of offences are if anything rather more lenient than those actually delivered by the English courts. For example, the public would discharge or caution more than twice as many drug offenders, 40 per cent more car thieves and 31 per cent more shoplifters than the courts actually do caution or discharge. A number of recent studies have also demonstrated that the more informed individuals are about the circumstances of individual cases, the more inclined they are to take a lenient view when it comes to sentencing. For example Seltzer and McCormick II (1987) found that simplistically worded questions about the death penalty for murder in general yielded greater support for that penalty than did concretely worded questions about particular types of murder e.g. 61.8 per cent voted 'yes' for the death penalty in general, but, somewhat surprisingly, only 42.8 per cent advocated it for rape-murder, and only 29.1 per cent for murder during the course of armed robbery.

Doob and Roberts (1984, 1988) show that over a long period of

Table 11.2   Effect of source of information on evaluation of the
sentence given to the accused

	Too harsh	About right	Too lenient	Total
Court-based information	52%	29%	19%	100%
Newspaper	13%	24%	63%	100%

Source: Doob and Roberts, 1984

time the Canadian public have felt that punishments were not severe
enough, especially for violent crimes. On the other hand, alternatives to prison were sought, 70 per cent agreeing that we should
explore other sanctions rather than build more prisons. The public,
in other words, are not punitive at all costs. As Hough et al. showed,
individual beliefs are imbued with misconceptions which fuel the
public's apparent punitiveness. Doob and Roberts (1988) found that
74 per cent overestimated how many crimes involved violence, 45
per cent seriously overestimated first offender recidivism, and 63
per cent said they were thinking of violent and repeat offenders
when saying that sentences were too lenient. Moreover, when asked
about alternative methods of controlling crime, the preferred ways
involved reducing employment, increasing social programmes and
increasing the use of non-custodial sentences, not building more
prisons.

Perhaps more importantly these authors show that there is
systematic neglect by newspapers of the reasons given by judges
for particular sentences. Newspapers create an image of judicial
leniency. When given more information – like, for example, court
documents – people are much more likely to agree that the actual
sentence meted out in a particular case was appropriate. In one
instance, after reading 2800 words in a newspaper about a particular case, a majority of one group of subjects (63 per cent) thought
the sentence too lenient (see table 11.2). After seeing court-based
information, 52 per cent of a different group of subjects thought
the sentence too harsh, a view subsequently supported by the Court
of Appeal. Indermauer's (1987) study in Western Australia also
indicates the importance of providing background characteristics
and details, if the public is to understand and approve of particular sentences. The interview studies of Blum-West (1985) indicate
why these findings should be as they are. When respondents were

asked to rate the seriousness of different crimes, they had a very stereotyped and serious instance in mind. When asked to decide those factors that would increase or decrease severity, they mentioned motive and circumstances as being important, the very factors that newspapers omit in their partial accounts of the sentencing decision.

Walker et al. (1988) confirm that in Australia, alternatives to imprisonment were welcomed by many respondents, a theme developed by McClelland and Alpert (1985). The latter found that probation was regarded as more akin to prison than a fine, a point noted by Frost and Stephenson (1989) in their study of views concerning electronic tagging. Tagging was highly regarded because it provided an acceptable alternative to imprisonment, especially in those cases where prisoners were on remand awaiting trial. Their experimental study indicated that if the public had its way, the introduction of tagging would result in reduced use of prison.

It seems clear that misinformation about the actual severity of judicial sentencing is a key factor in the apparent desire of the public for harsher sentences. Stalans and Diamond (1990) noted that although believing sentences for burglary are too lenient, their well-chosen sample of adults and jurors estimated the length of sentence to be substantially less than the minimum actually required in the state (Illinois) in question! However, what interested the investigators particularly was the possibility that overestimations of the severity of the typical burglary was associated with views of judicial leniency, a view that was substantially confirmed using both survey and experimental methods.

Conclusions

Thomas (1979) makes a simplifying distinction between just two competing models of sentencing. One emphasizes Equality as its guiding principle, the focus being on retribution and 'just deserts', or payment for misdeeds. This model suggests the appropriateness of a tariff, or recommended sentence for different offences. The second model emphasizes Variation according to individualized needs rather than an estimate of the severity of offence. This approach, which may be said to derive from Jeremy Bentham's utilitarian views, regards punishment as essentially an evil which can only be condoned when benefits can be demonstrated which outweigh the harm created (Bentham, 1879; Fletcher, 1978).

We have seen strong elements of both Equality and Variation in the sentencing policy of judges, and in the advice from the public, but overlaid with a pragmatic respect for what might be termed Criminal Appropriateness. Judicial practices vary from one jurisdiction and courtroom to another, but there is a consensus of findings endorsing the view that judges do have a hard core of Equalitarian respect for the severity of crime. This is incorporated as a key element in the construction of a typology of the offender that will lead to either a Criminal-appropriate, or Non-criminal-appropriate sentencing disposal. Other courtroom personnel – the police, the attorneys, and particularly the probation officer – play key roles in this process.

The public may also play its part, especially in well-publicized cases when judges may have an eye to the outpourings of media criticism that an apparently wayward sentence may occasion. The work on public attitudes that I have reviewed could well encourage judges in their Variation from the expected. For one thing, people differ quite markedly in their views, so that the response to judicial decisions is unlikely to be uniform. More importantly, the finding that offender, victim and sentencer characteristics all influence sentencing recommendations indicates an openness to deviation from Equality than can be safely indulged in the context of a coherent portrayal of the individual circumstances of the case. The finding that overestimation of the seriousness of the typical case coming up for judgement plays a key role in the public's concern about judicial leniency, and that insufficient information is given by news media to justify many judgements of the courts, should encourage judges, and magistrates to be more open and explicit about the reasons for their sentencing decisions. Most importantly, the results of many studies indicate that the development of coherent sentencing policies providing for more consistently humane treatment of offenders would most likely be welcomed by a frequently bemused and baffled public.

12

Procedure and the Distribution of Criminal Justice

Introduction: principles of justice outlined

Forensic social psychologists have normally distinguished between perceptions of *procedural* justice and distributive justice. 'Did I get a fair hearing?' and 'Was the sentence *deserved*?' are questions which respectively epitomize these two areas of concern.

Leventhal et al. (1980) endorse the view that a clear distinction should be made between procedural justice or 'the procedural systems that regulate the distribution of rewards and resources' (p. 169) and the distributive justice of the allocations of rewards generated by the procedures. Procedural and distributive issues are viewed as distinct but related features of organizational and social life generally. Any institution – a university or an industrial organization as well as the legal system – may be evaluated in terms of the justice of its procedural and distributive mechanisms for allocating rewards.

Principles of distributive justice were at issue in our discussion of sentencing. Three principles of distributive justice have been recognized by social psychologists as determinants of expectations in social exchanges. There is an *equality* rule which in relation to criminal justice suggests that those committing the same offence should be tested similarly. On the other hand the *contributions* rule suggests that individuals should be judged according to the extent of their personal responsibility for committing the crime in question. Yet another rule – that of *needs* – suggests that people should be punished in whatever way will lead to their reformation. Reconciling the conflicting implications of these rules is, as we have seen, a key issue in the sentencing of offenders.

In this chapter we focus mainly on questions of procedural justice. Leventhal et al. (1980) delineate five procedural concerns that characterize members of organizations. In particular, procedures should be (a) consistently applied to different individuals consistently over time. Decision-makers should be (b) unbiased, eschewing self-interest, and their judgements should be based on the (c) best available accurate information, Judgements should be (d) correctable, so that dubious decisions may readily be reviewed and if necessary reversed. The fifth and final procedural rule is that of (e) representativeness, and dictates that procedures at all stages must 'take into account the concerns and viewpoints of important individuals and subgroups in the population affected' (Leventhal et al., 1980, p. 196).

A brief review of the preceding chapters indicates that at every stage the psychology of criminal justice raises questions about the application of one or more of these principles. Conventional division of society into the criminal few and the law-abiding majority makes little psychological sense, a fact which exacerbates the arbitrary decision-making processes involved in the selection of suspects for criminal processing by victims, witnesses, police and prosecutors. Consistency is not a hallmark of the criminal justice system. Bias itself contributes to inconsistency, it being difficult if not impossible for decision-makers to remain uninfluenced by political, social and personal pressures and performances. Bias also undermines the requirement that the best available accurate information should inform decisions although it has also to be said that organizational and administrational inefficiencies hamper the activities of the police, defence, prosecutors and courts alike. Nor should one omit to mention that whatever the quality of the information presented to them, juries will not make consistent use of it.

Juries' decisions are, of course, notoriously uncorrectable, a structural fault that will surely be addressed by the Royal Commission that is presently examining our criminal justice system. As to representativeness, the conservatism that pervades all aspects of the formal processes of law has been amply demonstrated and is in any case too evident from daily newspaper reports for there to be any complacency on that score.

Against the background of our knowledge of decision-making in the criminal justice system, the main question raised at this point concerns the possibility that our system of criminal justice may be structurally flawed by virtue of its reliance on the adversarial system of combat between opposed parties. What psychological evidence is there on this issue? Can it be that we have much to learn from continental inquisitorial procedures? It is commonly asserted that the adversarial aim to win one's case is pursued at the expense of truth. Inquisitorial systems, it is said, aim to discover the truth, and directly discourage partisan distortions of reality. Alternatively it might be argued that the inherent conflict between prosecutors and defence and the intrinsic problems with ever knowing what truly happened in any case, means that differences in the quality of outcomes between different formal systems are likely to be more apparent than real.

I want first to review work on procedural justice which has directly addressed questions about what form of hearing or procedure people prefer. Are there formal aspects of a procedure that consistently influence judgements of fairness? How does the adversarial procedure stand in comparison with an inquisitorial form? What are the main components of procedural fairness? Then I wish to review studies which have explicitly drawn attention to problems of injustices, both procedural and distributive, in our criminal legal system, and finally I shall evaluate broadly the findings conveyed in the previous chapters in the light of expectations derived from accepted principles of fair procedure and social justice.

The adversarial system and theories of procedure

The determination of legal disputes by contest is seemingly enough called the adversarial system – sometimes the 'accusatorial' system – and is frequently contrasted with the so-called inquisitorial system, more typical of continental and Latin countries. In France, for example, the *juge d'instruction* is said largely to displace the advocates from centre stage (Clapham, 1981). From the outset, the *juge* takes over the role of examining witnesses, calling for evidence from police and whatever experts he or she chooses. The *juge* determines the 'facts' of the case, and decides what cases should go to trial, recording the steps taken and conclusions reached in a 'dossier' which, if the case is proceeded with, will dominate the trial and largely determine its outcome.

By way of contrast, in the adversarial system, 'The parties and their attorneys are . . . attitudinally and ethically committed to winning the contest rather than to some other goal, such as discovery of truth or fairness to the opposing side' (Goodpaster, 1987, p. 120). It follows that distortion of the truth is an unavoidable motive of the parties and their representatives. As Goodpaster, again puts it: 'This [adversary] process takes the general form of a dramatic contest aimed at shaping two mutually inconsistent interpretations of common data' (p. 120). The obvious temptation is for both sides to construct their cases by as cunning a selection and persuasive presentation of the facts as the constraints of legal procedure permit, in the context of as wholesale an attack on the veracity, motives and plausibility of the opposition as the trial judge will tolerate. Witnesses are victims of this frequently fascinating and sometimes spectacular contest.

It is not surprising that victims of crimes who, like witnesses, potentially face cross-examination in court, are frequently reluctant to press charges. Nor is it surprising that in general members of the public shun involvement in legal proceedings. After all, lawyers win cases by destroying the credibility of witnesses in the interests of establishing their preferred version of events. So far as I know, no studies have been carried out that compare the attitudes of citizens from countries espousing contrasting systems of criminal justice towards participation in courtroom proceedings. Such studies would be valuable. In the meantime, there have been extensive studies of laboratory simulations of contrasting procedures which have yielded provocative results. To these we now turn.

A theory of procedure: conflicts of interest and conflicts of truth

John Thibaut and Laurens Walker's book *Procedural Justice* (1975), has dominated subsequent discussion by psychologists of the merits of the adversary system. Their theory was later re-stated more explicitly in Thibaut and Walker (1978), and it is the later account that provides the basis for this discussion. The theory seeks to match types of dispute with procedural type. According to Thibaut and Walker, there are two main types of dispute: of 'Truth' and 'Justice' (see table 12.1). For example in scientific conflict, issues of truth are said to predominate. Essentially, the conflict is cognitive

Table 12.1 Types of dispute

		Conflict of Interest	
		Low	High
Cognitive Conflict	Low		'JUSTICE'
	High	'TRUTH'	['MIXED']

Source: After Thibaut and Walker, 1978

Table 12.2 Role of decision-maker in two procedural models

Trial Stage/Procedural System	Adversarial	Inquisitorial
I Development of issues	In the hands of the Parties/Decision-maker passive	Decision-maker active
II Investigation and Presentation of evidence	In the hands of the Parties/Decision-maker passive	Decision-maker active
III Determing outcomes	Decision-maker active	Decision-maker active

and will be decided by 'facts'. Conflicts of interest, on the other hand, predominate in Justice disputes, as in a civil trial where damages are claimed, or in a criminal court trial where punishment is demanded in return for harm done. The investigations of certain tribunals, where facts are determined in order to determine the outcome of a conflict of interest, are said to be of a 'mixed' character.

Table 12.2 portrays the two main procedural systems in legal trials, the principal difference being in the role played by the decision-maker. In the adversarial system, 'process control' is in the hands of the disputants themselves or of their representatives. They develop the issues and present the evidence. The decision-maker (the judge, or jury) is relatively inactive throughout this stage. In inquisitorial systems, on the other hand, the judge is active and directs proceedings in an 'authoritarian' way. Under both systems, however, the decision-maker is active in the final decision-making stage, when blame is attributed or the truth determined. In the view of Thibaut and Walker, civil and criminal disputes are predominantly justice disputes, for which the adversary system is preferable to the inquisitorial.

The evidence for this conclusion came largely from laboratory experiments, in which subjects expressed a preference for one procedure or another, or took roles in simulations of (civil) dispute resolution using different procedures. Clients of an adversarial system were more satisfied with verdicts, and rated the procedure as more fair, regardless of whether the verdict was advantageous to them personally. This was true not only of Americans, but also of French and other nationalities. In addition, the adversary system was shown, experimentally, to reduce the effects of 'expectancy bias' in decision-makers, whose prior opinions were more likely to change under the influence of arguments and views expressed in adversarial exchanges. The one seemingly negative finding is that although adversarial lawyers accumulate more of the available facts when their case is weak, they are less conscientious than they might be when they have a seemingly strong case. Self-serving lawyers apart, the adversarial system comes out tops.

There are reasons to believe that these conclusions are heavily influenced by the experimental laboratory materials and methods used in the authors' simulations. The legal issues studied were predominantly civil disputes in which the 'facts' themselves (e.g. the damage or nuisance caused) were not in dispute: what was contested was the legitimacy of the claims (conflicts of interests) arising from those facts. To be denied 'voice' in a pure conflict of interest must, indeed, be exceedingly frustrating. In practice, inquisitors may be less unrelenting than role-playing inquisitors following the experimenter's strict instructions.

More importantly criminal trials are essentially, and sometimes largely concerned with issues of truth, as well as conflicts of interest. At the stage of sentencing, the interests of the convict and society respectively are carefully weighed, and the degree of blameworthiness is assessed. The jury's prior task, however, is to determine where the truth lies and to assess the evidence in relation to the competing claims of two theories – not altogether unlike the evaluation of competing scientific claims, as it happens.

One compelling criticism of trial by jury is that in cases where evidence is complex, we can never be sure that evidence has been properly understood and appropriately evaluated because the jury has to give no account of its reasoning. As we saw in chapter 6, the assessment of blameworthiness is properly preceded by the attribution of cause and responsibility. The criminal trial inherently combines cognitive conflicts and conflicts of interest, and Thibaut and Walker (1978) admit that it is inappropriate to imagine that such mixed disputes are best adjudicated using merely one procedure. The tradition of research which has competitively evaluated so-called adversarial and inquisitorial forms of justice has demonstrated that observers and participants in mock proceedings condemn a procedure which denies them a voice, and which is thereby demonstrably unfair (see Lind et al., 1990). It has, however, contributed little or nothing to our evaluation of the relative advantages of legal systems conventionally said to incorporate adversarial or inquisitorial principles, as in comparisons say, between the respective merits of the English and French systems. Nor has it examined what actually happens in real-life adversarial systems.

The adversarial system in practice

In the wake of recently exposed serious miscarriages of justice in England, a Royal Commission has been established to examine critically the workings of the English adversarial criminal justice system. Ludovic Kennedy's (1964) view that, 'The tragedy of our courts is that means have come to count more than ends, form more than content, appearance more than reality' (p. 251), is now more frequently echoed in the press and within the legal profession, and an evaluation of the psychological evidence on the relative merits of the two systems is timely. Perhaps for too long the doubts and mixed feelings that many participants have experienced have been suppressed in the false hope that if ignored the faults will vanish and the merits of the adversarial system dazzle the beholder. Goodpaster (1987), for example, whilst admitting the doubts that exist, unashamedly states that the 'aim of this article is to articulate, elaborate and explore theories of American adversary criminal trial, *ultimately making the best case for our system*' (p. 118) [my italics]. Faults are excused primarily in the belief that the adversarial system defends the liberty of the citizen against 'the inevitable oppressive tendencies of government and official decision-making' (p. 153).

McConville and Baldwin (1981), on the other hand, argue that the whole process is fundamentally or structurally flawed, not because the process of trial is a sham, but because of what precedes the trial, or of what substitutes for the trial. Justice, they state, is largely *negotiated* in the interests more of the representatives and of the legal system than of the lawyers' clients. Let us see how they arrive at this conclusion.

In the great majority of prosecutions for criminal offences, suspects plead guilty. There is no trial in over 80 per cent of cases, and the appearance at court is merely to determine what sentence should be imposed on the supposedly contrite offender. Even in those cases which do lead to an appearance in court, deals may be struck by a process of plea bargaining which deprive both offender and victim of the opportunity to test their stories in a formal trial.

We are not concerned here with inadequacies in the adversary system arising from selective investigation and other malpractices by the police, which may lead to false confessions, or cynical decisions to plead Guilty because it is felt that, for whatever reason, there is no point in registering a plea of Not Guilty, a negative outcome to the trial being seen as a foregone conclusion. We are concerned more with those cases where the relationships between opposing lawyers and between lawyers and others within the criminal justice system lead to pressure being put on suspects to plead Guilty regardless of their feeling and preferences. In return for a Guilty plea, in the process called plea bargaining, the charges may be reduced in severity, and some promise given of lenient treatment in sentencing following discussions between respective lawyers and the presiding judge. In their book, *Negotiated Justice: pressures to plead guilty*, Baldwin and McConville (1977) documented such practices in the Birmingham Crown Court, and the authors came in for much opprobrium for so doing. Plea bargaining, openly acknowledged in the United States, was at the time commonly disavowed in England by many judges.

Baldwin and McConville demonstrated that there was a substantial number of defendants who changed their plea from Not Guilty to Guilty at the last minute before their trial was due to commence. Many reported that considerable pressure had been exerted on them by their lawyers who had emphasized in discussion with them that receiving a predictably lenient sentence without a trial was preferable to risking a likely heavier sentence at the conclusion of an expensive trial, whatever the chances might be of escaping conviction. The promises made were probably redeemed. Sentences imposed on matched defendants who either pleaded Guilty, Not Guilty or changed their plea from Not Guilty to Guilty, showed that late plea-changers were most favourably treated, and those who exercised their right to be regarded as Not Guilty until proven otherwise, paid heavily for their audacity.

A recent study (McLaughlin, 1990) indicates that plea bargaining may occur also in the magistrates' courts in England. He studied the role of Clerks to the Court. Their influence is decisive in many cases and their activities largely secretive. They negotiate changes in plea before cases are heard, and they influence magistrates' decision-making in private during the trial. In doing this they rely on the personal relationship and position of influence they have established with magistrates since the magistrate first received training, usually from the very same Clerks who continue to advise, and influence them.

There are strong parallels in other organized settings. Stephenson (1981) documented the tendency in industrial relations at plant level for chief negotiators on opposing sides to develop strong interpersonal bonds that enabled them to 'manage' the intergroup conflict satisfactorily at a public level without detriment to their continuing relationship. So it seems to be with relations between lawyers. McConville and Baldwin (1981) write as follows:

> By delivering a guilty plea, defence lawyers can cultivate good relations with the prosecutor (thereby facilitating long-term access to helpful information), increase their credibility with both prosecutor and judge (thereby strengthening their hand in the occasional contested case), and benefit financially from a rapid turnover of cases. The co-operative norms may be informal, but they may be enforced as effectively as any formal rules. Even the radical lawyer may find it extremely difficult not to be co-opted into this informal system, for an unwillingness to settle cases outside the courtroom with the prosecution and judge will render much of his work ineffective and result only in his clients being penalized. (p. 194)

Behind the facade and beneath the rhetoric of the vaunted adversary system lies an informal system of relationships and dealings in which those lawyers who do not co-operate are isolated and their clients disadvantaged. Clients find it baffling, but feel

234   *Procedure and the Distribution of Justice*

they have no choice but to comply. Ross (1980) in much the same way, but in a quite different context, distinguishes between 'tort law in action' and 'formal law', the former being 'more simple, liberal and inequitable' (p. 237). For example, when bodily injury is sustained in a motor accident, formal law prescribes that one or other is to blame. In practice, a negotiated sum is paid which relieves parties of the burden (and risk) of going to court where, after all, they might lose everything.

The crime of murder incites great public interest and plea bargaining in cases of murder is especially likely to evoke comment. In the United States there are degrees of murder. This invites plea bargaining, as does our distinction between murder and manslaughter. Pritchard (1986) argues that the tendency to engage in plea bargaining in homicide cases is essentially a *political* process, in which the prosecutor's perception of self-interest is paramount in their thinking, not the pursuit of justice. One principal factor affecting the prosecutor's judgement is the amount of public interest in a case. The greater the public interest, the more likely it is that there will be a public trial, principally because the prosecutor is under greater pressure to justify a decision not to proceed. Pritchard demonstrated this by showing that the amount of space given in newspapers reporting the murder was highly predictive of a case going to trial. Of course, other factors also influenced the decision to initiate plea bargaining: the acquaintance with the victim (more likely if suspect and victim had been acquainted); the suspect's prior record (less likely to negotiate if there is a record); and the initial charge (negotiations being less likely when charges were more serious). In all, 30 per cent of the variance was accounted for by these factors.

Alternatives to adversarial trial

Alternatives to conventional trial have been proposed which maintain an adversarial framework but which emphasize negotiation between the parties. It is not always profitable to make a sharp distinction between negotiations between two parties in dispute and quasi-judicial processes of mediation in which the mediator plays the role of catalyst of the negotiation rather than decision-maker in his or her own right (Morley and Stephenson, 1977; Morley et al., 1988). Mediation has been tried with success in certain civil disputes, for example disputes over child custody where the counsellor or mediator facilitates but does not impose an agreement (Zarski et al., 1985). The use of this technique is less pervasive in criminal disputes, although there are precedents in other cultures. Brown (1990) describes the interaction that took place in a Mexican community court that deliberately fostered a naturalistic and highly expressive exchange between contending parties alleging theft and/ or dishonesty. It seemed that the opportunity to give vent to feelings not normally expressed in polite society was welcomed by the protagonists, and served as a prelude to a mediated settlement that formed the basis of a written agreement that is legally binding.

Baskin and Sommers (1990) describe an evaluation of community-based mediation in the United States. State-planned mediation relies heavily on models of the courtroom trial, and the interaction is concentrated on evidence regarding past behaviour. By way of contrast, community-based mediation aims to give authority to the community itself, with the aim of improving future relationships not only between the contending parties but in relation to broader social changes. Although it seemed that the community-based model successfully shed the trappings and backward-looking ('evidence') orientation of traditional courtroom models, it was still the case that protagonists viewed the exercise as essentially a more socially acceptable extension of conventional courtroom practice. The advantages of the community-based model are clear in the case of the relatively trivial incidents that would otherwise have been the basis of criminal prosecutions. Indeed, avoiding the stigma of criminality was a foremost motive for co-operation in the project by potential suspects. The emphasis was securely placed by mediators on the future relationship, or 'neighbouring':

> Let's forget, right now, about the specifics in the past. You might just have to live with it. We have established that you have problems. We have to eliminate negative statements towards each other. That gets to be a habit. Defining each other in legal terms in not productive. You're neighbours and you don't have to be friends. But, you can be good neighbours.' (Baskin and Sommers, 1990, p. 264)

Contest or inquisition

Calls for change in this country from an adversarial to an inquisitorial system have been prompted by scandalous miscarriages of

justice. Unfortunately, little comparative research has been conducted which might facilitate an informed judgement about the
relative merits of so-called inquisitorial and adversarial systems.
The evidence reviewed in this book points to weaknesses at many
junctures in the criminal justice process, but many of these – the
unreliability of eye-witness testimony, hostile relations between
police and ethnic minorities, judicial biases and so on – are likely
to characterize both adversarial and inquisitorial systems. In practice, the social and political context of criminal investigation makes
such demands that different systems – whether adversarial or
inquisitorial – may well operate along very similar lines. Indeed,
Zuckerman (1991) in a review of police investigative procedures
in several European countries, suggests that differences in the role
played by the police in different systems are more apparent than
real. For example, the *juge d'instruction* in France is apparently apt
to delegate his or her powers to the police, and to accord great
weight to the police evidence when conducting his or her own
examination.

There is, nevertheless, a particular area of concern that is confined
to the English (and related) systems concerning the possible rami-
fications of jury decision-making on police practices. Zuckerman
(1991) asserts that it is faulty police performance that insistently
undermines our system of criminal justice. He suggests that improving police practice by closer monitoring and re-investigation
procedures is necessary because of the cognitive difficulties faced
by the police in constructing 'the truth' of what happened. The
practicality of his suggestions is a less important drawback to his
views than is the possibility that low standards of police performance are in large part determined not by cognitive failures but by
the need of police officers to render the outcomes of their labours
more predictable and acceptable given what they believe to be the
truth of the matter.

It may be that in Holland, for example, where a panel of three
judges delivers a verdict, the likelihood of obtaining a conviction
is no higher than it is in this country under the jury system. In
Holland, however, the judges have publicly to defend their verdicts,
whether of acquittal or conviction. Juries here have no such obligation. Moreover, as we have seen, although the conviction rate
may be moderately high, the question of who gets acquitted is an
extremely unpredictable affair.

We routinely impose on juries a task that is inappropriately

Table 12.3 Control and group-value models of procedural justice

Control Model (Thibaut and Walker, 1975)	Group-Value Model (Lind and Tyler, 1988)
Focus on short-term influence over Third Party	Focus on long-term relationship with legal authorities.
via Control over the process of Dispute Resolution	*via* Neutrality of decision-making procedure. Trust in third-party. Evidence of social standing.

undertaken by large teams, and the performance of which is not monitored and cannot ultimately be rationally evaluated. There may be good reasons for not abolishing the jury system, but I can think of no good reason for not reforming it.

The paramount importance of procedural fairness in law

Recent investigators have moved away from the comparison of ideal procedural types to examine directly the importance of procedural fairness in citizens' evaluations of their criminal justice system. Lind and Tyler (1988) propose what they call a Group Value model of procedural fairness which they contrast with the 'Control' model of Thibaut and Walker (see table 12.3). The Group Value model emphasizes the importance to individuals of their long-term relationship with legal authorities, in contrast to the short-term resolution of a particular dispute. Whereas Thibaut and Walker (1975) stressed influence and power over procedure, Lind and Tyler (1988) stress the symbolic relationship to the legal authorities, asking such questions as: Do the authorities show no bias? Do I trust them to do a good conscientious job? Do they treat me respectfully?

Tyler (1989) reports a test of these two models in a study of 652 Chicago citizens' encounters with the police and with the courts. Reports on appearances in court (22 per cent), of calls to the police for help (47 per cent), and on being stopped by the police (31 per cent) constituted the raw data. Independent variables were: Outcome Favourability; Control; Neutrality; Trust, and Standing. Neutrality, Trust and Standing were combined in a composite measure

Table 12.4 Variance unique to group-value, control and outcome variables in citizens' ratings of their encounters with the criminal justice system

	Aspects of Criminal Justice System Encounters			
	Procedural Justice in the encounter	Distributive Justice of particular outcome	Liking of Authorities dealt with	Beliefs about Justice of Authorities
Outcome Favourability	1	16	2	3
Control	1	0	1	0
Group-Value Variables	22	20	19	8

Note: High value = greater importance
Source: After Tyler, 1989

of Group Value for purposes of analysis. Dependent variables were Procedural Justice (ratings of fairness), Distributive Justice (had they got what they deserved?), Feelings towards the authorities (angry, frustrated or pleased) and Belief about Justice of the Authorities (in the past and in the future).

The results are portrayed in table 12.4. Group-Value variables were overwhelmingly important in ratings of procedural justice, less so in ratings of distributive justice and the other dependent variables where the outcome assumes more importance. Of the different components of Group Value, Trust and Group Standing were most consistently important, and minority group members placed consistently more stress on Group Standing than did whites. In all, the results indicate that in everyday encounters with the police and the courts, it is not so much influence and control, or even so much the actual decision taken by the authority that determines our satisfaction with the authorities, but the manner in which the encounter is handled: how unbiased, trustworthy and respectful the authorities were.

Tyler's study analysed reports by citizens of their experiences with the courts, and the police, but the majority of encounters involved the police. Other studies of wholly courtroom experiences have demonstrated how important it is that citizens actually judge the procedures to be fair, if they are to respect the court and the judges (Tyler, 1984). Yet other studies have also shown that general satisfaction may be directly affected in a similar way. Lind and Tyler (1988) for example, report the result of a study in which those whose cases had been sent to arbitration were asked about procedural fairness and their satisfaction with the outcome. Those who lost their cases were distinctly less dissatisfied when the procedures were thought to be 'fair'.

The distribution of criminal justice

The rehabilitative ideal has given way to the justice model as the predominant philosophy governing reform and change of the criminal justice system, and psychological scaling techniques are being applied to the thorny problems of ensuring that offence gravity becomes the central sentencing consideration (Pease, 1987, p. 41). Equality not needs determine what individuals are said to deserve when they have broken the law. Blameworthiness and harm done are to be assessed by objective standards, and punishments scaled accordingly. As Clarkson and Keating (1984) put it, 'blame plus harm equals criminal liability' (p. 576). How appropriate is this emphasis on 'deserved' punishment?

Cavender (1984) cogently criticizes the exclusive emphasis on retribution in sentencing. His main point is that abstract ideals of justice cannot be fairly applied without modification. We do not live in a society which is just, and our society falls short of those ideals of social organization that philosophers see as fundamental in a 'just' society, and as providing the moral basis for equal treatment. In practice, social disadvantage and injustice prevail. Proponents of the justice model fail to take such inequalities into account. As Cavender states, 'they avoid the fundamental issue of social justice within a social structure that generates inequality, and at the same time discard analyses that address these issues' (p. 212).

We have highlighted many social psychological processes that reinforce the socially divisive effects of a retributive policy. A crime becomes labelled as such by a tortuous decision-making process including the perpetrator, the victim, friends and relatives, the police, the lawyers and courts. At all points, stereotypes serve to ensure that 'hopeless criminal' cases are processed further whilst the 'respectable and respectful' are given the benefit of the doubt. The system operates, in other words, to confirm the socially successful in their respectability and the social failures in their criminality.

Of course, the system is not uniformly unresponsive to contributions and needs in its determination of justice. The work of Hilary Allen demonstrated that frequently great attention is paid to understanding the circumstances which lead women into criminality, and to re-directing them away from the criminal justice system and into the rather more sympathetic embrace of the medical and psychiatric services. The acknowledged use of various 'defences' in law – like that of duress – and the creation of distinct criminal acts that show special understanding of circumstances – like infanticide – recognize that there are occasions when there may be legitimate reasons for acting illegally. At present, however, the courts are strictly limited in the extent to which contextual factors can formally be taken into account. The number of special defences and of sub-categories of crime which acknowledge mitigating circumstances is small.

Despite today's dogmatic emphasis on retributive principles, recognition that two individuals may intentionally offend in similar ways, but be held to differ in blameworthiness (see chapter 6), sets the stage for reform of a system whose consequences are presently incompatible with principles of social justice. Biases in the process of selection of candidates for full criminal justice processing, from initial apprehension to conviction and sentencing, means that it is those whose criminal behaviour is most clearly excusable who are given the 'full treatment'. In logic, as Norrie (1986) points out, there is good reason to include a broad range of contextual factors in the operation of criminal justice. Commenting on the significance of the acceptable defence of 'duress', he states:

> once the significance of the context of reasoning is acknowledged in one situation, how is the law to distinguish between a context of threats, and a context of, say, bad social conditions, inadequate housing and education, unemployment, police harassment, and so on? Such conditions form the context for the bulk of crime, and the individual acting and reasoning within it is as irresponsible for the social environment as is the compelled individual for the threats imposed upon him or her. (p. 223).

Allen (1988) asks whether or not women will benefit in the long run by being treated less personally responsible for their criminal behaviour than men. She thinks not, but is inclined to the view that the practical answer to the problem of inequality is not to treat women less compassionately, but men more so (see also Allen, 1987). Inequality of treatment is camouflaged at all stages of decision-making in the criminal justice system. Allen (1987) brings to the fore the role of 'psychiatrization' in the sentencing process which, of course, may operate to protect social categories other than the female gender from harsher penalties. But at all stages – via the exercise of persuasive power by the offender, the timidity of victims, the discretion of police officers, the role of plea bargaining and the prejudice or incompetence of juries – a sifting process ensures that convicts may well perceive themselves to be deserving of sympathy.

Psychological research and criminal justice

Psychological research is used directly in two ways in the United States to influence the course of criminal justice. First, psychologists frequently testify in criminal trials as experts employed by one of the adversaries. Some of the problems that arise in this area were discussed in chapter 9 in the discussion of eyewitness testimony, the area in which psychologists are most frequently asked to testify (McCloskey et al., 1986). Second, appropriate bodies like the American Psychological Association have become involved in the presentation of evidence to the courts regarding the effect of procedural practices in criminal trials. The increasing rate of submission of *amicus curiae* or 'friends of the court' briefs by psychologists and psychological associations is described fully by Roesch et al. (1991). Acker (1990) suggests that psychologists should offer their services more systematically. The uninformed use of social science by Justices is extensive, and the potential contribution of psychologists is considerable, should they seek to take advantage of the available opportunities.

Not all commentators are enthusiastic about psychology's advisory contribution. One currently contentious issue concerns the alleged conviction proneness of 'death qualified' jurors, i.e. jurors selected because they have no principled objections to use of the death penalty in capital cases. Elliott (1991) criticizes the American Psychological Association's *amicus* brief in that instance because, he states, it was not constructed impartially and hence distorts the available evidence. Moreover, he suggests that the demands of adversarial justice make impartiality impossible and recommends that psychologists be reticent in future.

Elliott's views highlight the difficulties faced by psychologists who seek to establish more rational procedures – e.g. of questioning witnesses and of establishing facts – in the context of an assumed supremacy of the adversarial system. Suggested procedural changes will be challenged because they contravene established adversarial principles. One good example is the delay, seen both in the USA and in England, in creating an acceptable basis for the (non-adversarial) questioning of child witnesses, especially in cases of alleged sexual abuse, an issue discussed in chapter 5.

Far from recommending reticence, Rosen (1990) asks psychologists to question the right of lawyers to limit the scope of psychological research. He asserts that psychology's problem in this area has been its acceptance of the assumption that the law and legal decision-making should operate in a cultural vacuum, 'autonomously'. He takes as his starting point the contribution of psychologists to the question of media influences on legal decision-making. For example, Kassin (1984) suggested that the presence of cameras in the courtroom might adversely affect recall of witnesses, at least of those people who are sensitive to their public image, whereas Borgida et al. (1990) obtained data which suggested that cameras were no more detrimental than the presence of reporters; Greene (1990) reviewed evidence that wide publicity may affect the outcome of trials, and so on. Rosen, whilst accepting the worthiness of such research, regards it nevertheless as missing out an analysis of the possible benefits of publicity and, more importantly, as mistaken in its view that the law should operate autonomously, uninfluenced by cultural changes and insights: it is not psychology's job to sustain the independence of the law, rather, it should 'articulate and criticize the law's role in our social and cultural life.' (Rosen, 1990, p. 521).

The implication of this is that psychology should use its methodologies, theories and findings, to confront rather than merely reinforce established practice. Psychologists have traditionally taken for granted that contributing to the gradual improvement of existing procedures, structures and outcomes is the most it can aspire to, leaving quite unchallenged the 'autonomy' of the law. As this book has revealed, at each stage of criminal processing findings have been accumulated that seriously challenge conventional views and assumptions about the propriety of the system. This knowledge should be used to fuel critical evaluation of the law's activities.

References

Abramson, L Y, Seligman, M E P and Teasdale, J D (1978) Learned help-lessness in humans: critique and reformulation. *Journal of Abnormal Psychology*, 87, 49–74.

Acker, J R (1990) Social science in supreme court criminal cases and briefs: the actual and potential contribution of social scientists as amici curiae. *Law and Human Behavior*, 14, 25–42.

Adelson, J and O'Neil, R P (1966) Growth of political ideas in adolescence: the sense of community. *Journal of Personality and Social Psychology*, 4, 295–306.

Adler, F (1975) *Sisters in Crime: the rise of the new female criminal*. New York: McGraw Hill.

Agnew, R (1990) Adolescent resources and delinquency. *Criminology*, 28, 535–64.

Ajzen, I & Madden, T J (1986) Prediction of goal directed behaviour: attitudes, intentions and perceived behavioural control. *Journal of Experimental Social Psychology*, 22, 453–74.

Alicke, M D and Davis, T L (1989) The role of *a posteriori* victim information in judgements of blame and sanction. *Journal of Experimental Social Psychology*, 25, 362–77.

Allen, H (1987) *Justice Unbalanced: gender, psychiatry and judicial decisions*. Milton Keynes: Open University Press.

Allen, H (1988) One law for all reasonable persons? *International Journal of the Sociology of Law*, 16, 419–32.

Allen, H (1989) Fines for women: paradoxes and paradigms. In P Carlen and D Cook (eds) *Paying for Crime*, Milton Keynes: Open University Press.

American Psychiatric Association (1987) *Diagnostic and Statistical Manual of Mental Disorders*. Washington D. C.

Anderson, C A (1987) Temperature and aggression: effects on quarterly, yearly and city rates of violent and non-violent crime. *Journal of Personality and Social Psychology*, 52, 1161–73.

Andrews, D A, Robblee, M A, Saunders, R, Huartson, K, Robinson, D, Kiessling, J J and West, D (1987) Some psychometrics of judicial decision making: towards a sentencing factors inventory. *Criminal Justice and Behavior*, 14, 62–79.

Argeriou, M, McCarty, D & Blacker, E (1985) Criminality among individuals arraigned for drinking and driving in Massachusetts. *Journal of Studies on Alcohol*, 46, 525–30.

Aronson, E (1972) *The Social Animal*. San Francisco: Freeman.

Aronsson, K and Nilholm, C (1990) On memory and the collaborative construction and deconstruction of custody case arguments. *Human Communication Research*, 17, 289–314.

Aronsson, K, Jönsson, L and Linell, P (1987) The courtroom hearing as a middle ground: speech accommodation by lawyers and defendants. *Journal of Language and Social Psychology*, 6, 99–115.

Asch, S E (1951) Effects of group pressure upon the modification and distortion of judgements. In H Guetskow (ed.) *Groups, Leadership and Men*, Pittsburgh: Carnegie Press.

Atkinson, M and Drew, P (1979) *Order in Court: the organisation of verbal interaction in judicial settings*. London: Macmillan.

Baldwin, J and McConville, M (1977) *Negotiated Justice: pressures to plead guilty*. London: Martin Robinson.

Baldwin, J and McConville, M (1979) *Jury Trials*. Oxford: Clarendon Press.

Baldwin, J and McConville, M (1980) *Confessions in Crown Court Trials. Research Study No 5 Royal Commission on Criminal Procedure*. London: HMSO.

Bankston, W B, Jenkins, Q A L, Thayes-Doyle, C L and Thompson, C Y (1987) Fear of criminal victimisation and residential location: the influence of perceived risk. *Rural Sociology*, 52, 98–107.

Baskin, D R & Sommers, I (1990) Ideology and Discourse: some differences between state-planned and community-based justice. *Law and Human Behavior*, 14, 249–68.

Beach, W A (1985) Temporal density in courtroom interaction: constraints on the recovery of past events in legal discourse. *Communication Monographs*, 52, 1–18.

Bell, B E and Loftus, E F (1989) Trivial persuasion in the courtroom: the power of (a few) minor details. *Journal of Personality and Social Psychology*, 56, 669–79.

Ben-Ari, R and Amir Y (1988) Intergroup contact, cultural information and change in ethnic attitudes. In W Stroebe, A W Kruglanski, D Bar-Tal, and M Hewstone (eds) *The Social Psychology of Intergroup Conflict*. London: Springer-Verlag, 151–65.

Bennett, T and Wright, R (1984) *Burglars on Burglary: Prevention and the Offender*. Aldershot: Gower.

Bennett, W L & Feldman, M S (1981) *Reconstructing Reality in the Courtroom*. London: Tavistock.

Bentham, J (1879) *Introduction to the Principles of Morals and Legislation*. Oxford: Clarendon Press.

Berger, D E, Snortum, J R, Homel, R J, Hauge, R and Loxley, W (in press) Deterrence and prevention of alcohol-impaired driving in Australia, the United States, and Norway. *Justice Quarterly*.

Berliner, L and Conte, J R (1990) The process of victimisation: the victims perspective. *Child Abuse and Neglect*, 14, 29–40.

Biblarz, A, Barnowe, J T and Biblarz, D N (1984) To tell or not to tell: differences between victims who report crimes and victims who do not. *Victimology: an International Journal*, 9, 153–8.

Black, D (1976) *The Behavior of Law*. London: Academic Press.

Black, D (1983) Crime as social control. *American Sociological Review*, 48, 34–45.

Blackman, D E (1981) On the mental element in crime and behaviourism. In S Lloyd-Bostock (ed.) *Law and Psychology*. Oxford: SSRC Centre for Socio-Legal Studies, pp. 113–25.

Blasi, A (1980) Bridging moral cognition and moral action: a critical review of the literature. *Psychological Bulletin*, 88, 1–45.

Blumstein, A, Farrington, D P and Moitra, S (1985) Delinquency careers: innocents, desisters and persisters. In M Tonry and N Norris (eds) *Crime and Justice: an Annual Review of Research*. University of Chicago Press pp. 187–219.

Blumstein, A, Cohen, I and Farrington, D P (1988) Criminal career research. *Criminology*, 26, 1–35.

Blum-West, S (1985) The seriousness of crime: a study of popular morality. *Deviant Behavior*, 6, 83–98

Boice, R, Hanley, C P, Shaughnessy, P and Gansler, D (1982) Eyewitness accuracy: a general observational skill? *Bulletin of the Psychonomic Society*, 20, 193–5.

Bordens, K S and Horowitz, I A (1985) Joinder of criminal offences: a review of the legal and psychological literature. *Law and Human Behavior*, 9, 339–53.

Borgida, E, DeBono, K G and Buckman, L A (1990) Cameras in the courtroom: the effects of media coverage on witness testimony and juror perceptions. *Law and Human Behavior*, 14, 489–509.

Bowers, J M and Bekerian, D A (1984) When will post event information distort eyewitness testimony? *Journal of Applied Psychology*, 69, 466–72.

Box, S, Hale, C and Andrews, G (1988) Explaining fear of crime. *British Journal of Criminology*, 28, 340–56.

Bradley, G W (1978) Self-serving biases in the attribution process: a re-examination of the fact or fiction question. *Journal of Personality and Social Psychology*, 36, 56–71.

Brantingham, P J and Brantingham, P L (eds) (1981) *Environmental Criminology*. London: Sage.

Brigham, J C and Ready, D J (1985) Own-race bias in lineup construction. *Law and Human Behavior*, 9, 415–24.

Brown, A (1988) *Watching the Detectives*. London: Hodder & Stoughton.

Brown, B B (1985) Residential territories: cues to burglary vulnerability. *Journal of Architectural Planning and Research*, 2, 231–44.

Brown, B B and Altman, I (1983) Territoriality, defensible space and residential burglary: an environmental analysis. *Journal of Environmental Psychology*, 3, 203–20.

Brown, B B and Harris, P B (1989) Residential burglary victimisation: reactions to the invasion of a primary territory. *Journal of Environmental Psychology*, 9, 119–32.

Brown, I D (1975) Drivers' attitudes to the seriousness of road traffic offences considered in relation to the design of sanctions. *Accident Analysis and Prevention*, 7, 15–26.

Brown, P (1990) Gender, politeness, and confrontation in Tenejapa. *Discourse Processes*, 13, 123–41.

Brown, R (1965) *Social Psychology*. New York: Collier-Macmillan.

Brown, R J (1988) *Group Processes*, Ch. 4, Social influence in groups. Oxford: Blackwell, 90–123.

Brown, R and Herrnstein, R J (1975) *Psychology*. London: Methuen.

Brown, S E (1984) Police responses to wife beating: neglect of a crime of violence. *Journal of Criminal Justice*, 12, 277–88.

Budd, R D (1982) The incidence of alcohol use in Los Angeles County Homicide Victims. *American Journal of Alcohol Abuse*, 9, 105–11.

Bull, R and Clifford, B R (1984) Earwitness voice recognition accuracy. In G L Wells and E F Loftus (eds) *Eyewitness Testimony*. Cambridge: Cambridge University Press, 92–123.

Bull, R, Bustin, B, Evans, P and Gahagan, D (1983) *Psychology for Police Officers*. Chichester: Wiley.

Burney, E (1979) *J.P.: Magistrate, Court and Community* London: Hutchinson.

Burt, M (1983) Justifying personal violence: a comparison of rapists and the general public. *Victimology: an International Journal*, 8, 131–50.

Carlen, P (1974) Remedial routines for the maintenance of control in magistrates' courts. *British Journal of Law and Society*, 1, 101–17.

Carlen, P and Cook, D (eds) (1989) *Paying for Crime*. Milton Keynes: Open University Press.

Carroll, J S, Berkowitz, W T, Lurigio, A J and Weaver, F M (1987) Sentencing goals, causal attributions, ideology and personality. *Journal of Personality and Social Psychology*, 52, 107–18.

Cavender, G (1984) Justice, sanctioning and the justice model. *Criminology*, 22, 203–13.

Ceci, S J, Ross, D F and Toglia, M P (1987) Suggestibility of children's testimony: psycholegal implications. *Journal of Experimental Psychology: General*, 116, 38–49.

Central Statistical Office (1986) *Key Data*. London: HMSO.

Clapham, B (1981) Introducing psychological evidence in the courts: impediments and opportunities. In S. Lloyd-Bostock (ed.) *Psychology in Legal Contexts*. London: Macmillan, 95–106.

Clark, N K, Stephenson, G M and Rutter, D R (1986) Memory for a complex social discourse: the analysis and prediction of individual and group recall. *Journal of Memory and Language,* 25, 295–313.

Clarkson, C M V and Keating, H M (1984) *Criminal Law: Text and Materials.* London: Sweet and Maxwell.

Cohen, N (1991) Poor are 'vastly over-represented' in prison system. *The Independent,* 16 December.

Cohen, B-Z, Fishman, G and Soroka, J (1985) Judicial discretion and sentencing disparity in adult felony courts in Israel. *Journal of Criminal Justice,* 13, 99–115.

Cohn, E S and White, S O (1986) Cognitive development versus social learning approaches to studying legal socialization. *Basic and Applied Social Psychology,* 7, 195–209.

Colby, A (1983) A longitudinal study of child development. *Monographs of the Society for Research in Child Development,* 48, 1–124.

Coleman, A (1985) *Utopia on Trial.* London: Hilary Shipman.

Collins, J and Cox, B G (1987) Job activities and personal crime victimisation: implications for theory. *Social Science Research,* 16, 345–60.

Connolly, T (1987) Decision theory, reasonable doubt, and the utility of erroneous acquittals. *Law and Human Behavior,* 11, 101–12.

Conte, J R, Wolf, S and Smith, T (1989) What sexual offenders tell us about prevention: preliminary findings. *Child Abuse and Neglect,* 13, 293–301.

Corbett, C and Simon, F (1991) Police and public perceptions of the seriousness of traffic offences. *British Journal of Criminology,* 31, 153–64.

Corman, H, Joyce, T and Lovitch, N (1987) Crime, deterrence and the business cycle in New York City. *The Review of Economics and Statistics,* 695–700.

Cornish, D B and Clarke, R V (eds) (1986) *The Reasoning Criminal: rational choice perspectives on offending,* Introduction. New York: Springer, 1–16.

Cotton, J L (1986) Ambient temperature and violent crime. *Journal of Applied Social Psychology,* 16, 786–801.

Cox, T C and White, M F (1988) Traffic citations and student attitudes toward the police: an examination of selected interaction dynamics. *Journal of Police Science and Administration,* 16, 105–21.

Critchlow, B (1985) The blame in the bottle: attributions about drunken behaviour. *Personality and Social Psychology Bulletin,* 11, 258–74.

Croyle, J L (1983) Measuring and explaining disparities in felony sentences: courtroom group factors and race, sex, and socioeconomic influences on sentence severity. *Political Behaviour,* 5, 135–53.

Cullen, F T, Mathers, R A, Clark, G A and Cullen, J B (1983) Public support for punishing white-collar crime: blaming the victim re-visited? *Journal of Criminal Justice,* 11, 481–93.

Cusson, M and Pinsonneault, P (1986) The decision to give up crime. In D B Cornish and R V Clarke (eds) *The Reasoning Criminal*, New York: Springer-Verlag, 72–82.

Cutler, B L and Penrod, S D (1989) Moderators of the confidence-accuracy correlation in face recognition: the role of information in processing and base rates. *Applied Cognitive Psychology*, 3, 95–107.

Cutler, B L, Penrod, S D and Dexter H R (1989) The eyewitness, expert psychologist and the jury. *Law and Human Behavior*, 13, 311–32.

Cutler, B L, Penrod, S D and Dexter, H R (1990) Juror sensitivity to identification evidence. *Law and Human Behavior*, 14, 185–91.

Cutler, B L, Penrod, S, O'Rourke, T E and Martens, T K (1986) Unconfounding the effects of contextual cues on eyewitness identification accuracy. *Social Behaviour*, 1, 113–34.

Cutler, B L, Penrod, S D and Martens, T K (1987) Improving the reliability of eyewitness identification: putting context into context. *Journal of Applied Psychology*, 72, 629–37.

Dalby, J T (1985) Criminal liability in children. *Canadian Journal of Criminology*, 27, 137–45.

Dane, F C and Wrightsman, L S (1982) Effects of Defendants' and Victims' Characteristics on Jurors' Verdicts. In N L Kerr and R M Bray (eds) *The Psychology of the Courtroom*, London: Academic Press, 83–115.

Danet, B and Bogoch, B (1980) Fixed fight or free-for-all? An empirical study of combativeness in the adversary system of justice. *British Journal of Law and Society*, 7, 36–60.

Davies, P W, and Crequer, N (1991) Targeting 'criminal children' attacked. *The Independent*, 16 September, 2.

Davis, G E, and Leitenberg, H (1987) Adolescent sex offenders. *Psychological Bulletin*, 101, 417–27.

Davis, J H (1989) Psychology and Law: the last 15 years. *Journal of Applied Social Psychology*, 19, 199–230.

Davis, J H, Kerr, N L, Atkin, R S, Holt R and Meek, D (1975) The decision process of 6- and 12-person juries assigned unanimous and two-thirds majority rules. *Journal of Personality and Social Psychology*, 32, 1–14.

Decker, S H and Wagner, A E (1982) The impact of patrol staffing on police–citizen injuries and dispositions. *Journal of Criminal Justice*, 10, 375–82.

Deffenbacher, K A (1980) Eyewitness accuracy and confidence: Can we infer anything about their relationship?. *Law and Human Behavior*, 4, 243–60.

Deffenbacher, K A (1991) A maturing of research on the behaviour of eyewitnesses. *Journal of Applied Cognitive Psychology*, 5, 377–402.

Deffenbacher, K A and Loftus, E F (1982) Do jurors share a common understanding concerning eyewitness behaviour?. *Law and Human Behavior*, 6, 15–30.

Dent, H R and Stephenson, G M (1979) An experimental study of the effectiveness of different techniques of questioning child witnesses. *British Journal of Social and Clinical Psychology*, 18, 41–51.

Denton, K and Krebs, D (1990) From the scene to the crime: the effect of alcohol and social context on moral judgement. *Journal of Personality and Social Psychology*, 59, 242–8.

Deusinger, I M (1986) Questioning convicted burglars: a contribution to crime prevention. In H Wegener, F Lösel and J Haisch (eds), *Criminal Behavior and the Justice System: Psychological Perspectives*, New York: Springer Verlag, 118–16.

Diamond, S S (1990) Revising images of public punitiveness: sentencing by lay and professional English magistrates. *Law and Social Inquiry*, 191–221.

Dickinson, J and Emler, N (1992) Developing conceptions of work. In J Hartley and G M Stephenson (eds) *Employment Relations*, Oxford: Basil Blackwell, 19–43.

Dijkstra, W (1987) Interviewing style and respondent behaviour. *Sociological Methods and Research*, 16, 309–34.

Dillehay, R C and Nietzel, M T (1985) Juror experience and jury verdicts. *Law and Human Behavior*, 9, 179–91.

Dodder, R and Hughes, S P (1987) Collegiate drinking behaviour: a test of neutralization theory. *Journal of Alcohol and Drug Education*, 33, 73–85.

Doob, A N and Roberts, J V (1984) Social psychology, social attitudes and attitudes towards sentencing. *Canadian Journal of Behavioural Science*, 16, 269–80.

Doob, A N and Roberts J (1988) Public punitiveness and public knowledge of the facts: some Canadian surveys. In N Walker and M Hough (eds) *Public Attitudes to Sentencing: Surveys from five countries*, Aldershot: Gower, 111–33.

Douglas, R (1989) Does the magistrate matter? Sentencers and sentence in the Victorian Magistrates' Courts. *Australian and New Zealand Journal of Criminology*, 22, 40–59.

Drass, K A and Spencer, J W (1987) Accounting for pre-sentencing recommendations: typologies and probation officers' theory of office. *Social Problems*, 34, 277–93.

Dunford, F W, Huizinga, D, and Elliott, D S (1990) The role of arrest in domestic assault: the Omaka Police experiment. *Criminology*, 1990, 28, 183–206.

Dunstan, R (1980) Context for coercion: analysing properties of courtroom 'questions'. *British Journal of Law and Society*, 7, 61–77.

Dutton, D G (1986) Wife assaulters' explanations for assault: the neutralization of self-punishment. *Canadian Journal of Behavioural Science*, 18, 381–90.

Egan, D, Pittner, M and Goldstein, A G (1977) Eyewitness identification: photographs vs live models. *Law and Human Behavior*, 1, 199–206.

Ehrlich, I (1982) The market for offences and the public enforcement of laws: an equilibrium analysis. *British Journal of Social Psychology*, 21, 107–20.

Eisenstein, J and Jacob, H (1977) *Felony Justice: an organisational analysis of criminal courts.* Boston: Little, Brown & Co.

Elliott, R (1991) Social science data and the APA: the Lockhart brief as a case in point. *Law and Human Behavior*, 15, 59–76.

Ellis, H (1984) Practical aspects of face memory. In G L Wells and E F Loftus (eds) *Eyewitness Testimony*, Cambridge: Cambridge University Press, 12–37.

Ellsworth, P C (1991) To tell what we know or wait for Godot? *Law and Human Behavior*, 15, 77–90.

Emler, N (1984) Differential involvement in delinquency: towards an interpretation in terms of reputation management. *Progress in Experimental Personality Research*, 13, 173–239.

Emler, N P and Hogan, R (1981) Developing attitudes to law and justice: an integrative review. In S S Brehm, S M Kassin, and F X Gibbons (eds), *Developmental Social Psychology*, New York: Oxford University Press, Ch. 14, 298–314.

Emler, N P, Heather, N and Winton, M (1978) Delinquency and the development of moral reasoning. *British Journal of Social and Clinical Psychology*, 17, 325–31.

Emler, N, Ohana, J and Moscovici, S (1987) Children's beliefs about institutional roles: a cross-national study of representations of the teacher's role. *British Journal of Educational Psychology*, 57, 266–37.

Emler, N, Reicher, S and Ross, A S (1987) The social context of delinquent conduct. *Journal of Child Psychology and Psychiatry*, 28, 99–109.

Erez, E (1984) Self-defined 'desert' and citizens' assessment of the police. *The Journal of Criminal Law and Criminology*, 75, 1276–99.

Ewing, C P (1990) Psychological self-defense: a proposed justification for battered women who kill. *Law and Human Behavior*, 14, 579–94.

Eysenck, H J (1960) Learning theory and moral values in children. *British Journal of Educational Psychology*, 30, 11–21.

Eysenck, H J (1964) *Crime and Personality*, London: Routledge.

Eysenck, H J and Eysenck, S B G (1978) Psychopathy, personality and genetics. In R D Hare and D Schalling (eds) *Psychopathic Behaviour*, Chichester: Wiley, 197–223.

Farrington, D P (1981) Psychology and Police Interrogation. *British Journal of Law and Society*, 8, 97–107.

Farrington, D P (1986) Stepping stones to adult criminal careers. In D Olweus, J Block and M R Yarrow (eds) *Development of anti-social and pro-social behaviour: research, theories and issues*, New York: Academic Press, 359–84.

Farrington, D P (1989) Self-reported and official offending from adolescence to adulthood. In M W Klein (ed.) *Cross-national research in self-reported crime and delinquency*, Dordrecht, Netherlands: Kluwer, 399–423.

Farrington, D P (1990) Implications of criminal career research for the prevention of offending. *Journal of Adolescence*, 13, 93–113.

Farrington, D P and West, D J (1990) The Cambridge Study in delinquent development: a long-term follow-up of 411 London males. In J H Kerner and G Kaiser (eds) *Criminality: Personality, Behaviour and Life History*, London: Springer-Verlag 115–38.

Farrington, D P and Hawkins, J D (1991) Predicting participation, early onset and later persistence in officially recorded offending. *Criminal Behaviour and Mental Health*, 1, 1–33.

Farrington, D P and West, D J (in press) The Cambridge study in delinquent development: a long-term follow-up of 411 London males' in Kaiser, G and Kerner, J H (eds) *Criminality: Personality, Behaviour, Life History*, Heidelberg: Springer-Verlag.

Farrington, D P, Biron, L and LeBlanc,M (1982) Personality and delinquency in London and Montreal. In J Gunn and D P Farrington (eds) *Abnormal Offenders, Delinquency and the Criminal Justice System*, Chichester: Wiley, 153–201.

Farrington, D P, Gallagher, B, Morley, L, St Ledger, R J and West, D J (1986) Unemployment, school leaving and crime. *British Journal of Criminology*, 26, 335–56.

Farrington, D P, Snyder, H N and Finnegan, T A (1988) Specialisation in juvenile court careers. *Criminology*, 26, 461–87.

Feeney, F (1986) Robbers as decision-makers. In D B Cornish and R V Clarke (eds) *The Reasoning Criminal*, New York: Springer-Verlag, 53–71.

Feldman, M P (1977) *Criminal Behaviour: a psychological analysis*. London: Wiley.

Feldman-Summers, S and Ashworth, C (1981) Factors related to intentions to report a rape. *Journal of Social Issues*, 37, 53–70.

Feldman-Summers, S and Norris, J (1984) Differences between rape victims who report and those who do not report to a public agency. *Journal of Applied Social Psychology*, 14, 562–73.

Ferguson, T (1952) *The Young Delinquent in his Social Setting*. London: Oxford University Press.

Ferraro, K H (1989) Policing women battering. *Social Problems*, 36, 61–74.

Fielding, N G and Fielding, J (1991) Police attitudes to crime and punishment: certainties and dilemmas. *British Journal of Criminology*, 31, 39–53.

Fincham, F D and Jaspars, J M (1980) Attribution of responsibility: from man the scientist to man as lawyer. *Advances in Experimental Social Psychology*, 13, 81–138.

Finckenbauer, J O and Kochis, D S (1984) Causal theory and the treatment of juvenile offenders: A case study. *Advances in Forensic Psychology and Psychiatry*, 1, 49–63.

Fischer, G J (1987) Hispanic and Majority student attitudes toward forcible date rape as a function of differences in attitudes towards women. *Sex Roles*, 17, 93–101.

Fishbein, M and Ajzen, I (1975) *Belief, Attitude, Intention and Behavior* Reading, MA: Addison-Wesley.

Fisher, R P, Gieselman, R E and Amador, M (1989) Field test of the cognitive interview: enhancing the recollection of actual victims and witnesses of crime. *Journal of Applied Psychology*, 74, 722–7.

Fletcherm G P (1978) *Rethinking Criminal Law*, Boston: Little, Brown and Company.

Fletcher, G P (1987) Law and morality: a Kantian perspective. *Columbia Law Review*, 87, 533–58.

Ford, D A (1983) Wife battery and criminal justice: a study of victim decision making. *Family Relations*, 32, 463–75.

Frazier, P A (1990) Victim attributions and post-rape trauma. *Journal of Personality and Social Psychology*, 59, 298–304.

Freiberg, A (1988) The State as a victim of crime. *Australian and New Zealand Journal of Criminology*, 21, 20–30.

Frey, D, Rogner, O, Schuler, M and Korte, C (1985) Psychological determinants in the convalescence of accident patients. *Basic and Applied Social Psychology*, 6, 317–28.

Frost, S M and Stephenson, G M (1989) A simulation study of electronic tagging as a sentencing option. *The Howard Journal of Criminal Justice*, 28, 91–104.

Fulero, S M and Penrod, S D (1990) Attorney jury selection folklore: what do they think and how can psychologists help? *Forensic Reports*, 3, 233–59.

Gacono, C B and Meloy, J R (1988) The relationship between cognitive style and defensive processes in the psychopath. *Criminal Justice and Behaviour*, 15, 472–83.

Gallatin, J and Adelson, J (1971) Legal guarantees of individual freedom: a cross-national study of the development of political thought. *Journal of Social Issues*, 27, 93–108.

Galvin, J and Polk, K (1983) Attrition in case processing: is rape unique? *Journal of Research in Crime and Delinquency*, January, 126–54.

Garner, T and Rubin, D L (1986) Middle class blacks' perceptions of dialect and style shifting: The case of Southern attorneys. *Journal of Language and Social Psychology*, 5, 33–48.

Gauld, A and Shotter, J (1977) *Human Action and its Psychological Investigation*. London: Routledge & Kegan Paul.

Gebotys, R J and Roberts, J V (1987) Public views of sentencing: the role of offender characteristics. *Canadian Journal of Behavioural Science*, 19, 479–88.

Geiselman, R E and Padilla, J (1988) Cognitive interviewing with child witnesses. *Journal of Police Science and Administration*, 16, 236–42.

Geiselman, R E, Fisher, R P, MacKinnon, D P and Holland, H L (1985) Eyewitness memory enhancement in the police interview: cognitive retrieval mnemonics versus hypnosis. *Journal of Applied Psychology*, 70, 401–12.

Gerdes, E P, Dammann, E J and Heilig, K E (1988) Perceptions of rape victims and assailants: effects of physical attractiveness, acquaintance and subject gender. *Sex Roles*, 19, 141–53.

Gibb, F (1989) Consistency in Sentencing. *The Times*, 10 March.

Gibling, F and Davies, G (1988) Reinstatement of context following exposure to postevent information. *British Journal of Psychology*, 79, 129–41.

Gilligan, C (1982) *In a Different Voice*. London: Harvard University Press.

Glueck, S and Glueck, E T (1950) *Unraveling juvenile delinquency*. Cambridge, Mass.: Harvard University Press.

Goffman, E (1952) On cooling the mark out: some aspects of adaptation to failure. *Psychiatry*, 15, 451–63.

Goldyn, L (1981) Gratuitous language in appellate cases involving gay people: 'Queer baiting from the bench'. *Political Behavior*, 3, 31–48.

Goodman, G S, Levine, M, Melton, G B and Ogden, D W (1991) Child witnesses and the confrontation clause: the American Psychological Association. Brief in *Mayland v. Craig. Law and Human Behavior*, 15, 13–31.

Goodman, L A and Kruskal, W H (1954) Measures of association for cross classifications. *Journal of American Statistical Association*, 49, 732–64.

Goodpaster, G (1987) On the theory of American Adversary Criminal Trial. *Journal of Criminal. Law and Criminology*, 78, 118–54.

Gottfredson, D M, Gottfredson, S D and Conly, C H (1989) Stakes and risk: incapacitative intent in sentencing decisions. *Behavioural Sciences and the Law*, 7, 91–106.

Gottfredson, M R (1984) *Victims of Crime: the dimensions of risk*. London: HMSO (HORS No. 81).

Gottfredson, M and Hirschi, T (1988) Science, public policy and the career paradigm. *Criminology*, 26, 37–56.

Grabosky, P N, Braithwaite, J B and Wilson, P R (1987) The myth of community tolerance toward white-collar crime. *Australian and New Zealand Journal of Criminology*, 20, 33–44.

Graham, J (1988) *Schools, disruptive behaviour and delinquency: a review of research*. London: HMSO.

Grant, A (1987) Videotaping police questioning: A Canadian experiment. *Criminal Law Review*, 375–83.

Grant, J D, Grant, J and Toch, H (1982) Police-Citizen conflict and decisions to arrest. In Konečni & Ebbeson, *The Criminal Justice System: a Socio-Psychological Analysis*, San Francisco: Freeman, 133–58.

Greenberg, M S, Wilson, C E, Ruback, R B and Mills, M K (1979) Social and emotional determinants of victims crime reporting. *Social Psychology Quarterly*, 42, 364–72.

Greenberg, M S, Ruback, R B and Westcott, D R (1982) Decision making by crime victims: a multimethod approach. *Law and Society Review*, 17, 47–84.

Greene, E (1990) Media effects on jurors. *Law and Human Behavior*, 14, 439–50.

Greene, E and Loftus, E F (1984) What's new in the news? The influence of well-publicized news events on psychological research and court-room trials. *Basic and Applied Social Psychology*, 5, 211–21.

Greene, E and Loftus, E F (1985) When crimes are joined at trial. *Law and Human Behavior*, 9, 193–207.

Gudjonnson, G H (1984a) Attribution of blame for criminal acts and its rela-tionship with personality. *Personality and Individual Differences*, 5, 53–8.

Gudjonsson, G (1984b) A new scale of interrogative suggestibility. *Per-sonality and Individual Differences*, 5, 303–14.

Gudjonsson, G (1984c) Interrogative suggestibility: comparison between 'false confessors' and 'deniers' in criminal trials. *Medical Science and Law*, 24, 56–60.

Gudjonsson, G H (1989) The effects of suspiciousness and anger on sug-gestibility. *Medical Science and the Law*, 29, 229–32.

Gudjonsson, G and Clark, N K (1986) Suggestibility in Police Interroga-tion: A Social Psychological Model. *Social Behaviour*, 1, 83–104.

Gudjonsson, G and Hilton, M (1989) The effects of instructional manipu-lation on interrogative suggestibility. *Social Behaviour*, 4, 189–93.

Gudjonsson, G and Lebegue, B (1989) Psychological and psychiatric as-pects of a coerced-internalized false confession. *Journal of the Forensic Science Society*, 29, 261–9.

Gudjonsson, G and Lister, S (1984) Interrogative suggestibility and its relationship with self-esteem and control. *Journal of the Forensic Science Society*, 99–110.

Gudjonsson, G and MacKeith, J A C (1988) Retracted confessions: legal, psychological and psychiatric aspects. *Medical Science and Law*, 28, 187–94.

Haan, N, Smith, M B and Block, J (1968) Moral reasoning of young adults: political-social behavior, family background, and personality correlates. *Journal of Personality and Social Psychology*, 10, 183–201.

Hale, D C (1988) Fear of crime and quality of life: a test of Garofolo and Laub's model. *Criminal Justice Review*, 13, 13–19.

Hamilton, V L (1978) Who is responsible? Towards a *social* psychology of responsibility attribution. *Social Psychology* 41, 316–28.

Hamilton, V L and Sanders, S J (1983) Universals in judging wrongdoing: Japanese and Americans compared. *American Sociological Review*, 48, 199–211.

Hampson, S E (1982) Criminal Personality. In *The Construction of Person-ality: an introduction*, London: Routledge & Kegan Paul, 249–80.

Hans, V P and Vidmar, N (1982) Jury Selection. In N L Kerr and R M Bray (eds) *The Psychology the Courtroom*, London: Academic Press, 39–82.

Hargreaves, D H (1967) *Social relations in a secondary school*. London: Routledge.

Hargreaves, D H (1980) Classrooms, Schools and Juvenile Delinquency. *Educational Analysis*, 2, 75–87.

Hargreaves, D H (1981) Schooling for delinquency. In L Barton and S Walker (eds) *Schools, Teachers and Teaching*, Lewes: The Falmer Press, 9–25.

Harris, S, Mussen, P and Rutherford, E (1976) Some cognitive, behavioural, and personality correlates of maturity of moral judgement. *Journal of Genetic Psychology*, 128, 123–35.

Hart, H L A and Honoré, A M (1978) Causation in the Law. In H Morris (ed.) *Freedom and Responsibility: Readings in philosophy and law*. Stanford: Stanford University Press, 325–42.

Hassinger, J (1985) Fear of crime in public environments. *Journal of Architectural and Planning Research*, 2, 289–300.

Hastie, R, Penrod, S D and Pennington, N (1983) *Inside the Jury*. Cambridge, Mass: Harvard University Press.

Hathaway, S R and McKinley, J C (1942) *Minnesota Multiphasic Personality Inventory*. Minneapolis: University of Minnesota Press.

Haugaard, J J, Repucci, N D, Laird, J and Nauful, T (1991) Children's definitions of the truth and their competency as witnesses in legal proceedings. *Law and Human Behavior*, 15, 253–71.

Hayward, L R C (1981) Psychological consequences of being the victim of a crime. In S M Lloyd-Bostock (ed.) *Law and Psychology*, London: SSRC, 61–6.

Heath, L (1984) Impact of newspaper crime reports on fear of crime: multimethodological investigation. *Journal of Personality and Social Psychology*, 47, 263–76.

Heider, F (1958) *The Psychology of Interpersonal Relations*. New York: Wiley.

Hoffman, P B and Hardyman, P L (1986) Crime seriousness scales: public perception and feedback to criminal justice policymakers. *Journal of Criminal Justice*, 14, 413–31.

Hogarth, J (1971) *Sentencing as a Human Process*. Toronto: University of Toronto Press.

Holdaway, S (1983) *Inside the British Police*. Oxford: Blackwell.

Hollin, C R (1989) *Psychology and Crime* London: Routledge.

Holstein, J A (1985) Jurors' interpretation and jury decision making. *Law and Human Behavior*, 9, 83–100.

Holstein, J A (1988) Court ordered incompetence: conversational organisation in involuntary commitment hearings. *Social Problems*, 35, 458–73.

Home Office, *Police and Criminal Evidence Act 1984 (s66): Codes of Practice*. London: HMSO.

Home Office (1989) *Tackling Crime*. London: HMSO.

Home Office (1990) *Crime, Justice and Protecting the Public Cm. 965*. London: HMSO.

Hope, T (1986) Crime, community and the environment. *Journal of Environmental Psychology*, 6, 65–78.

Horai, J and Bartek, M (1978) Recommended punishment as a function of injurious intent, actual harm done, and intended consequences. *Personality and Social Psychology Bulletin*, 4, 575–8.

Hough, M (1987) 'Offenders' choice of target: findings from victim surveys. *Journal of Quantitative Criminology*, 3, 355–69.

Hough, M, Moxon, D and Lewis, H (1987) Attitudes to punishment: findings from the British Crime Survey. In D C Pennington and S Lloyd-Bostock (eds) The Psychology of Sentencing, Oxford: Centre for Socio-Legal Studies, 117–30.

Howard, J A (1984a) Societal influences on attribution: blaming some victims more than others. *Journal of Personality and Social Psychology*, 47, 494–505.

Howard, J A (1984b) The 'normal' victim: the effects of gender stereotypes on reactions to victims. *Social Psychology Quarterly*, 47, 270–81.

Howarth, E (1986) What does Eysenck's psychoticism scale really measure? *British Journal of Psychology*, 77, 223–27.

Huizinga, D and Elliott, D S (1987) Juvenile offenders: prevalence, offender incidence, and arrest rates by race. *Crime and Delinquency*, 33, 206–23.

Indermauer, D (1987) Public perception of sentencing in Perth, W.A. *Australian and New Zealand Journal of Criminology*, 20, 163–83.

Irving, B (1980) *Police Interrogation: a case study of present practice*. London: HMSO Research Study No. 2 Royal Commission on Criminal Procedure.

Irving, B and Hilgendorf, L (1980) *Police Interrogation: The Psychological Approach*. London: HMSO Research Study No. 1 Royal Commission on Criminal Procedure.

Irving, B and McKenzie, B (1988) *Regulating Custodial Interviews*. London: The Police Foundation.

Jackson, B S (1990) *Law, Fact and Narrative Coherence*. Merseyside: Deborah Charles Publications.

Jackson, M N (1988) Lay and professional perceptions of dangerousness and other forensic issues. *Canadian Journal of Criminology*, 30, 215–29.

Jaffe, P, Wolfe, D A , Telford, A and Austin, G (1986) The impact of police charges in incidents of wife abuse. *Journal of Family Violence*, 1, 37–49.

Jaffe, P, Wilson, S K and Saxe, L (1987) Court testimony of child sexual abuse victims: emerging issues in clinical assessments. *Canadian Psychology*, 28, 291–5.

Jenkins, J (1990) I think it was that man there. *The Independent*, 24 August, 21.

Jermier, J M, Gaines, J and McIntosh, N J (1989) Reactions to physically dangerous work: A conceptual and empirical analysis. *Journal of Organizational Behaviour*, 10, 15–33.

Jones, D P H (1987) The evidence of a 3-year old child. *Criminal Law Review*, 677–81.

Jones, E E and Nisbett, R E (1972) The actor and the observer: divergent perceptions of the causes of behaviour. In E E Jones, D E Kanouse,

H H Kelley, S Valins and B Weiner (eds) *Attribution: Perceiving the causes of behaviour*, Morristown, NJ: General Learning Press.

Junger, M (1990) Studying ethnic minorities in relation to crime and police discrimination. *British Journal of Criminology*, 30, 493–502.

Jurkovic, G J (1980) The juvenile delinquent as a moral philosopher: a structural-developmental perspective. *Psychological Bulletin*, 88, 709–27.

Kalven, H and Zeisel, H (1966) *The American Jury*. Chicago: University of Chicago Press.

Kapardis, A and Farrington, D P (1981) An experimental study of sentencing by magistrates. *Law and Human Behavior*, 5, 107–21.

Kassin, S M (1984) TV cameras, public self-consciousness, and mock juror performance. *Journal of Experimental Social Psychology*, 20, 336–49.

Kassin, S M, Ellsworth, P C and Smith, V L (1989) The general acceptance of psychological research on eyewitness testimony. *American Psychologist*, 44, 1089–98.

Kassin, S M, Williams, L N and Saunders, C L (1990) Dirty tricks of cross-examination: the influence of conjectural evidence on the jury. *Law and Human Behavior*, 14, 373–84.

Kelley, H H (1973) The process of causal attribution. *American Psychologist*, 28, 107–28.

Kelman, H C and Hamilton, V L (1989) *Crimes of Obedience: towards a social psychology of authority and responsibility*. London: Yale University Press.

Kempf, K L and Austin, R L (1986) Older and more recent evidence on racial discrimination in sentencing. *Journal of Quantitative Criminology*, 2, 29–48.

Kennedy, L (1964) *The Trial of Stephen Ward*. Harmondsworth: Penguin Books.

Kennedy, L W and Forde, D R (1990) Routine activities and crime: an analysis of victimization in Canada. *Criminology*, 28, 137–52.

Kerr, N L (1982) Trial participants' behaviors and jury verdicts: an exploratory field study. In V J Konečni and E B Ebbeson (eds) *The Criminal Justice System: a Socio-Psychological Analysis*, San Francisco: Freeman, 258–90.

Kidd, R F (1985) 'Impulsive bystanders': why do they intervene? In D P Farrington and J Gunn (eds) *Reactions to crime: the public, the police, courts and prisons*, Chichester: Wiley, 21–39.

King, M (1986) *Psychology in and out of court*. London: Pergamon.

Kitzinger, C (in press) Justice: A Patriarchal Value? Chapter 3 in *Feminist Morality*. Milton Keynes: Open University Press.

Kohlberg, L (1981) *The philosophy of moral development: moral stages and the idea of justice*. San Francisco: Harper & Row.

Kolvin, I, Miller, F J W, Fleeting, M and Kolvin, P A (1988) Social and parenting factors affecting criminal-offence rates. *British Journal of Psychiatry*, 152, 80–90.

Konečni, V J and Ebbeson, E B (1979) External validity of research in legal psychology. *Law and Human Behaviour*, 3, 389–90.

Konečni, V J and Ebbeson, E B (1982) The Sentencing Decision. In V J Konečni and Ebbeson (eds) *The Criminal Justice System*, 293–32.

Konečni, V J, Mulcahy, E M and Ebbeson, E B (1980) Prison or mental hospital: factors affecting the processing of persons suspects of being 'mentally disorded sex offenders'. In P D Lipsitt and B D Sales (eds) *New Directions in Psycholegal Research*, N.Y.: van Nostrand Reinhold, 85–124.

Koss, M P, Gidycz, C A and Wisniewski, N (1987) The scope of rape: incidence and prevalence of sexual aggression and victimization in a national sample of higher education students. *Journal of Consulting and Clinical Psychology*, 55, 162–70.

Koss, M P and Dinero, T E (1989) Discriminant analysis of risk factors for sexual victimization among a national sample of college women. *Journal of Consulting and Clinical Psychology*, 57, 242–50.

Krahé, B (1988) Attributions to victims of rape. *Journal of Applied Social Psychology*, 18, 50–58.

Kramer, G P, Kerr, N L and Carroll, J S (1990) Pre-trial publicity, judicial remedies, and jury bias. *Law and Human Behavior*, 14, 409–38.

Krebs, D L, Denton, K, Carpendale, J I, Vermevlen, S, Bartek, S and Bush, A (1989) The many faces of moral judgement. In M A Luszcg and T Nettlebeck (eds) *Psychological Development: perspectives across the life-span*, North-Holland: Elsevier, 97–105.

Kühlhorn, E (1990) Victims and offenders of criminal violence. *Journal of Quantitative Criminology*, 6, 51–9.

Kurzon, D (1985) How lawyers tell their tales. *Poetics*, 14, 467–81.

Lacey, N, Wells, C and Meure, D (1990) *Reconstructing Criminal Law: critical perspectives on crime and the criminal process*. London: Weidenfeld and Nicolson.

Larzelere, R E and Patterson, G R (1990) Parental management: mediator of the effect of socioeconomic status on early delinquency. *Criminology*, 28, 301–23.

Lassiter, G D and Irvine, A A (1986) Videotaped confessions: the impact of camera point of view on judgements of coercion. *Journal of Applied Social Psychology*, 16, 268–76.

Latané, B, Williams, K and Harkins, S (1979) Many hands make light the work: the causes and consequences of social loafing. *Journal of Personality and Social Psychology*, 37, 822–32.

Launay, G (1987) Victim-Offender reconciliation. In B J McCurk, D M Thornton and M Williams (eds) *Applying Psychology to Imprisonment*, London: HMSO 273–302.

Launay, G and Murray, P (1989) Victim/Offender groups. In M Wright and B Galaway (eds) *Mediation and Criminal Justice*, London: Sage, 113–31.

Laycock, G (1984) *Reducing burglary: a study of chemists' shops*. Home Office Crime Prevention Unit: Paper No 1.

Laycock, G (1985) *Property marking: a deterrent to domestic burglars?* London: Home Office.

Le Van, E A (1984) Nonverbal communication in the courtroom: attorney beware. *Law and Psychology Review*, 8, 83–104.

Leach, C (1979) *Introduction to Statistics: a nonparametric approach for the social sciences*. Chichester: Wiley.

LeDoux, J C and Hazelwood, R R (1985) Police attitudes and beliefs towards rape. *Journal of Police Science and Administration*, 13, 211–20.

Lerner, M J (1980) *The Belief in a Just World*. New York: Plenum.

Leschied, A D W and Wilson, S K (1988) Criminal liability of children under twelve: a problem for child welfare, juvenile justice or both? *Canadian Journal of Criminology*, 30, 17–29.

Lester, D (1991) Crime as opportunity: a test of the hypothesis with European homicide rates. *British Journal of Criminology*, 31, 186–91.

Leventhal, G S, Karuza, J Jr, and Fry, W R (1980) Beyond Fairness: a theory of allocation preferences. In G Mikula (ed.) *Justice and Social Interaction*, Vienna: Hans Huber, 167–218.

Levi, M (1991) Regulating money laundering. *British Journal of Criminology*, 31, 109–25.

Levine, M D (1987) Attention deficits: the diverse effects of weak control systems in childhood. *Pediatrics Annals*, 16, 117–31.

Lind, E A (1982) The Psychology of Courtroom Procedure. In N L Kerr and K M Bray (eds) *The Psychology of the Courtroom*, London: Academic Press, 13–37.

Lind, E A and O'Barr, W M (1979) The social significance of speech in the courtroom. In H Giles and R St Clair (eds) *Language and Social Psychology*, Oxford: Blackwell, 66–87.

Lind, E A and Tyler, T R (1988) *The Social Psychology of Procedural Justice*. London: Plenum Press.

Lind, E A, Erikson, B E, Conley, J and O'Barr, W M (1978) Social attributions and conversation style in trial testimony. *Journal of Personality and Social Psychology*, 36, 1558–67.

Lind, E A, Kanfer, R and Earley, P C (1990) Voice, control, and procedural justice: instrumental and non-instrumental concerns in fairness judgements. *Journal of Personality and Social Psychology*, 59, 952–9.

Lindsay, R C L and Wells, G L (1983) What do we really know about cross-race identification? In S Lloyd-Bostock and B R Clifford (eds) *Evaluating Witness Evidence*, Chichester: Wiley, 219–33.

Linz, D G and Penrod, S (1984) Increasing attorney persuasiveness in the courtroom. *Law and Psychology Review*, 8, 1–47.

Lisak, D and Roth, S (1988) Motivational factors in nonincarcerated sexually aggressive men. *Journal of Personality and Social Psychology*, 55, 795–802.

Liska, A E, Sanchirico, A and Reed, M D (1988) Fear of crime and constrained behaviour: specifying and estimating a reciprocal effects model. *Social Forces*, 66, 827–37.

Lloyd-Bostock, S (1983) Attributions of cause and responsibility as social phenomena. In J Jaspars, F D Fincham and M Hewstone (eds) *Attribution Theory and Research*, London: Academic Press, 261–89.

Loftus, E F and Davies, G M (1984) Distortions in the memory of children. *Journal of Social Issues*, 40, 51–67.

Loftus, E F and Ketcham, K (1983) The malleability of eyewitness accounts. In S Lloyd-Bostock and B R Clifford (eds) *Evaluating Witness Evidence*, Chichester: Wiley 159–71.

Loftus, E F, Loftus, G R and Messo, J (1987) Some facts about 'weapon focus'. *Law and Human Behavior*, 11, 55–62.

Losley, J, Kuhl, A F and Roberg, R R (1985) Relationship of nontraditional sex-role attitudes to severity of women's criminal behaviour. *Psychological Reports*, 56, 155–8.

Lott, J R Jr (1987) Juvenile delinquency and education: a comparison of public and private provision. *International Review of Law and Economics*, 7, 163–75.

Lupfer, M B, Cohen, R and Bernard, J L (1987) The influence of moral reasoning on the decisions of jurors. *Journal of Social Psychology*, 127, 653–67.

Lurigio, A J and Carroll, J S (1985) Probation officers' schemata of offenders: content, development and impact on treatment decisions. *Journal of Personality and Social Psychology*, 48, 1112–26.

Luus, C A E and Wells, G L (1991) Eyewitness identification and the selection of distractors for line-ups. *Law and Human Behavior*, 15, 43–57.

Lynch, J P (1987) Routine activity and victimisation at work. *Journal of Quantitative Criminology*, 3, 283–300.

Maass, A and Köhnken, G (1989) Eyewitness identification: simulating the 'weapon effect'. *Law and Human Behavior*, 13, 397–408.

MacCoun, R J and Kerr, N L (1988) Asymmetric influence in mock jury deliberation: jurors' bias for leniency. *Journal of Personality and Social Psychology*, 54, 21–33.

Macdonald, J E and Gifford, R (1989) Territorial cues and defensible space theory: the burglar's point of view. *Journal of Environmental Psychology*, 9, 193–205.

Macrae, C N and Shepherd, J W (1989) Do criminal stereotypes mediate juridic judgements? *British Journal of Social Psychology*, 28, 189–91.

Maddock, J W (1988) Child reporting and testimony in incest cases: comments on the construction and reconstruction of reality. *Behavioral Sciences and the Law*, 6, 201–20.

Maguire, M (1988) Effects of the PACE provisions on detention and questioning. *British Journal of Criminology*, 28, 19–43.

Maguire, M (1981) Victims of residential burglary. In S M Lloyd-Bostock (ed.) *Law and Psychology*, London: SSRC 67–83.

Malinowski, C I and Smith, C P (1985) Moral reasoning and moral conduct: An investigation prompted by Kohlberg's theory. *Journal of Personality and Social Psychology*, 49, 1016–27.

262 *References*

Malpass, R S and Devine, P G (1983) Measuring the Fairness of Eyewitness Identification Lineups. In S Lloyd-Bostock and B R Clifford (eds) *Evaluating Witness Evidence*, Chichester: Wiley 81–102.

Markoulis, D (1989) Political involvement and socio-moral reasoning: testing Emler's interpretation. *British Journal of Social Psychology*, 28, 203–12.

Marks, K (1991) Wife who killed gets probation. *The Independent*, 14 December.

Maxfield, M G (1987) Lifestyle and routine activity theories of crime: empirical studies of victimisation, delinquency and offender decision-making. *Journal of Quantitative Criminology*, 3, 275–82.

Maynard, D W (1982) Defendant attributes in plea bargaining: notes on the modeling of sentencing decisions. *Social Problems*, 29, 347–60.

McBarnet, D (1981) Magistrates' courts and the ideology of justice. *British Journal of Law and Society*, 8, 181–97.

McCabe, S and Purves, R (1974) *The Shadow Jury at Work*. Oxford: Blackwell.

McCleary, R, Nienstedt, B C and Erven, J M (1982) Uniform crime reports as organizational outcomes: three time series experiments. *Social Problems*, 361–72.

McClelland, K A and Alpert, G P (1985) Factor analysis applied to magnitude estimates of punishment seriousness: patterns of individual differences. *Journal of Qualitative Criminology*, 1, 307–18.

McCloskey, M, Egeth, H and McKenna, J (1986) The experimental psychologist: the ethics of expert testimony. *Law and Human Behavior*, 10, 1–13.

McConville, M and Baldwin, J (1981) *Courts, Prosecution and Conviction*. Oxford: Oxford University Press.

McCord, J (1990) Crime in moral and social contexts – the American Society of Criminology, 1989, Presidential Address. *Criminology*, 28, 1–26.

McCord, W and McCord, J (1956) *Psychopathy and Delinquency*. London: Grune & Stratton.

McCord, W and McCord, J (1959) *The Origins of Crime*. New York: Columbia University Press.

McCord, J and Otten, L (1983) A consideration of sex roles and motivation for crime. *Criminal Justice and Behaviour*, 10, 3–12.

McFatter, R M (1978) Sentencing strategies and justice, effects of punishment philosophy on sentencing decisions. *Journal of Personality and Social Psychology*, 36, 1490–500.

McFatter, R M (1986) Sentencing disparity: perforce or perchance? *Journal of Applied Social Psychology*, 16, 150–64.

McGraw, K M (1985) Subjective probabilities and moral judgements. *Journal of Experimental Social Psychology*, 21, 501–18.

McKinnon, D P, O'Reilly, K E and Geiselman, R E (1990) Improving eyewitness recall for licence plates. *Applied Cognitive Psychology*, 4, 129–40.

McLaughlin, H (1990) Court clerks: advisers or decision-makers? *British Journal of Criminology*, 30, 358–370.

McNamee, S M (1977) Moral behaviour, moral development and motivation. *Journal of Moral Education*, 7, 27–31.

Memon, A and Bull, R (1991) The Cognitive Interview: its origins, empirical support, evaluation and practical implications. *Journal of Community and Applied Social Psychology*, 1, 291–307.

Meyer, C B and Taylor, S E (1986) Adjustment to rape. *Journal of Personality and Social Psychology*, 50, 1226–34.

Miethe, T D, Stafford, M C and Sloane, D (1990) Lifestyle changes and risks of criminal victimisation. *Journal of Quantitative Criminology*, 6, 357–76.

Milgram, S (1974) *Obedience to Authority*. London: Tavistock.

Miller, A (1991) *Banished Knowledge: facing childhood injuries*. London: Virago.

Miller, J G (1984) Culture and the development of everyday social interaction. *Journal of Personality and Social Psychology*, 46, 961–77.

Mills, H (1990) Probation Officers' call for end to sentencing 'lottery'. *The Independent*, 23 January.

Mills, H and O'Sullivan, J (1991) Experts criticise sex abuse trial procedure. *The Independent*, 20 November.

Mingay, D (1987) The effect of hypnosis on eyewitness memory: reconciling forensic claims and research findings. *Applied Psychology: an International Review*, 36, 163–83.

Minor, W W (1984) Neutralization and the hardening process. *Social Forces*, 62, 994–1001.

Mitchell, J and Dodder, R A (1983) Types of neutralization and types of delinquency. *Journal of Youth and Adolescence*, 12, 307–18.

Mitchell, J, Dodder, R A and Norris, T D (1990) Neutralization and delinquency: a comparison by sex and ethnicity. *Adolescence*, 25, 487–97.

Moffitt, T E (1990) Juvenile delinquency and Attention Deficit Disorder: Boys' developmental trajectories from age 3 to 15. *Child Development*, 61, 893–910.

Moffitt, T E and Silva, P A (1988) IQ and delinquency: a direct test of the differential detection hypothesis. *Journal of Abnormal Psychology*, 97, 330–3.

Morash, M (1982) Relationships of legal reasoning to social class, closeness to parents, and exposure to a high level of reasoning among adolescents varying in seriousness of delinquency. *Psychological Reports*, 50, 755–60.

Morawetz, T (1986) Reconstructing the criminal defences: the significance of justification. *Journal of Criminal Law and Criminology*, 77, 277–307.

Morgan, M and Grube, J W (1991) Closeness and peer group influence. *British Journal of Social Psychology*, 30, 159–69.

Morley, I and Stephenson, G M (1977) *The Social Psychology of Bargaining*. London: George Allen and Unwin.

Morley, I E, Webb, J and Stephenson, G M (1988) Bargaining and arbitration in the resolutions of conflict. In W Stroebe, A W Kruglanski, D Bar-Tal and M Hewstone (eds), *The Social Psychology of Intergroup Conflict*, Berlin: Springer-Verlag, 117–34.

Morris, A (1987) *Women, Crime and Criminal Justice*. Oxford: Blackwell.

Morris, P (1980) *Police Interrogation: review of literature*. London: HMSO Research Studies No 3 Royal Commission on Criminal Procedure.

Morse, S J (1990) The misbegotten marriage of psychology and bad law. *Law and Human Behavior*, 14, 595–618.

Moscovici, S and Nemeth, C (1974) Social influence II: Minority influence. In C Nemeth (ed.) *Social Psychology: classic and contemporary integrations*, Chicago: Rand McNally, 217–49.

Moser, G (1988) Vandalism in urban public telephones. In D. Canter, J C Jesuino, L Soczka and G M Stephenson (eds) *Environmental Social Psychology*, Dordrecht: Kluwer, 66–75.

Moston, S (1987) The suggestibility of children in interview studies. *First Language*, 7, 67–78.

Moston, S, Stephenson, G M and Williamson, T (1992) The effects of case characteristics on suspect behaviour during police questioning. *British Journal of Criminology*, 32, 23–40.

Muehlenhard, C L and Hollabaugh, L C (1988) Do women sometimes say no when they mean yes? The prevalence and correlates of women's token resistance to sex. *Journal of Personality and Social Psychology*, 54, 872–9.

Naylor, B (1989) The child in the witness box. *Australian and New Zealand Journal of Criminology*, 22, 82–94.

Nemeth, C (1983) Sex differences and decision making in juries. In H H Blumberg, P Hare, V Kent and M Davies (eds) *Small Groups and Social Interaction*, Chichester: J Wiley, Vol. 1, 69–77.

Nemeth, C (1986) Social Psychology and Trial by Jury. In Berkowitz, L A (ed.) *Survey of Social Psychology*, London: Holt, Rinehart and Winston, 430–47.

Newman, O (1972) *Defensible Space*, New York: Macmillan.

Nisan, M and Koriat, A (1989) Moral justification of acts judged to be morally right and acts judged to be morally wrong. *British Journal of Social Psychology*, 28, 213–25.

Norrie, A (1986) Practical reasoning and criminal responsibility: a jurisprudential approach. In D B Cornish and R V Clarke (eds) *The Reasoning Criminal*, New York: Springer-Verlag, 217–30.

O'Barr, W M (1982) *Linguistic Evidence: Language, Power and Strategy in the Courtroom*, London: Academic Press.

O'Rourke, T E, Penrod, S D, Cutler, B L and Stuve, T E (1989) The external validity of eyewitness identification research: generalising across subject populations. *Law and Human Behavior*, 13, 385–95.

Orne, M T, Soskis, D A, Dinges, D F and Orne, E C (1984) Hypnotically induced testimony. In Wells, G L and Loftus, E F (eds) *Eyewitness Testimony*, Cambridge: Cambridge University Press, 171–213.

Orsagh, T (1985) The judicial response to crime and the criminal: a utilitarian perspective. *Journal of Quantitative Criminology*, 1, 369–86.

Oswald, M E (1990) Justification and goals of punishment and the attribution of responsibility in judges. Paper presented at 2nd European Conference on Law and Psychology, Erlangen-Nürnberg, 13–15 September.

Oyserman, D and Markus, H R (1990) Possible selves and delinquency. *Journal of Personality and Social Psychology*, 59, 112–25.

Paternoster, R and Iovanni, L (1986) The deterrent effect of perceived severity: a re-examination. *Social Forces*, 64, 751–77.

Pearson, R (1976) Women defendants in magistrates' courts. *British Journal of Law and Society*, 3, 265–73.

Pease, K (1987) Psychology and Sentencing in D C Pennington & S Lloyd-Bostock (eds) *The Psychology of Sentencing: approaches to consistency and disparity*, Oxford: Centre for Socio-Legal Studies, 36–45.

Peele, S (1990) Does addiction excuse thieves and killers from criminal responsibility? *International Journal of Law and Psychiatry*, 13, 95–101.

Penman, R (1987) Discourse in Courts: cooperation, coercion and coherence. *Discourse Processes*, 10, 201–18.

Penman, R (1990) Facework and politeness: multiple goals in courtroom discourse. *Journal of Language and Social Psychology*, 9, 15–38.

Pennington, N and Hastie, R (1986) Evidence evaluation in complex decision making. *Journal of Personality and Social Psychology*, 51, 242–58.

Pennock, M (1988) Delinquency: a question of justification, denial and excuse. Final year project. Institute of Social and Applied Psychology University of Kent, Canterbury, Kent.

Penrod, S, Loftus, E and Winkler, J (1982) The Reliability of Eyewitness Testimony: a psychological perspective. In N L Kerr and R M Bray (eds) *The Psychology of the Courtroom*, London: Academic Press, 119–68.

Philips, S U (1985) Strategies of clarification in judges' use of language: from the written to the spoken. *Discourse Processes*, 8, 421–36.

Phillips, L and Votey, H L (1981) Crime generation and economic opportunities for youth. In *The Economics of Crime Control*, London: Sage, 151–71.

Piaget, J (1932) *The Moral Judgement of the Child*. London: Routledge and Kegan Paul Ltd.

Pogrebin, M R, Poole, E D and Regroli, R M (1986) Stealing money: an assessment of bank embezzlers. *Behavioural Sciences and the Law*, 4, 481–90.

Police and Criminal Evidence Act (1984) London: HMSO.

Pritchard, D (1986) Homicide and bargained justice: the agenda-setting effect of crime news on prosecutors. *Public Opinion Quarterly*, 50, 143–59.

Pugh, M D (1983) Contributory fault and rape convictions: loglinear models for blaming the victim. *Social Psychology Quarterly*, 46, 233–42.

Pynoos, R S and Spencer, E (1986) Witness to Violence: the child interview. *Journal of the American Academy of Child Psychiatry*, 25, 306–19.

Rafky, D M (1977) The cognitive gap between the police and the policed:

an exploratory study in attitude organisation. *Law and Human Behavior*, 1, 63–77.

Raine, A and Venables, P H (1981) Classical conditioning and socialisation – a biosocial interaction. *Personality and Individual Differences*, 2, 273–83.

Reicher, S and Emler N (1985) Delinquent behaviour and attitudes to formal authority. *British Journal of Social Psychology*, 24, 161–8.

Reicher, S and Emler, N (1987) The difference between acquiescing and not disagreeing. *British Journal of Social Psychology*, 26, 95.

Reming, G C (1988) Personality characteristics of supercops and habitual criminals. *Journal of Police Science and Administration*, 16, 163–7.

Renwick, S and Emler, N (1984) Moral reasoning and delinquent behaviour among students. *British Journal of Social Psychology*, 23, 281–3.

Resick, P A (1987) Psychological effects of victimization: implications for the criminal justice system. *Crime and Delinquency*, 33, 468–78.

Reskin, B F and Visher, C A (1986) The impacts of evidence and extra legal factors in jurors' decisions. *Law and Society Review*, 20, 423–38.

Reynolds, D (1976) When pupils and teachers refuse a truce: the secondary school and the creation of delinquency. In G Maugham and G Pearson (eds) *Working Class Youth Culture*, London: Routledge and Kegan Paul, 124–37.

Robinson, D N (1980) *Psychology and Law: can justice survive the social sciences?* Oxford: Oxford University Press.

Robinson, W P (1990) Academic achievement and self-esteem in secondary schools: muddles, myths and reality. *Educational Research and Perspectives*, 17, 3–21.

Roesch, R, Golding, S L, Hans, V P and Repucci, N D (1991) Social Science and the Courts: the role of amicus curiae briefs. *Law and Human Behavior*, 15, 1–11.

Rose, V M and Randall, S C (1982) The impact of investigator perceptions of victim legitimacy on the pressing of rape/sexual assault cases. *Symbolic Interaction*, 5, 23–36.

Rosen, R E (1990) Liberal battle zones and the study of law and the media. *Law and Human Behavior*, 14, 511–21.

Ross, D F, Dunning, D, Toglia, M P and Ceci, S J (1990) The child in the eyes of the jury: assessing mock jurors' perceptions of the child witness. *Law and Human Behavior*, 14, 5–23.

Ross, H L (1980) *Settled out of court: the social process of insurance claims adjustment.* New York: Aldine.

Rossi, P H, Simpson, J E and Miller, J L (1985) Beyond crime seriousness: fitting the punishment to the crime. *Journal of Quantitative Criminology*, 1, 59–90.

Rowe, D C, Osgood, D W and Nicewander, W A (1990) A latent trait approach to unifying criminal careers. *Criminology*, 28, 237–70.

Rush, C and Robertson, J (1987) The utility of information to the sentencing decision. *Law and Human Behavior*, 11, 147–55.

Saks, M J (1977) *Jury Verdicts.* Lexington, Mass.: D C Heath.

Saks, M J and Hastie, R (1978) *Social Psychology in Court.* London: van Nostrand.

Samenow, S E (1984) *Inside the Criminal Mind.* New York: Times Books.

Sampson, R J (1987) Does an intact family reduce burglary risk for its neighbours? *Sociology and Social Research,* 71, 204–7.

Sampson, R J and Wooldredge, J D (1987) Linking the micro- and macro-level dimensions of lifestyle-routine activity and opportunity models of predatory victimisation. *Journal of Quantitative Criminology,* 3, 371–93.

Sanders, A (1987) Constructing the case for the prosecution. *Journal of Law and Society,* 14, 229–53.

Sanders, G S and Chiu, W (1988) Eyewitness errors in the free recall of actions. *Journal of Applied Social Psychology,* 18, 1241–59.

Saunders, D G and Skze, P B (1986) Attitudes about woman abuse among police officers, victims, and victim advocates. *Journal of Interpersonal Violence,* 1, 25–42.

Saywitz, K, Jaenicke, C and Camparo, L (1990) Children's knowledge of legal terminology. *Law and Human Behavior,* 14, 523–35.

Scarman, Lord (1986) Letter to *The Times,* 7 October.

Schönbach, P (1987) Accounts of men and women for failure events: applications of an account-phase taxonomy. In G R Semin and B Krahé (eds) *Issues in Contemporary Germany Social Psychology,* London: Sage, 97–118.

Schönbach, P (1990) *Account Episodes: the management or escalation of conflict,* Cambridge: Cambridge University Press.

Scott, R L and Tetreault, L A (1987) Attitudes of rapists and other violent offenders towards women. *Journal of Social Psychology,* 127, 375–80.

Scully, D and Marolla, J (1984) Convicted rapists' vocabulary of motive: excuses and justifications. *Social Problems,* 31, 530–44.

Scully, D and Marolla, J (1985) 'Riding the Bull at Gilley's': Convicted rapists describe the rewards of rape. *Social Problems,* 32, 251–63.

Sebba, L and Nathan, G (1984) Further explorations in the scaling of penalties. *British Journal of Criminology,* 23, 221–49.

Seltzer, R and McCormick II, J P (1987) The impact of crime victimisation and fear of death on attitudes towards death penalty defendants. *Violence and Victims,* 2, 99–114.

Shapland, J and Cohen, D (1987) Facilities for victims: the role of the police and the courts. *Criminal Law Review,* 1987, 28–38.

Shaver, K G (1986) *The Attribution of Blame.* New York: Springer-Verlag.

Shaver, K G and Drown, D (1986) On causality, responsibility and self-blame: a theoretical note. *Journal of Personality and Social Psychology,* 50, 697–702.

Shiner, R A (1990) Intoxication and responsibility. *International Journal of Law and Psychiatry,* 13, 9–35.

Shireman, C H and Reaver, F G (1986) *Rehabilitating Juvenile Justice.* New York: Columbia University Press.

Shultz, T R and Wright, K (1985) Concepts of negligence and intention in the assignment of moral responsibility. *Canadian Journal of Behavioural Science*, 17, 97–108.

Silbert, M H and Pines, A M (1983) Early sexual exploitation as an influence in prostitution. *Social Work*, 28, 285–9.

Simester, A P and Simester, D I (1990) Analysing sexual offence sentences: an empirical approach. *Australian and New Zealand Journal of Criminology*, 23, 269–83.

Simpson, A W B (1984) *Cannibalism and the Common Law*. London: Chicago University Press.

Singer, S I (1988) The fear of reprisal and the failure of victims to report a personal crime: *Journal of Quantitative Criminology*, 4, 289–302.

Skogan, W G (1981) On attitudes and behaviours. In D A Lewis (ed.) *Reactions to Crime*, London: Sage, 19–45.

Smeaton, G and Byrne, D (1987) The effects of R-rated violence and erotica, individual differences, and victim characteristics on acquaintance rape proclivity. *Journal of Research in Personality*, 21, 171–84.

Smith, D A (1987) Police response to interpersonal violence: defining the parameters of legal control. *Social Forces*, 65, 767–82.

Smith, D J (1983) *Police and People in London III: a survey of police officers*, London. Policy Studies Institute No. 620.

Smith, M D (1987) Changes in the victimisation of women: is there a new female victim'? *Journal of Research in Crime and Delinquency*, 24, 291–301.

Smith, M E (1988) 'We help our people to become good citizens': persuasion and the 'morally defective'. *International Journal of Moral and Social Studies*, 3, 59–93.

Smith, T F (1985) Law talk: juveniles' understanding of legal language. *Journal of Criminal Justice*, 13, 339–53.

Smith, D J and Gray, J (1983) *Police and People in London IV: The police in action*, London. Policy Studies Institute No. 621.

Smith, D J and Tomlinson, S (1989) *The School Effect*. London: Policy Studies Institute.

Smith, D A, Visher, C A and Davidson, L A (1984) Equity and discretionary justice: the influence of race on police arrest decisions. *The Journal of Criminal Law and Criminology*, 75, 234–49.

Smith, V L, Kassin, S M and Ellsworth, P C (1989) Eyewitness accuracy and confidence: Within- versus Between-subjects correlations. *Journal of Applied Psychology*, 74, 356–9.

Snarey, J, Reiner, J and Kohlberg, L (1985) The Kibbutz as a model for Moral Education: a longitudinal cross-cultural study. *Journal of Applied Developmental Psychology*, 6, 151–72.

Snyder, R J (1986) Gambling swindles and victims. *Journal of Gambling Behavior*, 2, (1), 50–57.

Softley, P (1980) Police Interrogation: An Observational study in four police stations. *Research Study no. 4. Royal Commission on Criminal Procedure*, London: HMSO.

Sommer, R (1987) Crime and vandalism in university residence halls: a confirmation of defensible space theory. *Journal of Environmental Psychology*, 7, 1–12.

Sparks, P and Durkin, K (1987) Moral reasoning and political orientation: the context sensitivity of individual rights and democratic principles. *Journal of Personality and Social Psychology*, 52, 931–6.

Sparks, R F, Genn, H G and Dodd, D J (1977) *Surveying Victims*, Chichester: Wiley.

Spencer, J W (1988) The role of text in the processing of people in organisations. *Discourse Processes*, 11, 61–78.

Spielberger, C D, Kling, J K and O'Hagan, E J (1978) Dimensions of Psychopathic personality: antisocial behaviour and anxiety. In R D Hare and D Schalling (eds) *Psychopathic Behaviour: approaches to research*, Chichester: John Wiley, 23–46.

Stafford, E and Hill, J (1987) The tariff, social inquiry reports and the sentencing of juveniles. *British Journal of Criminology*, 27, 411–20.

Stalans, L J and Diamond, S S (1990) Formation and change in lay evaluations of criminal sentencing. *Law and Human Behavior*, 14, 199–214.

Steiner, I D (1972) *Group Process and Productivity*. London: Academic Press.

Stephenson, G M (1981) Intergroup bargaining and negotiation. In H Giles and J C Turner (eds) *Intergroup Behaviour*, Oxford: Blackwell, 168–98.

Stephenson, G M (1984) Accuracy and confidence in testimony: a critical review and some fresh evidence. In D J Muller, Blackman and Chapman (eds) *Psychology and Law*, Chichester: Wiley, 229–48

Stephenson, G M (1990) Should collaborative testimony be permitted in courts of law? *The Criminal Law Review*, May, 302–14.

Stephenson, G M and Kniveton, B (1991) Unconscious suggestion in identification evidence: an inadvertent rediscovery of the experimenter effect. Unpublished manuscript. ISAP: University of Kent, UK, CT2 7LZ.

Stephenson, G M and Moston, S (1993) Attitudes and assumptions of police officers when questioning criminal suspects. British Psychological Society, *Issues in Criminological and Legal Psychology*, Aspects of Police Interviewing, No. 18, 30–6.

Stephenson, G M, Kniveton, B H and Wagner, W (1991) Social influences on remembering: intellectual, interpersonal and intergroup components. *European Journal of Social Psychology*, 21, 463–75.

Stephenson, G M, Clark, N K, and Wade, G S (1986) Meetings make evidence? An experimental study of collaborative and individual recall of a simulated police interrogation. *Journal of Personality and Social Psychology*, 50, 1113–22.

Stets, J E and Pirog-good, M A (1987) Violence in dating relationships. *Social Psychology Quarterly*, 50, 237–46.

Stewart, J E II (1980) Defendant's attractiveness as a factor in the outcome of criminal trials: an observational study. *Journal of Applied Social Psychology*, 10, 348–61.

Stokes, R and Hewitt, J P (1976) Aligning actions. *American Sociological Review*, 41, 838–49.

Stradling, S G, Tuohy, A P and Harper, K J (1990) Judgemental asymmetry in the exercise of police discretion. *Applied Cognitive Psychology*, 4, 409–21.

Sullivan, P S, Dunham, R G and Alport, G P (1987) Attitude structures of different ethnic and age groups concerning police. *Journal of Criminal Law and Criminology*, 78, 177–93.

Summit, R C (1983) The child sexual abuse accommodation syndrome. *Child Abuse and Neglect*, 7, 177–93.

Sykes, G M and Matza, D (1957) Techniques of neutralization: a theory of delinquency. *American Sociological Review*, 22, 664–70.

Tanford, S, Penrod, S, and Collins, R (1985) Decision Marking in Joined Criminal Trials: The influence of Charge Similarity, Evidence Similarity and Limiting Instructions. *Law and Human Behavior*, 9, 319–37.

Tapp, J L and Kohlberg, L (1971) Developing senses of law and justice. *Journal of Social Issues*, 27, 65–91.

Tennen, H and Affleck, G (1990) Blaming others for threatening events. *Psychological Bulletin*, 108, 209–32.

Thorndyke, P W (1977) Cognitive structure in comprehension and memory of narrative discourse. *Cognitive Psychology*, 9, 77–110.

Thibaut, J and Walker, L (1975) *Procedural Justice*. Hillside, N J: Erlbaum.

Thibaut, J and Walker, L (1978) A Theory of Procedure. *California Law Review*, 66, 541–66.

Thomas, D A (1979) *Principle of Sentencing* (2nd ed). London: Heinemann.

Thurman, Q C (1984) Deviance and the neutralization of moral commitment: an empirical analysis. *Deviant Behavior*, 5, 291–304.

Tuck, M and Riley, D (1986) The theory of reasoned action: a decision theory of crime. In D B Cornish and R V Clarke (eds) *The Reasoning Criminal*, New York: Springer, 156–69.

Tucker, A, Mertin, P and Luszcz, M (1990) The effect of a repeated interview on young children's eyewitness testimony. *Australian and New Zealand Journal of Criminology*, 23, 117–24.

Tutt, N and Giller, H (1989) The elimination of custody. *Issues in Criminological and Legal Psychology*, 14, 33–48.

Twining, W (1983) Identification and misidentification in legal processes: redefining the problem. In S Lloyd-Bostock and B R Clifford (eds) *Evaluating Witness Evidence*, Chichester: Wiley, 255–83.

Tyler, T R (1984) The role of perceived injustice in defendants: evaluations of their courtroom experience. *Law and Society Review*, 18, 51–74.

Tyler, T R (1989) The psychology of procedural justice: a test of the group-value model. *Journal of Personality and Social Psychology*, 57, 830–8.

Tyler, T R and Rasinski, K (1984) Comparing psychological images of the social perceiver: role of perceived informativeness, memorability and affect in indicating the impact of crime victimization. *Journal of Personality and Social Psychology*, 46, 308–29.

Valdés, G (1986) Analysing the demands that courtroom interaction makes upon speakers of ordinary English: toward the development of a coherent descriptive framework. *Discourse Processes*, 9, 269–303.

van Voorhis, P (1986) The utility of Kohlberg's theory of moral development among adult probationers in a restitution field setting. *Genetic, Social and General Psychology Monographs*, 111, 101–26.

Visher, C A (1983) Gender, police arrest decisions, and notions of chivalry. *Criminology*, 21, 5–28.

von Hirsch, A (1985) *Past or future crimes: deservedness and dangerousness in the sentencing of criminals*. Manchester: Manchester University Press.

von Hirsch, A and Jareborg, N (1989) Sweden's sentencing statute enacted. *Criminal Law Review*, 275–81.

Wagenaar, W A (1988a) *Identifying Ivan: a case study in legal psychology*. London: Harvester Wheatsheaf.

Wagenaar, W A (1988b) The proper seat: a Bayesian discussion of the position of expert witnesses. *Law and Human Behavior*, 12, 499–510.

Wakefield, H and Underwager, R (1989) Evaluating the child witness in sexual abuse cases: interview of inquisition? *American Journal of Forensic Psychology*, 7, 43–69.

Walker, L E A (1989) Psychology and violence against women. *American Psychologist*, 44, 695–702.

Walker, J, Collins, M and Wilson, P (1988) How the public sees sentencing: an Australian survey. In N Walker and M Hough (eds) *Public Attitudes to Sentencing: surveys from five countries*, Aldershot: Gower, 149–59.

Walker, T G and Main, E C (1973) Choice shifts in political decision-making. *Journal of Applied Social Psychology*, 3, 39–48.

Walster, E (1966) Assignment of responsibility for an accident. *Journal of Personality and Social Psychology*, 3, 73–9.

Walton, M D (1985) Negotiation of responsibility: judgements of blameworthiness in a natural setting. *Developmental Psychology*, 21, 725–36.

Ward, D (1990) Society, as embodied by a jury, can decide. *The Independent*, 10 February.

Warr, M (1987) Fear of victimisation and sensitivity to risk. *Journal of Quantitative Criminology*, 3, 29–46.

Warren, A, Hulse-Trotter, K and Tubbs, E C (1991) Inducing resistance to suggestibility in children. *Law and Human Behavior*, 15, 273–85.

Watkins, J G (1989) Hypnotic hyperamnesia and forensic hypnosis: a cross-examination. *American Journal of Clinical Hypnosis*, 32, 71–83.

Weaver, F M and Carroll, J S (1985) Crime perceptions in a natural setting by expert and novice shoplifters. *Social Psychology Quarterly*, 48, 349–59.

Webb, J (1990) Arbitration Work and the Feasibility of Final-offer Arbitration. *Social Behaviour*, 5, 117–25.

Webb, V J and Marshall, I H (1989) Response to criminal victimization by older Americans. *Criminal Justice and Behavior*, 16, 239–59.

Webster, T M, King, H N and Kassin, S M (1991) Voices from an empty chair: the missing witness inference and the jury. *Law and Human Behavior*, 15, 31–43.

Weiss, G (1990) Editorial: Hyperactivity in Childhood. *The New England Journal of Medicine*, 323, 1413–5.

Wells, G L (1978) Applied Eyewitness Testimony Research: System Variables and Estimator Variables. *Journal of Personality and Social Psychology*, 36, 1546–57.

Wells, G L and Murray, D M (1984) Eyewitness Confidence. In G L Wells and E Loftus (eds) *Eyewitness Testimony*, Cambridge: Cambridge University Press, 155–70.

West, D J (1984) The victim's contribution to sexual assault. In J Hopkins (ed.) *Perspectives on Rape and Sexual Assault*, London: Harper & Row, 1–14.

West, D J and Farrington, D P (1973) *Who becomes delinquent?* London: Heinemann.

West, M A (1986) Moral evaluation and dimensions of violence. *Multivariate Behavioural Research*, 21, 229–51.

White, J L, Moffitt, T E, Earls, F, Robins, L and Silva, P A (1990) How early can we tell? Predictors of childhood conduct disorder and adolescent delinquency. *Criminology*, 28, 507–33.

White, R (1989) Making ends meet: young people, work and the criminal economy. *Australian and New Zealand Journal of Criminology*, 22, 136–50.

Wikström P H (1990) Age and crime in a Stockholm cohort. *Journal of Quantitative Criminology*, 6, 61–84.

Wilkins, L T (1984) *Consumerist Criminology*. London: Heinemann.

Willander, J L (1988) The relationship between attention problems in childhood and antisocial behavior eight years later. *Journal of Child Psychology and Psychiatry*, 29, 53–61.

Willemsen, T M and van Schie, E C M (1989) Sex stereotypes and response to juvenile delinquency. *Sex Roles*, 20, 623–38.

Williams, L M and Farrell, R A (1990) Legal response to child sexual abuse in day care. *Criminal Justice and Behaviour*, 17, 284–302.

Williams, L S (1984) The classic rape: when do victims report? *Social Problems*, 31, 459–67.

Williamson, T M (1993) From Interrogation to Investigative Interviewing; Strategic Trends in Police Questioning. *Journal of Community and Applied Social Psychology*, 3, 89–99.

Wilson, G D (1973) *The Psychology of Conservatism*. New York: Academic Press.

Wilson, H (1987) Parental supervision re-examined. *British Journal of Criminology*, 27, 275–30.

Wilson, J Q and Herrnstein, R J (1985) *Crime and Human Nature*. New York: Simon and Schuster.

Wilson, P R and Gorring, P (1985) Social antecedents of medical fraud and over-servicing: what makes a doctor criminal? *Australian Journal of Social Issues*, 20, 175–87.

Windle, M, Barnes, G M and Welte, J (1989) Causal models of adolescent substance use: an examination of gender differences using distribution-free estimates. *Journal of Personality and Social Psychology*, 56, 132–42.

Winkel, W, Koppelaar, L and Vrij, A (1988) Creating suspects in police–citizen encounters: two studies on personal space and being suspect. *Social Behaviour*, 3, 307–19.

Wirtz, P V and Harrell, A V (1987) Victim and crime characteristics, coping responses and short- and long-term recovery from victimization. *Journal of Consulting and Clinical Psychology*, 55, 866–71.

Wodak, R (1980) Discourse analysis and courtroom interaction. *Discourse Processes*, 3, 369–80.

Wolfgang, M E, Figlio, R M and Sellin, T (1972) *Delinquency in a Birth Cohort*. Chicago: Chicago University Press.

Yarmey, A D (1984) Age as a factor in eyewitness memory. In G L Wells and E Loftus (eds) *Eyewitness Testimony*, Cambridge: Cambridge University Press, 142–54.

Yochelson, S and Samenow, S E (1976) *The Criminal Personality: Volume 1: A Profile for Change*. New York: Jason Aronson.

Yochelson, S and Samenow, S E (1977) *The Criminal Personality Volume 2: The Change Process*. New York: Jason Aronson.

Yuille, J C and Cutshall, J L (1986) A case study of eyewitness memory of a crime. *Journal of Applied Psychology*, 71, 291–301.

Zarski, L P, Knight, R and Zarski, L J (1985) Child custody disputes: a review of legal and clinical resolution methods. *International Journal of Family Therapy*, 7, 96–106.

Zuckerman, A (1991) Miscarriage of Justice and Judicial Responsibility. *The Criminal Law Review*, 492–500.

Author Index

Subject Index